The Whiteness
of Child Labor Reform
in the New South

D1002858

The Whiteness
of Child Labor Reform
in the New South

SHELLEY SALLEE

The University of Georgia Press

ATHENS AND LONDON

© 2004 by the University of Georgia Press
Athens, Georgia 30602
All rights reserved
Set in New Baskerville by J. Jarrett Engineering, Inc.
Printed and bound by Thomson-Shore
The paper in this book meets the guidelines for
permanence and durability of the Committee on
Production Guidelines for Book Longevity of the
Council on Library Resources.

Printed in the United States of America
07 06 05 04 03 C 5 4 3 2 1
07 06 05 04 03 P 5 4 3 2 1

Library of Congress Cataloging-in-Publication Data

Sallee, Shelley, 1967–
The whiteness of child labor reform in the New South /
Shelley Sallee.
p. cm.
Includes bibliographical references and index.
ISBN 0-8203-2448-5 (hardcover : alk. paper)
— ISBN 0-8203-2570-8 (pbk. : alk. paper)
1. Child labor—Southern States. 2. Social movements—
Southern States. 3. Social movements—United States.
4. White supremacy movements—Southern States. I. Title.
HD6250.U5 S687 2004   331.3′1′089034075—dc21
2003011158

British Library Cataloging-in-Publication Data available

For Wallis, Hank, and Kate

CONTENTS

ACKNOWLEDGMENTS

SINCE THIS BOOK is a revised dissertation, its content is a product of an academic journey, and its publication as a book reflects a more intimate history of a busy family and work life. My gratitude to specific individuals who made this project possible extends beyond these brief acknowledgments. My thanks goes to those who inspired me to embark on the journey, to those who offered guidance and advice along the way, and to those who supported me to the end.

Many who have inspired are often embedded in the bibliography—authors I have never met—but those most important to my academic career were the teachers and scholars who challenged me to address historical problems. As a high school student in Cookeville, Tennessee, an area I often had in mind as I studied the New South and southern poverty, my history teacher and father, Jack Sallee, taught me to be interested in historical interpretations and the power of history to illuminate our humanity for better or worse. At Smith College, R. Jackson Wilson asked the best questions for making his students think like historians, and Dan and Helen Horowitz encouraged my interest in pursuing graduate studies. My friend Jane Elkind Bowers also figures in the story at this point, for she and I together followed the path from Smith to graduate school at the University of Texas at Austin. A breakfast with Dan Horowitz and Debbie Cottrell, another graduate-student friend and Smith administrator, at my ten-year college reunion revitalized my commitment to turning my dissertation into this book.

While I was reading for major exams, several scholars shaped my decision to take up the topic of child labor in the South. Megan Seaholm, who served on my oral exam committee, shared her time and passion for the fields of women's history, labor history, and the Progressive Era. When I mentioned my dissertation topic, she appreciated my interest in looking at a reform that women were heavily involved with in the New South. Neil Foley, my dissertation advisor, offered the theory and interest in "whiteness" that helped me make sense of the racialized rhetoric that permeated so many of my sources. Jacquelyn Dowd Hall, who helps so many graduate students, probably doesn't even remember evaluating my dissertation proposal during a history conference at the University of North Carolina at Chapel Hill, but she offered valuable criticism. In a fleeting conversation at Vassar College during a Berkshire Conference of Women Historians, Glenda Gilmore encouraged me to contact established scholars for comment on papers I hoped to present at conferences. Elizabeth Hayes Turner was one such scholar who offered help for a conference panel at the Southern Women's Historical Association conference in Charleston. After that paper presentation, Marjorie Julian Spruill's praise motivated me more than she could know. More recently Kriste Lindenmeyer's suggested readings were critical to revisions made in the last two chapters.

My dissertation committee's expertise made the defense one of the most meaningful moments of my graduate experience. This conversation with Neil Foley, David Shearer Bowman, Robin Kilson, Deslie Deacon, and Kevin Kenny led to a significant revision of the introduction and the formulation of the idea of a transregional reform culture. While any shortcomings are my own, this book is better because of their input. The committee's investment in my work and a university fellowship for a year of research were critical to the completion of the dissertation.

The community of graduate students in my program, some whose support extends well beyond our experience together as students, deserves credit. Byron Hulsey, Thomas Clarkin, Jon Lee, Carol Keller, Beth Boyd, Mitty Myhr, Cindy Gladstone, and I discussed our work, read chapters, and celebrated milestones along the way to publication. Christy Sample Wilson responded with enthusiasm years later when I called for help with manipulating census data into charts and tables. Also deserving of more thanks than this acknowledgment can offer is Suzanne Hurley, who helped edit the manuscript notes and kept me sane while finalizing the bibliography, and Caroline Chamberlain, who donated precious time to copy material from the Florence Kelley Papers in the New York Public Library. Their friendship is a precious treasure of graduate school.

Behind every book by a parent are caregivers. To the many students who babysat for me, the St. Stephen's preschool staff, and Kathy Fitzpatrick Sallee I owe a special thank you. To St. Stephen's Episcopal

School I am eternally grateful for creating an environment where I can combine teaching and family life so seamlessly. Lastly, to my husband Wallis Goodman I owe a category of gratitude that extends beyond child care and domestic chores to one of advocacy for the worth of unpaid academic work. He never faltered in his support for my pursuit of publication. He also entered pages of census data into spreadsheets for the analysis in chapter 2. We have both been liberated by the completion of this project.

The University of Georgia helped by sending the manuscript to experts who offered critical advice for revision. Copyeditor Ellen Goldlust-Gingrich polished the manuscript. For their support, professionalism, and expertise I am grateful.

*The Whiteness
of Child Labor Reform
in the New South*

INTRODUCTION

In 1900, the New South was a region of contradictions, struggling to live up to southern boosters' overblown promises. It was a capital-poor region banking on industrial and commercial development. It was a land accustomed to slogans of white unity yet was rent by class divisions—Populist and Republican insurgencies and distinctions between "crackers" and the "better sort" of white exposed white unity as an untidy myth. It was a region that promised democracy "for whites only" yet disfranchised certain white men. It was a region riddled with racial violence yet advertising racial tranquillity. In the wake of slavery, war, and Reconstruction, the South had been reunited with the rest of the nation in name but not fully in spirit.

This book argues that northern and southern reformers camouflaged the contradictions of the New South by inventing fictions of whiteness. Progressives manipulated these myths to ease sectional differences that thwarted southern reform efforts. To borrow and revise a phrase from C. Vann Woodward, "Progressivism for whites only" was more than an exclusion of blacks from white-sponsored reform; rather, it was an insistence on whiteness as essential to American identity and critical to the politics of reform.[1] Reformers dealt with the rise of a white working class by recategorizing the children of marginalized poor whites. As poor whites became a "white trash" working class, reformers invented the "forgotten child" as the country's most promising white, the purest Anglo-Saxon. In the face of apparent disparities between southern white haves and have-nots and between a rapidly modernizing North and an impoverished, rural South, reformers promoted white supremacy as a basis for bringing the New South in line with minimal national standards of child welfare.

Through a serious examination of race and reformers, many of whom historians have labeled racial moderates, a new interpretation of Progressivism emerges that helps answer why socially forward-looking white

1

reformers appear so backward on the issue of race. This book shows how political incentives and interregional relationships made reformers such as Jane Addams and Florence Kelley unlikely accomplices in Jim Crow segregation and the politics of white supremacy. The only language in the New South more powerful than that of industrial progress was the rhetoric of white supremacy. Reformers applied their own brand of Progressive white supremacy in their efforts to nudge an impenetrable one-party system in the South toward minimal child welfare and compulsory education standards.

White Progressives promoted fictions of whiteness in the southern anti–child labor campaign for a number of reasons. Class-conscious Progressives seeking a return to a less economically divided social order turned to a politics of racial solidarity to avoid inflaming latent class antagonisms. Reformers created links between race and citizenship rights in the early twentieth century as class divisions threatened to undermine democracy for all whites. In addition, the "whiteness" of reform encouraged a spirit of regional reconciliation. Making whiteness a basis for citizenship rights created common ground between white northerners and southerners. Northern reformers made concessions to white supremacy in the South in exchange for support for national reform goals. What I call a transregional white middle class emerged during the Progressive Era, with members judging themselves by their own cosmopolitan ideals, pressuring the South to judge itself by these modern standards, and interpreting their local conditions for leading Progressive child welfare organizations.

It was not a given that reform would emphasize race over class when it came to white child laborers. In fact, Samuel Gompers and the American Federation of Labor initiated the southern anti–child labor campaign with class rather than race as a primary organizing principle. Gompers was responding to organized labor's outrage regarding southern competition's effect on northern textile wages. Organized labor recognized that child labor was cheap labor, and children comprised more than 22 percent of the textile labor force in the South, compared to 6 percent in New England.[2] As long as such a disproportionate number of children worked in the mills, southern wages would remain low, potentially undermining wage gains in the Northeast.

Organized labor defined the dominant rhetoric of the child labor problem in terms of class. Birmingham's *Labor Advocate* urged child labor reform as part of a larger radical labor politics. Faced with intransigent politics in a virtually one-party region and given his gendered view of trade union goals, however, Gompers curtailed radical labor politics on the issue of child labor in the name of broadening support for child labor laws. He decided to use a language and an approach that he believed would appeal to the white middle class, already proven allies in northern state campaigns for protective legislation. Gompers chose to send a well-educated Englishwoman, Irene Ashby, to Alabama to make child labor into a humanitarian issue divorced from class politics. He focused on Alabama, where the budding cotton textile industry had more northern ownership than did industries in the rest of the Piedmont. Gompers encouraged Ashby to play race cards—for example, warning that poor white children were going to work while black children were going to school. Gompers made a concerted effort to mute labor's voice, undermining the position of radical labor politics in favor of middle-class, sentimental, racialized reform. His southern strategy was typical of his pragmatism and was based on a number of considerations explored in this work.

Ashby's success was a real coup. Gompers saw her as the perfect agent for winning the "sentimental" types over to labor's side without having them recognize which team they were joining. The larger, unintended consequence of turning the fight over to "the sentimental, the Christian, the noble, the public spirited citizens," as he informed textile union leaders he had done, was that white middle-class reformers publicized the problem within their own prevailing ideas about race, family, and gender.[3] Reformers diminished the connections among child labor, fair wages and hours, and labor's right to organize.

The first white middle-class reformers to take up the cause in Alabama racialized the child labor problem to cover the widening class factions among whites and to avoid haunting, controversial injustices exposed by organized labor. Early southern reformers laid an ideological groundwork for the whiteness of child labor reform out of their own views of racial order. White southern Progressives wanted a stable social order and believed that divisions among whites and crossrace alliances fueled social chaos. Reformers' visions of white supremacy conformed to their ideal of social order even though their racial rhetoric sounded much like that of the politicians for whom the reformers had only contempt. Southern Progressives were appalled at the political corruption in the

South and despised the manipulation of lower-class white voters. Even more frightening to Progressives was racial violence, especially lynching.

Progressives adopted some of the rhetoric of white supremacy to promote their vision of social order for the New South. This southern Progressive vision included improving the status of marginalized whites. Against a backdrop of corruption, violence, and social unrest, reformers considered divisions among whites a root of social disorder and lamented the declining power of the "better sort" of white men. Reformers invested in racial solidarity to confront growing class divisions.[4] Progressives' concerns about class divisions not only were real but also were based on the impact of industry and declining agricultural opportunities on the status of poor whites. The currency of the term *cracker* suggested the declining status of poor whites. Even though manufacturers touted the reliability and superiority of a native white workforce, industry also benefited from a derogatory stereotype that fostered a southern attitude that mill work, regardless of the hours and conditions, was good enough for this inferior type of white family. *Cracker* no longer referred to a backwoods farmer who cracked corn but to a racially inferior white who had become "the lowest element among the white people."[5]

Characterizations of crackers as lazy and ignorant relegated them to the justifiably impoverished. Manufacturers played to attitudes that the cracker families they hired had sunk so low that mere employment was a form of uplift. In contrast, reformers saw the *cracker* label as a dangerous development that would inhibit democratic progress and foster greater class and race conflict. As one concerned citizen put it, "The division between [mill people] and other people is widening all the time . . . permitting things to continue that unfit [mill workers] more and more for better service in life." To overcome this division among whites, reformers drew on dominant racial ideologies about Anglo-Saxon superiority, injecting urgency into their arguments by using eugenics narratives that warned about racial deterioration among neglected whites. Reformers removed children from categories such as *poor whites, mountain whites, low whites,* and *crackers*—terms that increasingly dubbed them inferior—and began referring to "our pure Anglo-Saxon stock," "noble though undeveloped people of the mountains and hills," and simply "the unstarted."[6] New South Progressives resurrected myths about an old "classless" South to combat New South class strife.

When Southern Progressives reconstructed myths about white unity, they made race an "organizing principle" for the restoration of order among whites and between the races. Edgar Gardner Murphy, head of the Alabama Child Labor Committee (ACLC), a founder of the National Child Labor Committee (1904), and the ideologue of the early southern child labor movement, identified race as the key to controlling unruly whites. He explained the need for racial solidarity and uplift within each race in his acclaimed 1909 book, *The Basis of Ascendancy*. When he addressed "the double basis of our race security," he exposed his concern about unruly whites by arguing that each race had to rid itself of its "vicious elements," "its own forces of irresponsibility"—the whites he blamed for lynchings and racial violence.[7]

To address "irresponsibility," Murphy turned to men he considered models of responsibility. He recruited men into child labor reform from education reform circles and from the Southern Society, a group of prominent, white Montgomery men committed to studying the "race problem." These men reflected a fundamental shift away from philanthropists' earlier commitments to African American education and toward a focus on whites first. As racial moderates, these reformers saw themselves as restoring order and ending racial violence with the hope that white society would tolerate "appropriate" advances for African Americans. Murphy's men were racial paternalists who blamed racial friction and rowdy class strife on ignorance and economic distress among white southerners. Murphy, reflecting his concern regarding growing class fissures, called poor whites "plain people" in a concerted effort to avoid drawing attention to their lower class and racial status as defective whites.[8]

Progressives such as Murphy did not view disfranchisement clauses in southern states' new constitutions as mechanisms solely for eliminating African Americans from the voting polity. Murphy and other southern Progressives understood restoring good government to mean removing "irresponsible" elements—both white and black. This interest in controlling irresponsible whites fueled the next generation of reform ideas. In 1901, when Alabama debated suffrage requirements, Murphy favored enfranchisement of educated African Americans, such as his acquaintance Booker T. Washington. But because Murphy blamed plain whites for provoking racial violence, working their children, tramping from town to town and across the countryside, and falling prey to irresponsible demagogues or disorderly biracial alliances such as the Populists, he advocated the disfranchisement of illiterate white men.[9]

At the same time, Murphy was a Progressive and saw himself as an advocate of democratization in the New South, and although he wrote off lower-class white fathers as irresponsible, he wanted to save their children. "In the promise of the forgotten child of the people, the enlarging democracy finds its charter," he declared. Murphy felt that the only hope for solving the race problem and creating good government, a classic goal of order-oriented Progressives, was "control of our white population," an impossible task "if the children of this state are kept, by the operation of our factory conditions, from the schooling, which our Negroes are eagerly seeking."[10] Closing the mill door and opening the school door became synonymous with salvaging white southern manhood. Murphy started in Alabama, and this book follows the development of reform specifically in that state while placing Alabama reform in the larger context of the southern and national reform movements, both of which Murphy initially helped to shape.

As a variety of Progressives analyzed and addressed the southern child labor problem and mobilized an interregional coalition of child welfare experts to campaign for reform, race defined the terms of the debate, putting manufacturers, who already claimed to value the whiteness of their workforce, on the defensive. The child labor reform campaign provoked posturing among employers, who, regardless of their actual treatment of workers, had a growing investment in exaggerating their concern for unfortunate whites. Moreover, the focus on whites defined the terms of the national debate, making it possible for northerners and southerners to work together without southern suspicion that "outsiders" were intervening out of an interest in African Americans' rights.

The national child labor movement saw the New South as shackled by an intransigent politics that was unresponsive to social and humanitarian problems. Not only did the South have weaker laws and the highest proportion of child labor in the textile industry, but the region's backwardness also threatened to retard reform everywhere. Although reform that focused on whites did not significantly improve the socioeconomic situation of thousands of impoverished white cotton mill families, it did affect public debate and the contours of Progressivism. It helps explain how and why such well-intentioned reformers, ahead of their time on social reform, reinforced notions of white supremacy.

The centrality of the "southern problem" in child labor reform suggests that at least in Alabama, the rise of women's activism on this issue intersected with male reform efforts in ways that traditional studies of the rise of women's reform culture overlook. Like the phrase *separate spheres,* the recent thesis regarding "two Progressive Eras," which contrasts "the cultural politics of men" with the more reformist "cultural politics of women," overemphasizes the separateness of women's reform. Child labor reform in Alabama shows that left alone, the state's organized clubwomen might not have mounted a significant reform movement.[11] On the one hand, the trajectory of white middle-class women using separate-sphere ideology to justify more public activity is apparent in Alabama, where white middle-class women became increasingly involved in public life in the name of needy children. On the other hand, child labor reform in Alabama illuminates the importance of distinguishing between women's public activity and their political action with a legislative agenda.

Clubwomen were some of the first people in Alabama to address the needs of poor cotton mill children with free kindergartens and some of the last, behind organized labor and the ACLC, to demand strict child labor laws. Murphy's all-male ACLC mounted the initial legislative campaign. Despite the declaration of female child labor reformer Conradine Skaggs McConaughy that "if we believe in the supremacy of the Caucasian race we must then be up and doing," the racially charged motives and rhetoric of Murphy and his men were not promoted by the women Progressives who joined the cause as extensively as by the men.[12] The whiteness of reform, however, created an important breakthrough for white Alabama women who wanted to become true Progressive activists by paving the way for them to be part of a larger network of politicized women.

The whiteness of reform ultimately facilitated the interregional reconciliation that was characteristic of the Progressive Era. In Alabama, this reconciliation—a product of male and female reform culture and northern and southern reform agendas—was a necessary step so that the state's organized women could become the kind of leaders associated with a distinct female Progressive politics. A by-product of the whiteness of child labor reform was that it strengthened white southern women's activism, enabling them to overcome some of the regional conservatism that characterized their early interest in poor white children. As northern white Progressives sacrificed older philanthropic concerns regarding African American education and adopted white-focused reform to apply leverage on the South, suspicions of outside influence subsided in southern states, including Alabama. The national movement was determined to bring the South up to a minimal national standard so that reform elsewhere could advance. Southerners were pressured to do more, and a minority of eager Alabama reformers sought help from leading Progressive groups. White, middle-class women organized around child-centered service goals were the likely agents of regional reconciliation on the child labor issue. A transregional, white middle class with women as some of its most visible, active agents developed a modern child welfare vision.

Evidence of the role that the whiteness of reform and women's activism played in regional reconciliation during this period was apparent at the National Child Labor Committee's 1911 annual conference in Birmingham, a festival of regional reconciliation. This was the first national meeting after the release of the U.S. Bureau of Labor report titled *Woman and Child Wage-Earners in the United States.* The report exposed the depth of sectional disparity on child labor and education conditions. The 1911 meeting addressed the sectional disparity at the heart of the issue but did so not by dwelling on themes of southern backwardness but rather with a spirit of regional reconciliation promoted by celebrated Progressive Theodore Roosevelt. Roosevelt urged conservation of the South's "children crop." Illuminating the role of the whiteness of southern child labor reform, Roosevelt urged southerners to get in step with the nation. If northerners protected the children of "Slovacs, Poles, Italians, French-Canadians, Portuguese, [and] Greeks," the southerners, he declared, should protect their "own flesh and blood."[13] Roosevelt was warmly received, and the occasion involved much mutual backslapping and congratulations among white northern and southern reformers.

The 1911 Birmingham meeting strengthened white Alabama women's ties to national reform circles and transformed the agenda of Alabama's women leaders. Both Addams and Kelley addressed the meeting, and Kelley forged a lasting relationship with local reformer Nellie Kimball Murdoch. Kelley and the National Consumers' League provided Murdoch with support that was critical to Alabama women Progressives' ability to overcome regional conservatism and to champion a minimal national standard of child welfare.

Kelley understood how to make labor reform appeal to moral and family issues that were traditional concerns of middle-class white women. By 1915 Alabama's female-dominated reform movement not only demanded stronger child labor and compulsory education laws but also advocated the eight-hour day for women and children, something that Murphy and the ACLC had never dared to do. The shift from conservatism to Progressivism in Alabama women confirms arguments that women's organizations used "gender-specific" arguments to offer an unprecedented challenge to "the dominance of capitalist values." This new call for an eight-hour workday for all women and youth workers was a significant advance from the early steps of the all-male ACLC and reflected the development of the national anti–child labor movement and a transregional Progressive culture. This network of national associations was especially critical because child labor reform was more controversial than other forms of civic improvement that scholars have shown that southern women initiated. Significantly, these Alabama women, connected to a larger Progressive network, also followed Kelley's lead and demanded recognition of workers' right to organize and of women's right to vote as part of this pursuit of better child welfare laws.[14]

This new transregional middle-class culture promoted a child welfare agenda in the name of middle-class women's special knowledge about child development, family, and the sanctity of the home, claiming that the reformers' standards were modern standards. While limited in its scope, the 1919 creation of the Alabama Child Welfare Department (CWD) reflected this new middle-class culture and the influence of women and gender in shaping it.

Local reformers such as Loraine Bedsole Bush, head of the Alabama Child Welfare Department, took their cues from the U.S. Children's Bureau and the National Child Labor Committee. At the same time, these women had begun to pride themselves on their knowledge of local problems and their ability to serve as mediators between their home state and national Progressive groups. They adopted a children-first strategy and in some cases broke with the past and tried to extend the state's protection to African American children as well as whites. But the CWD ultimately remained locked into a whites-first reform mode, publicizing the department with the image of well-scrubbed, healthy white children "saved" from the mill in what the reformers hoped would be the beginning of greater public support of poor families.[15]

The whiteness of southern child labor reform changes interpretations of white Progressivism, replacing an acceptance of racism as a blanket explanation for the focus on "whites only" with a more complex understanding of reformers' political investments in race-based arguments. Reformers' racial attitudes and strategies show white southerners' various interpretations of white supremacy and the regional and national forces that supported race as the defining character of the New South's social order. Alabama Progressives who despised white supremacy's violence and corruption nevertheless racialized reform in a way that reinforced notions of white superiority and competition between the races. In an effort to compel the South to join a campaign for a national standard for child labor and compulsory education, white northern Progressives united with southern Progressives, putting a premium on whiteness as a criterion for citizenship rights and government protection. Public welfare was white welfare by the time white Alabama women working with the National Child Labor Committee established the CWD. Indeed, this emphasis on the whiteness of the South's child laborers gave rise to a white transregional Progressive culture willing to ignore the plight of African Americans in the name of progress in the South.

Mill Men

MANUFACTURERS HIRED CHILDREN along with their parents as a family package. Mill men hired adult laborers at low wages and found that children provided the bonus of elasticity and adaptability. Children could be hired and fired as needed to expand or contract the labor force. Reformers, however, did not believe that children should fulfill this need for cheap, flexible labor and publicized the plight of these young, predominantly white laborers, demanding that the public see them as white children full of the potential that their Anglo-Saxon racial heritage allegedly promised. The child labor reform movement put mill men on the defensive. Although the textile industry in both the North and the South used paternalism to attract and retain workers—often families—the child labor reform movement increased manufacturers' incentive to invent propaganda of paternalism that was not based in reality.[1]

Once reformers identified industry as exploiting white children, mill men had to explain themselves, developing elaborate justifications for their labor practices and drawing on myths about the noblesse oblige of the southern elite that were popular in an age of nostalgia for the Old South. When Progressives charged that "the new slavery of the mills is worse than the old slavery of the cotton fields," southern mill men responded by claiming that they were helping those who could not help themselves. No longer able to dismiss workers as undeserving "crackers" or as poor whites who were better off in the mills than in the fields, mill men created a more positive public image by arguing that employing poor whites would enable them to pull themselves up by their bootstraps.

Employment was uplift. Mill propaganda justified child labor as part of a phase of the South's regeneration. Broadus Mitchell's *The Rise of Cotton Mills in the South,* published in 1921 and the premier book on the topic until recent decades, attributed a philanthropic interest to mill men's motivations for developing the cotton textile industry in the South. Mitchell's study of South Carolina mills found that "the use of children was not avarice then, but philanthropy, not exploitation, but generosity and cooperation and social-mindedness." Mitchell apparently took at face value mill men's overblown rhetoric about their interest in their workers' welfare. Similar to slaveholders' development of a proslavery argument in response to the growth of a radical abolitionist movement, mill interests in the New South had an incentive for a public relations elaboration of paternalism when the child labor reform movement put them on the defensive. Mitchell's work testifies to the effectiveness of this defense in a context barren of good choices for the rural poor.[2]

One of the most blatant examples of textile manufacturers' propaganda to counter the anti–child labor movement appeared in 1912. Thomas Dawley Jr., a former U.S. Bureau of Labor investigator hired by manufacturers to tell their side of the story, published *The Child That Toileth Not: The Story of a Government Investigation* in an attempt to discredit the nineteen-volume Bureau of Labor report *Woman and Child Wage-Earners in the United States.* Progressives heralded the report as proof that stronger child labor laws were needed; conversely, manufacturers despised it and used their influence in the U.S. Senate to try to block the confirmation of Charles P. Neill as commissioner of labor because the report had been prepared under his direction. These efforts to derail Neill's nomination failed, but industry leaders tried to undermine the report by hiring Dawley to publish their version of the situation. The mythical southern mill man in Dawley's account was a simple farmer who "scraped together $500" and convinced a "Yankee machine man" to help open a cotton mill. The Yankee reaped unprecedented profits, while the mill invigorated the defeated southern community.[3]

In response to Progressives' efforts to prove the debilitating effects of child labor, Dawley argued that cotton mills enhanced rather than stunted children's development. Child laborers, he argued, transformed their parents' condition of despair and the moral depravity that allegedly followed from their lack of work. He maintained that the mills provided children the chance to be industrious yet allowed them time to enjoy the countryside and to seek an education. In contrast to the moral bankruptcy he reported finding in moonshine-laced mountain enclaves where poor whites had no opportunities, he found bucolic scenes of robust white mill children "enjoying the warm spring sunshine." Dawley played on stereotypes of uneducated, rural whites to argue that mill men were saving children from the "white trash" lifestyle of their parents. Not all mill propaganda was as transparent as Dawley's, but his work demonstrates a link between efforts to pass stricter child labor laws and mill owners' investment in exaggerating their interest in social uplift. Although he personally condemned the cotton manufacturers' actions, David Clark, editor of the *Southern Textile Bulletin,* admitted that companies in North Carolina had purchased and circulated "a considerable number" of copies of Dawley's book.[4]

The truth about mill men and child laborers was more complicated than either Dawley's portrayal or reformers' propaganda. Mill men were town men, not farmers. They were neither particularly evil nor especially benevolent. They were primarily businessmen interested in the commercial life of their towns or in finding a lucrative southern investment for their North-based companies. They used various forms of paternalism to attract and keep workers who were, according to recent scholarship, autonomous and free laborers, *not* bound to an "industrial plantation," as defenders of southern exceptionalism have suggested. In 1894, the *Manufacturers' Record* announced "Alabama's Awakened interest in Cotton Manufacturing": the mill men saw themselves as leaders in this new form of economic opportunity in the region. The textile journal declared, "Alabama ought to give the Carolinas a good close race for first position." The number of working spindles, the measure of production capacity, increased by 62.3 percent between 1880 and 1890 in Alabama. Between 1895 and 1900, twenty-one new mills were built in the state, with a total capitalization of $7.5 million.[5]

In Alabama, mills were built as part of towns, following a pattern that scholars have found in the Carolinas. By building mills near towns, operators had access to advanced communications and transportation systems.[6] Most of Alabama's cotton mills consequently were located in the northern half of the state, where towns had developed around the coal and iron ore industries.

The men who built the mills had ties to organized commercial interests and knew how to raise local funds for mill building as well as how to collaborate with outside investors. Alabama's mill men comprised a mix of local elites and established northern textile interests. In 1893, two of the state's leading citizens, Braxton Bragg Comer and Rufus Rhodes, organized the Birmingham Commercial Club to promote the town, and by 1895 the club boasted about two hundred members among Birmingham's population of more than twenty-six thousand. Many of the same names that appeared in columns about Commercial Club members surfaced in society columns as well, and these men focused on building up their town rather than on uplifting the poor. The club's committee on factories recommended in 1895 that laws be changed to attract cotton mills, and the organization's women's auxiliary "vowed to find ten women to take $100 stock in the cotton mill" planned for Avondale, on the city's outskirts. A study of Gadsden, a town that had a little more than six thousand people in 1890, showed that mill men were politically diverse and spanned generations but were bound together by marital ties, common church affiliations, and membership in secret associations and Masonic lodges.[7]

Such local support for mill construction in Alabama is important because the textile industry was one of the few New South industries known for being homegrown at a time when regional commercial development relied heavily on outside investors. Studies of mill building in the Carolinas emphasize the significance of local funding and local men. Although Alabama mills had local support, it was by no means the whole picture. Even when most stockholders in a company were local, they often controlled less than half of the common stock. For example, a majority of the Dallas Mills stockholders lived in Huntsville, but they controlled only 16.7 percent of the company's common stock.[8]

More than in the Carolinas, outside investment was largely responsible for the growth of Alabama's cotton textile industry. The upsurge in cotton spindles in Alabama occurred from 1895 to 1900, when northern textile men, hurt by the 1893 depression, were most interested in the advantages that the South provided. Northeastern manufacturers made highly publicized exploratory trips to the South, and although the idea of a "mill exodus" was an exaggeration, New England manufacturers looked for ways to shift their production of coarse cotton goods to the South. The 1900 U.S. census reported, "There are now single establishments in Massachusetts which pay annually a larger sum in wages than the entire cost of labor in Southern cotton mills in 1880." There was relatively little industry in the New South and growing concern over labor costs in the Northeast, and the South had huge development potential. In Alabama in particular, New England manufacturers were responsible for the upsurge in the state's cotton manufacturing capacity; by 1900, three northeastern manufacturers owned 48 percent of the state's cotton spindles.[9]

All mill men were primarily businessmen, but they were also complicated men with unique motivations. For example, Howard Gardner Nichols, a Massachusetts manufacturer who established a cotton mill in Gadsden, Alabama, had a real social vision as well as a business plan. In fact, the "familiar paternalism" he practiced by offering housing, schools, and land for gardens was good business.[10] Nichols's vision was shaped by the model mill villages of an earlier industrial age, which had been replaced by the more troublesome phase of conflict between capital and labor in the Northeast. Nichols, a privileged northerner with financial security that upstart southern manufacturers lacked, could afford to approach mill building with a social vision and needed to provide incentives to attract and retain workers in a rural part of northern Alabama. Braxton Bragg Comer of Alabama, by contrast, was preoccupied with breaking into the industry and did not leave any record of early concern about social uplift. His Avondale Mills near Birmingham became the only prominent locally owned mills. Comer had little money to promote any ambitions of social uplift that he might privately have held, and because his mills were located near Birmingham, they had less difficulty attracting and retaining a workforce.

A New North in the New South

The Massachusetts-based Dwight Manufacturing Company (DMC) opened a branch mill in Alabama City, near Gadsden, in 1895. Four stories high, the mill covered three city blocks and housed twenty-five thousand spindles and eight hundred looms. The mill virtually created Alabama City. In many respects, this mill typified the industry's shift to the South, resulting from eager collaboration among northern and southern commercial interests. Gadsden's mayor, Reuben Alexander Mitchell, helped the DMC lobby the Alabama legislature to support the repeal of an 1887 law restricting women and children to eight hours work per day for manufacturing purposes and banning the employment of children under age fourteen. The measure's repeal in December 1894 sealed the decision of Dwight's president, Thomas Jefferson Coolidge, to open a mill in Alabama City. "Labor," Coolidge claimed, "is the greatest savings of all."[11]

Nichols grafted his social idealism onto Dwight's business interests during his tenure as the DMC agent in Alabama City from January 1895 until the summer of 1896, when he was crushed to death by a falling electric generator. A young, earnest man from a New England family with a history of donating to Christian missionaries, Nichols prided himself on his vision for a model mill village, which had become a thing of the past in Massachusetts. He sought freedom from restrictive labor laws and believed that an orderly, well-developed mill village would deter labor agitation.[12]

Nichols had followed his father into cotton manufacturing in Chicopee, Massachusetts, but growing conflict between labor and capital had changed the business. Nichols said that "labor agitation" was a direct cause of the company's decision to "come South," complaining that "labor agitators, largely foreigners, have been weaving a web of oppressive laws around cotton manufacturing industries. . . . Laws are made which are of no real benefit to operatives, but of great annoyance to manufacturers." To the devoted Protestant, staunch Republican, Harvard-educated Nichols, Massachusetts looked like an industrial experiment gone awry, and the South could be romanticized as a place to begin anew. The Republican vision—societal progress fueled by free labor and small-scale capitalist growth tempered by Protestant ethics and a commitment to democratic ideals—appeared powerless against the increasing class conflict, ethnic strife, and urban alienation in Massachusetts. In Nichols's view, "alien-born citizens" and "religious intolerance" were exacerbating social problems in the North, while popular culture encouraged him to see the relatively undeveloped South and its nonimmigrant rural population in romantic terms. Nichols's letters illustrate his tendency to romanticize the South: "This is Sunday afternoon," he wrote to his parents. "I am sitting on the highest ledge on the eastern side of Lookout Mountain, overlooking the country for miles around." He had heard "a very interesting sermon . . . at our little church." From the sermon, "Help from the hills," he recalled the line, "I will lift up mine eyes unto the hills, from whence cometh my help."[13] Nichols saw himself as an industrial pioneer, bringing opportunity to the region.

Nichols wanted to create a respectable, orderly mill village, as pure as Gadsden's natural surroundings, where his version of Christian conduct prevailed. The village would be centered on the church and would have public schools and a library. He banned saloons and concealed weapons in the hopes of creating an orderly community of satisfied workers. In contrast to the uniformity of typical mill housing, Nichols planned Victorian cottages in different colors and styles, with ample room for gardens. The 350 cottages around the mill rented for one dollar a month, three dollars less than homes in Gadsden.[14] In 1902 the *Gadsden Times-News* praised the company for building "its operatives a beautiful church and library building, with 1,000 or more volumes, a handsome school, which is free, and a bathing pond with a number of bath rooms." The newspaper thought that the DMC provided "every comfort which [operatives] could find in a great city, and everything is free for them." The teacher in the mill village recalled Nichols as a man who liked to discuss "the ways and means to uplift his people." She held that he envisioned "a model city with model operatives" and suggested that he was unusual. She feared that the schoolhouse and other plans would be a "disappointment" in his successors' hands.[15]

Nichols's vision was good business in a period when it was difficult to attract and retain workers, who often saw the mills as stopgap employers —during the summertime, families frequently returned to farming. Nichols's last letter to his father suggested that his cottages were tools to attract workers. In 1898, R. A. Mitchell, a former Gadsden mayor who became the DMC's Alabama manager after Nichols's death, reported to the Massachusetts office that despite his advertising efforts, it was difficult to recruit labor when the weather was good: "Most of the laboring class are now engaged picking cotton, and there will no doubt be a scarcity of laborers for two or more weeks," he concluded. That same year, Mitchell also complained of labor competition with other mills. While there had been "no systematic exodus of operatives," he indicated that during the "summertime the mill populations in this section" moved often and were vulnerable to being attracted to Avondale and Cordova, which were "making strenuous efforts to get help."[16]

Nichols's Alabama City mill village was as close to a model village as any in Alabama. But the village, which manufacturers would later present as evidence in support of their good social intentions, was compromised when it did not also make good business sense. Managers' letters after Nichols's death show that business exigencies impinged on plans for the village. When the mill could cut costs by building cheaper housing for more transient labor, it did so. Interim agent Charles H. Moody, a native of Georgia, advised the DMC that if the company built more cottages, "it would be well to build a cheaper grade, such as were built for the negroes, as they seem to be quite popular with a certain class of help." Another manager, O. B. Tilton, advocated following through on Nichols's plans for a reading room only because it was "the very best thing . . . to provide for [the workers] before any mischief can be introduced by outside influences." Tilton fired the female teacher with whom Nichols had discussed his plans for uplift and instead hired "a preacher who could do both jobs." And while the mill under Nichols had provided for a woman "in very destitute circumstances" with two sick children and an infant, Tilton informed the city that "the Dwight Company have reached a point where they consider their duties to her have been fulfilled" and withdrew support.[17]

In their quest for an orderly village with an orderly workforce, Dwight managers instituted a nightly nine o'clock curfew for the Alabama City mill village, enforced, as was the ban on alcohol, by a policeman hired by the mill. As in the case of earlier efforts in model New England mill towns such as Lowell, Massachusetts, such paternalism was designed to keep out the undesirables and to attract a higher class of labor. While some workers appreciated mill efforts to encourage respectability and to keep out the riffraff, mill management exacted a price from its employees. Workers who sought to organize politically to oppose the mill-supported ticket for municipal offices, which included mill superintendent Charles H. Moody, were ordered to stop or lose their jobs, and those who did not comply were fired.[18]

The Avondale Mills and a Hard-Driving Southern Businessman

A comparison between Alabama entrepreneur Braxton Bragg Comer, who built the Avondale Mills near Birmingham, and the DMC's Nichols suggests that paternalism was practiced only when it made business sense. Comer did not have the business incentives to create a model mill village that Nichols and Mitchell had in Gadsden, and contrary to the old versions of mill men as uniquely interested in social uplift, Comer was too busy and too financially strapped to give the subject much thought until child labor reformers challenged him. Nichols's privileged background and association with a well-established firm enabled him to consider larger social plans that more hard-pressed southern entrepreneurs could not afford. If Nichols was preoccupied with a vision for a model mill village to promote his Christian values and to keep labor agitators at bay, Comer was preoccupied with earning his capitalist credentials.

Braxton Bragg Comer came from a privileged background but, unlike Nichols, who could follow his father into cotton manufacturing, Comer had to make his own way after the Civil War, and by the time he became president of the Avondale Mills, Comer was a hard-driving businessman, "the highest type of the modern *bourgeoisie*." The son of a Barbour County planter who owned more than sixty slaves, Comer chose a new direction when the family's plantation floundered after his father's death in 1858 and the Civil War. Educated at the University of Alabama at Tuscaloosa and at Emory and Henry College in Virginia, Comer looked for new means of wealth and status after he returned to Alabama in the 1870s. In 1885, he developed a wholesale grocery and commission business in Anniston. Five years later, he moved to Birmingham and went into the banking and gristmill business. By the 1890s, he was president of City National Bank and Birmingham Corn and Flour Mills.[19]

As a result of his business dealings in Birmingham, Comer was an ideal candidate to serve as a local representative for David Trainer and E. E. Trainer, textile men from Pennsylvania who initiated plans for the construction of a four-story brick mill with thirty thousand spindles and one thousand looms. Birmingham newspapers supported Comer's effort "to build the mill with home money and run it with home money." Comer encouraged a few business leaders to get the movement for a cotton mill under way: "Capital is like a flock of sheep, timid by nature," he argued, "but let one break through a wire fence into a rich pasture and the flock will go through, even if they lose some wool in the attempt."[20]

While Comer eventually succeeded in establishing the only Alabama firm to achieve prominence in the industry, during the early stages of organizing Avondale Comer was insecure about his new position and resented northern intervention. Using his Birmingham Commercial Club contacts, Comer convinced B. F. Roden, president of the Avondale Land Company, to donate the site for the enterprise, and Comer subscribed to ten thousand dollars in stock. He put his reputation on the line by assuring prospective backers that "we can build and run a mill cheaper than" would be possible in the Carolinas. Given his level of commitment, Comer was angry when he received the first order for fabric from a northeastern selling agency that expected a low price because of connections to northern stockholders. The Trainers withdrew their support of Comer after he refused to sell at the lower price.[21]

The conflict almost cost Comer his job. Northeastern stockholders would have fired Comer if Frederick Jenks of the Jenks Machinery Company in Pawtucket, Rhode Island, had not intervened. Jenks had installed more than one hundred thousand dollars worth of machinery at the mill and held enough stock that his vote preserved Comer's position. The loss of the Trainers' support imperiled the mill's finances, and a number of local citizens exacerbated the problem by reneging on their promised subscriptions. But Comer resolved to persevere, vowing, "I'll run this cotton mill as long as I can borrow a dollar," even turning to a Wall Street banker for a loan. Comer at first ran the mill with little financial security and with only two other men in the office to help him, purchasing cotton himself. The experience left Comer bitter about the power of outsiders over his position, and he later channeled his frustration over dependence on eastern men and their money into a political career based on attacking eastern-controlled railroads, trusts, and corporations.[22]

Comer subsequently claimed that he had started Avondale Mills "at the request of the Chamber of Commerce to help give employment to those badly in need of it in the young and struggling city of Birmingham," but records of the early years of Avondale show a predominant concern with establishing himself rather than his city or its unemployed. Private documents show a man absorbed in keeping his business afloat. After Comer became governor in 1906 and turned the operation of the mill over to his son, Donald, B. B. Comer continued to micromanage the mill with profit as his primary concern. Exchanges between the two men show a struggle to compete in the industry. Governor Comer was not interested in a model village to replace the large tenements that housed the six hundred "mostly boys, girls and women" who worked for him. With the Avondale Mills located near Birmingham and thus having easier access to laborers, Comer lacked an incentive for paternalism. He sponsored no private projects of social uplift for children and women in his mills. He was, however, very concerned about other details. He ad-

vised his son on upgrading the machinery, curtailing or expanding production, and selling the cloth in New York. The hard lessons from his
early experiences with northeastern buyers stayed with Comer, who
warned his son that the buyers "will do their best to make you cut prices."
Comer's advice to another son summed up his business philosophy:
"Trust nobody."[23]

Privately, the Comers were not concerned about the welfare of child
laborers but rather worried that child labor might become a source of
conflict within their workforce. Donald Comer hesitated to tell his father
about the "air of dissatisfaction in the mills." One worker had complained that the manager was running the automated machines that
spun cotton into yarn too fast, thereby "working [the employee's] children to death." Even though the senior Comer might have wanted to
know more about trouble that could potentially disrupt his workforce,
his son's letter suggests that the governor would not have worried about
a child being overworked: Donald wrote, "I will not listen to any more
of them and will not quote any more of their troubles to you." The Comers also reportedly used harsh tactics with disgruntled employees. When
a fired worker refused to move out of his house, the Comers responded
by sending a crew to remove the roof. Braxton Bragg Comer had insti-
gated violence that kept Republicans from the polls in the 1870s, used
the state militia to break strikes in the coal mining industry, and organized opposition to the earliest child labor laws.[24]

Homegrown Mills

Mill men in Florence, Alabama, came closer than others in their state
to the classic profile of local businessmen with close ties to their communities. Florence was touted for the success of its "home cotton mill
project," in which "the small contributions of home citizens" and local
entrepreneurs raised the capital for Cherry Mill, which had twelve thousand spindles, and Ashcraft Mill, which started with only three thousand
spindles. But local money did not translate into a particular concern for
the plight of Florence's mill workers. The founder of the Cherry Cotton
Mill, Noel Franklin Cherry, was the son of a large cotton planter from
Hardin County, Tennessee. Cherry had gone into the mercantile business in Tennessee and Mississippi during Reconstruction and was interested in linking his textile business with the new wave of economic

growth that accompanied Florence's boom days in the 1890s. In 1872, he and his brother, W. H. Cherry, organized the Mountain Mills Cotton Mill Company, located in the countryside near Florence. They subsequently moved the mill to Florence to have access to railroads and reopened as the Cherry Cotton Mill in 1893 with the help of Florence's "new men." Noel Cherry's partners, Nial Childs Elting and Charles M. Brandon, typified Florence's new commercial class: Elting had moved to Florence from New York in 1889 to start the First National Bank; Brandon had come to Florence after his father became a railroad superintendent.[25]

Cherry hoped to make Florence a textile hub and encouraged the industry's growth there by helping the Ashcraft brothers break into the business. When the Ashcrafts started an integrated mill where spinning and weaving occurred under the same roof, Cherry became a chief subscriber of stock, although the Ashcraft Mill remained a family business. Cyrus W. Ashcraft, John Thomas Ashcraft, and Erister Ashcraft were the chief officers, and another brother, Lee, served on the board of directors. All other board members were from Florence, except for one man from Charlotte, North Carolina, and one from Savannah, Tennessee.[26]

The Ashcrafts, whose father had been a Clay County farmer and machinist, built a cotton oil company in 1898. In 1899, they expanded their business into a tripartite complex: an oil mill, a cotton ginnery, and a spinning and weaving factory. John Thomas Ashcraft and Cyrus Ashcraft graduated from the State Agricultural and Mechanical College at Auburn. After coming to Florence in 1889 to work as a teacher, John, who had earned a degree in engineering, became a lawyer and provided counsel for Florence businesses. Head of his graduating class in 1888, Cyrus served as president of the Ashcraft Mill. A local newspaper reported the brothers' belief that good southern men should put all of "their means and their skill and their energies into such industries."[27]

As small enterprises, the Cherry and Ashcraft mills did not attempt to create model mill villages. Textile workers lived in Sweetwater, an area of East Florence near the mills on Sweetwater Creek. The Ashcraft Mill provided limited, poor-quality housing for operatives. While Florence propaganda literature characterized "Cotton Mill Hill" as a place where "happiness and contentment reign . . . supreme," the homes were small, clapboard buildings divided by an internal wall to make duplexes rented at twenty-five cents a room. Only mill managers had individual houses.[28]

In the early phase of mill building in Florence, uplift of mill families was not a preoccupation of the mill men.

Mill Men as Town Leaders

Local newspapers presented mill men as town leaders in terms of their commercial contributions, not their social investment in improving workers' lives. In the 1890s, mill men faced no social pressure to help their poor white employees. These businessmen were celebrated simply for their commercial contributions. In Florence, "special industrial editions" of the newspapers featured Noel Cherry, John Ashcraft, and Cyrus Ashcraft as ambassadors of industrial development. A similar industrial edition of the *Birmingham News* praised Braxton Bragg Comer for winning the "full confidence of directors and stockholders and the industry" and for turning a profit "contrary to expectation." The newspaper considered the impact on the workers only by noting that to manufacture fine cloth, Comer's mill had to "train all its help." The *News* said nothing about how the mill provided for operatives other than the assertion that since "pure spring water" was "piped through the mill and village for the use of the help," the village was "cleaner than any in the state."[29]

To point out that mill men were more interested in proprietary progress than philanthropy is not to suggest that they were "old meanies," as Broadus Mitchell accused his critics of portraying the manufacturers. Mill men were profit minded and understood the benefits of a family labor system. At the same time, they believed that they were doing great things for their towns, helping local merchants, bolstering property values, increasing the population, generating real estate booms, and stimulating other industries.[30]

As long as no one questioned mill men's labor practices or defined community progress in terms of greater social and economic progress for the poor, mill men did not often concern themselves with the condition of their employees. Promoters praised mill entrepreneurs primarily for the benefits their efforts would bring to proprietary interests. The *Birmingham News* declared that, "impelled by self-interest and a mutual pride in the upbuilding of the town, the Eastern people, the native land owners and those who invested in the mill vied with each other in the excellence of the improvements they have placed upon their respective properties." When Alabama newspapers emphasized what mills would do for the "community," the writers were referring to what the commercial interests viewed as beneficial.[31]

Mill promoters assumed that employment was benefit enough for laborers and enthused about the jobs created and business stimulated. The *Gadsden Times-News* declared, "Stop and think what [a mill] means for Gadsden and Etowah county! At present nearly 1,000 people are employed in one capacity or another, and the mill is a little city of over 2,000 people. . . . It means work for hundreds of laborers in erecting the plant." During the early 1890s, Alabama newspapers rarely presented cotton mills as means for indigent women and children to sustain themselves. One exception occurred in 1895, when the *Birmingham News* reported that the mills had "given employment every working day in the year to women and children, who else had been [burdens] upon their communities." Newspapers more often stressed the wealth that employment opportunities created for a town. Upon mentioning that the Dwight Mill "would furnish employment for hundreds of thousands of hands," the *Gadsden Tribune* declared that the firm would "create wealth on a greater scale than any other manufacturing interest has ever done." When Dwight shipped silver dollars to Gadsden to meet workers' payrolls, merchants were delighted that laborers might become customers who could pay in cash rather than rely on credit, as many farmers did between harvests. The *Anniston Hot Blast* indicated the potential consumer role imagined for operatives: "Beyond the dividends is the business sustained by the operatives."[32]

These dialogues conform to what Paul M. Gaston has called the "New South creed." The New South creed showed great faith in the ability of "a new economic and social order based on industry and scientific, diversified agriculture" to transform the region into a prosperous, harmonious region. Mill men in the 1890s reflected this creed and were not preoccupied with their philanthropic responsibilities or with "cooperation and social-mindedness."[33] Their community status did not depend on civic-mindedness. With the exception of young northern idealist Howard Gardner Nichols, Alabama's mill men in the 1890s were celebrated as businessmen in a region hungry to prove its competitive capabilities. Organized commercial interests embraced mill entrepreneurs as men of progress because mill building was viewed as in the interest of the property-owning townspeople. Until anti–child labor voices arose, mill operators did not have to worry about proving their social consciousness. In fact, they were men in good standing. When the anti–child labor movement developed and questioned their labor practices, they had a long textile history of paternalism to exaggerate for public relations purposes and a New South creed that bolstered the idea that economic progress brought social progress.

Factory Families

On July 3, 1900, a crowd of "half a thousand people" gathered "to witness the initial run" of brown sheeting, a coarse cotton cloth manufactured by the Ashcraft Cotton Mill. Town boosters billed the day as "Factory Day." Guests toured Florence industries after a bugle-announced welcome at the mill. Factory Day was the prelude to the town's Fourth of July celebration, which included the "old fiddlers'" jamboree at the fairgrounds. The *Florence Herald*'s coverage of the two-day celebration reflected the strength of the town's growing commercial class culture, which emphasized commercial development. A "new industrial club," formed two weeks later, continued Factory Day's celebration of industrial progress.[1]

The fanfare celebrated factory and commercial development rather than factory workers. Workers, who had the Fourth of July off, joined the crowd of two thousand at the fairgrounds. Some operatives may have performed in the old fiddlers' contest. Leroy Brewer, Percy Gooch, John Banes, and Claude Morrison from the factory district of East Florence had formed a string band the previous year. A crew from the pump factory won the tug of war, and other workers may have participated in the wheelbarrow race, potato race, boys' bicycle race, or the "fat men's race." Workers in East Florence had a reputation for drinking "fresh mountain dew," a habit that the *Florence Herald* reported was kept under control for the celebration. Not a "single case of drunkenness or disorderly conduct" disturbed the town.[2] Factory Day celebrated the new town culture, but references to the factory district, with its fiddlers, "dew" drinkers, and concerns about unruly behavior, suggested that the town's commercial class recognized factory workers as a separate class.

The real nature of the emerging class of white wage workers is hard to glean from middle-class oriented newspaper coverage of Factory Day or from reports written by politically motivated reformers. In contrast to the pictures of family disintegration and premature marriages later drawn by reformers, census data show a range of household formations with the common theme of strong kinship networks. Children often remained part of their parents' households well into young adulthood, delaying marriage and procreation. Once young adults married, unmarried siblings or aging parents often became a part of these new households. Families with children too young to work in the mill were the most likely to take in boarders. Census data suggest how children constituted a part of poor families' economic and social strategies. Child labor not only was a carryover from the agricultural traditions of the region but also remained critical for working-class family autonomy and even male independence. Before the rise of a southern anti–child labor movement, workers and employers accepted child labor as the norm, even if they harbored concerns about it. Private letters reveal that mill men organized to stamp out the earliest signs of efforts to limit child labor.

Factory Day's suggestion of underlying class divisions is important for understanding the misleading nature of racial slogans about white unity and white supremacy when it came to the position of southern mill workers. In keeping with the standards of the day, these workers were predominantly white, and race shaped interactions between employees and employers. When reformers began to charge mill men with hurting poor whites, mill interests mythologized race as a key to social harmony between white capitalists and their native-born white workforce. Whiteness, in reality, meant more to the workers than to their employers. Despite propaganda about the virtues of workers' whiteness, mill men were fundamentally interested in cheap labor, not the whiteness of their labor force, and showed interest in hiring nonwhite labor. Conversely, white workers were protective of their claims to whiteness. Instead of creating racial harmony with employers, the issue of race generated conflict between the two groups. Labor militancy, rare in late-nineteenth-century Alabama textile mills, surfaced when employers threatened workers' sense of racial custom and job security with the possibility of hiring African Americans.

New South Mill Families

Wage laborers were a small minority of Alabama's population at the turn of the twentieth century. Of the state's total 1900 population of 1,828,697, only 2.9 percent were wage earners in manufacturing establishments. In comparison, wage earners comprised 17.7 percent of Massachusetts' population. The cotton textile industry was the third-largest employer of wage laborers in Alabama nationally behind the iron and steel industry and the lumber industry. Even after the industrial boom in East Florence, which brought iron, steel, and cotton production to the area, wage earners constituted only 9.2 percent of the town's population. Cotton mill laborers comprised only a small minority of the state's population but were significant for their growing numbers. The U.S. census reported that Alabama's wage-earning class had increased by just over 200 percent between 1890 and 1900.[3]

Cotton mill wage laborers, in particular, were conspicuous because they were white. Although cotton mills hired African Americans for outdoor work, native-born white farm families from Alabama, Tennessee, and Georgia formed the majority of the textile workforce and the majority of the population in mill towns. A photograph taken at the Dwight Mills in Alabama City shows black and white workers, but the African Americans in the photograph likely lived in a nearby community. The 1900 census shows only five households in Alabama City headed by African Americans and a total of only twenty-one African Americans. Most of these blacks identified themselves as washerwomen, servants, and day laborers, although one man was a teamster and may have worked for the mill. African Americans may have commuted from surrounding areas for outdoor jobs, but Alabama City was a white town. The state also had few immigrant workers: Avondale, on the outskirts of Birmingham, boasted one of Alabama's largest mills but had only 33 foreign-born citizens out of a total population of 3,060, and only 90 of Florence's more than 6,000 citizens had been born outside the United States. Thus, immigrant labor was not a significant option in these New South mill villages.[4]

Mill agents recruited native-born whites from the surrounding areas.

The Winters, Robinet, and Roberts families were typical of Florence's new workforce, rural whites who represented the first generations in their families to live in town. Natives of Alabama, Joseph Winters and his two daughters, Susan, age seventeen, and Estelle, age fourteen, worked in the mill while his wife, Sarah, worked at home. Andrew Robinet and his family moved to Florence from Tennessee. He worked in the local wagon shop, and his wife worked at home, while his three oldest daughters, ages sixteen through twenty-five, worked in the cotton mill. Cauman Roberts also worked at the wagon works as a wheel builder. Originally from Indiana, he married an Alabama woman named Annie, and they had five children. Their thirteen- and fourteen-year-old daughters worked as spinners in the Florence cotton mills.[5]

Mill families were working families. While the mother might work at home, the men and children of various ages were expected to work for wages in mills or other nearby industries. In Alabama City, most male heads of household worked with their children in the Dwight Mill, whereas Florence's mills were smaller and men found work elsewhere. According to the 1900 census, of the 233 male heads of households in Alabama City in 1900, 155 worked for the cotton mill, 65 worked elsewhere, and 13 had no occupation listed. The Jones family was typical. The thirty-seven-year-old father worked in the mill, while his wife was at home with their youngest children. Their nineteen-, seventeen-, thirteen-, and eleven-year-old children worked in the mill, and their eight- and nine-year-olds attended school. Ten years later, the patterns remained the same. Dilard Mathies was a spinner in the Alabama City mill. His oldest daughter, Eva, age thirteen, also worked as a spinner, while Mattie, his wife, worked at home and cared for their three youngest children. Wiley Dinnas had a skilled position in the cotton mill. His wife, Annie, took care of their four youngest children and worked at home. Their other four children, ages twelve through sixteen, worked in the mill. The Dinnas and Jones families were larger than the average southern textile family, which included 5.1 persons. Alabama City's male-headed households averaged 6 members, and female-headed households averaged 7. At the Dwight Mill, 66.5 percent of male-headed households had 6 or more members, and only about 10 percent of families in Alabama City had only very young children (age nine or under). While some of the large household size is explained by the addition of boarders, large families with employable children were the norm.[6]

The 1900 census data from Alabama City suggest that mill workers waited until they reached their twenties and early thirties to marry and have children, and 30 percent of the town's cotton mill households included children age twenty-one or older living with their parents. The ages of the male heads of households offer further evidence of delayed marriage: of the 233 male heads of household, 53 were under age thirty, 20 were twenty-three or younger, and only 1 was under twenty. Marriage and procreation were delayed because family responsibilities and poverty caused young couples to have difficulty establishing independent households.[7]

The 1910 U.S. Bureau of Labor study of women and child laborers, the most comprehensive accounting of textile workers, showed a rise in the proportion of men in the industry. The change resulted from the growth of the family labor system in the southern textile states and the significant increase in southern industry. Children continued to work in the mills into adulthood, providing a stable supply of trained workers and increasing the number of male workers. By 1905 men comprised 45.5 percent of the textile labor force in the southern states, increasing in absolute numbers from 4,633 in 1880 to 54,621 in 1905. Women comprised 31.6 of the workforce, growing from 7,587 in 1880 to 37,918 in 1905. Over this period, the number of child laborers increased from 4,097 to 27,571, making them 22.9 percent of the labor force in 1905, down slightly from 25 percent in 1900.[8]

At the Dwight Mill in Alabama City, children represented a significant component of the labor force. Children fifteen years old or younger comprised 29.5 percent of the Dwight workforce in 1900, and eight- to thirteen-year-olds made up 20 percent of the employees. These numbers are based on every person identified as working for the cotton mill in 1900 in census records for Alabama City. If managers and bookkeepers were excluded from the total, the percentage of children would rise slightly. Most children worked, and even those who were not employed rarely attended school. As figure 2 shows, children not at work did not necessarily attend school. Although sixty-two Alabama City children aged fifteen or younger were in school, ninety-four neither attended school nor worked. The first Alabama factory inspector's report in 1909 confirms this youthful character of mill workers throughout the state, finding that four hundred of Lannett Mills' one thousand employees were between the ages of twelve and eighteen. Younger children not on the payroll likely could be found in the mill as unpaid "helpers." The shortage of immigrants and skilled older women, along with the large size of southern families, contributed to the increase of children as a proportion of the workforce.[9]

Throughout the last decade of the nineteenth century, southern states had the highest proportion of child laborers of any section. The southern cotton mills employed more than 60 percent of all children under sixteen years of age in the U.S. textile industry in 1900. Alabama's mills, which were predominately yarn mills where only spinning was required, tended to have a greater percentage of child laborers because spinning required less skill than weaving. A 1912 investigation found that Alabama had the highest percentage of children ages twelve and thirteen in the mills. The U.S. Bureau of Labor report found that of the Alabama mills investigated, 92 percent of twelve- and thirteen-year-olds in mill families were employed, compared with 44.9 percent of North Carolina's children of those ages. Data from the Dwight Mill support these statistics. In 1900, 86 percent of the twelve- and thirteen-year-olds in Alabama City who lived in cotton mill households worked in the mill.[10]

Married women with children rarely worked in the cotton mills. One study found that even when the father's contribution to household income was questionable, only 13 percent of married women worked in the textile industry. Analysis of the 1900 census data regarding the Dwight Mill population supports this finding: of the 221 wives in cotton mill families, 207 listed no occupation; the remaining 14 women worked in the cotton mill, and most of these workers had no children. Of the 50 female heads of cotton mill households, only 9 worked outside the home, 8 of them in the mill. The women and girls in the mills were young and single. Slightly more than 60 percent of all female employees were under the age of twenty-one. In a typical Alabama City household headed by a woman, Mary Broom, whose youngest child was two and who was not employed outside the home, was the head of a six-member household that also included her twenty-three-year-old son, who was a mill employee, and his wife. Mary's daughters, Lola and Mary, ages sixteen and fourteen, also worked in the mill. Women in Florence followed the same trend. Jane Jones and her sister did not work in the Florence cotton mill after Jane's husband died, but Jane's four grown daughters worked at the mill and supported their mother and aunt with the help of their brother, a farmhand. Jones lived near Cornelia Fields, also head

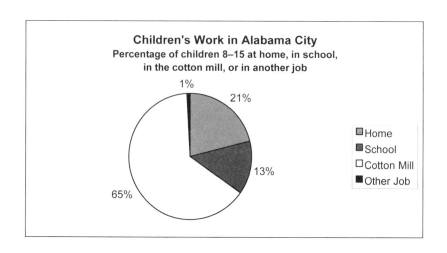

Children's Work in Alabama City
Percentage of children 8–15 at home, in school, in the cotton mill, or in another job

1%
21%
13%
65%

- Home
- School
- Cotton Mill
- Other Job

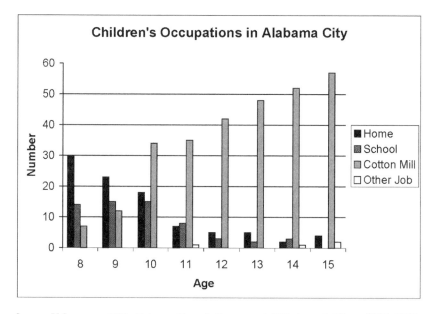

Children's Occupations in Alabama City

- Home
- School
- Cotton Mill
- Other Job

Number

Age

Source: U.S. census, 1900, Alabama, Etowah County, e.d. 165, sheets 1–27, pp. 273A–296B.

of her household. Fields's two oldest daughters, eighteen-year-old Jackie and fifteen-year-old Lurnett, worked in the mill. Their twelve-year-old sister likely would soon join them at work.[11]

Mill families worked in the mills because this employment offered steady wages, unlike the uncertainty of farming. Agricultural opportunities were declining in Alabama and Georgia in the late 1890s. Although mill wages were low, if multiple family members worked for wages, the overall economic gain could be greater than when the entire family worked on a farm. In many cases the families had been "eking out . . . a wretched existence from small and barren patches of land" before coming to the mill. Whatever housing, schooling, and wages the mills offered did not have to be of high quality to be an improvement over extreme poverty. In the mountain regions of Alabama, Tennessee, and Georgia, from which a part of the labor force of the cotton mills was recruited, investigators found "hard conditions of life." Of the 844 families surveyed in such rural areas, 487 owned the small farms on which they lived, while 357 rented. Five hundred seventy-six of the families' houses consisted only of one or two rooms, with multiple persons sleeping in one room. The U.S. Bureau of Labor report described the houses as "of the most primitive character and destitute of the simplest necessary conveniences": 279 lacked even a single window, and more than 90 percent lacked indoor toilets.[12]

From the 1890s through the early 1900s, some of the farm families who became mill workers continued to think of themselves as struggling farmers even as they became factory laborers. Mill work could be a new strategy to support old agricultural ways. It was not uncommon for fathers to continue to farm while daughters worked in the mill. Samuel Kelly, his wife, and two of his daughters were tenant farmers while Mattie, his youngest daughter, was a spinner in Florence. Other families worked temporarily in the mills while waiting until conditions improved for farming, and employers complained of families leaving seasonally. By the early 1910s, however, the U.S. Bureau of Labor concluded that it was becoming unusual for families to spend long periods of time away from the cotton mills "after having once worked in them."[13]

Between 1900 and 1910 mill workers became an identifiable working class in which even the skilled workers were socially separate from the commercial class. The *Florence Herald* recognized this division between the working class and middle class by having a separate section on industrial East Florence, "The News from East Florence," that maintained the distinctions by providing social and other news for the skilled workers. For example, the column included the announcement that the "boss spinner at the Cherry Cotton Mills, Herbert L. Holden, is the proudest man in East Florence. He has a new baby girl." In addition, the paper reported that J. E. Yon of Edgefield, North Carolina, was coming to be "boss carder," the manager of the room where raw cotton was carded or brushed before being spun. "The News from East Florence" rarely identified unskilled women, youths, or male laborers. An ordinary mill woman might make the column if she fell sick or died from the measles, mumps, or pneumonia, common health problems: Rosa L. Darby made the news because she died at the age of twenty. Ordinary workers could also write themselves into the town newspaper by violating social norms. "A man by the name of Price" made the news when his "mind became unbalanced on Cherry Hill" and he "destroyed the furniture in his house, running his wife and children off."[14]

When the *Florence Herald* reported on ordinary workers, the paper was patronizing. For example, when reporting layoffs at the Cherry Mill, on one hand columnist Max Halifax acknowledged a "badly demoralized" night force, raising a question about the validity of the employers' excuse that the workers had been fired for "unsatisfactory work." On the other hand, the columnist ultimately sided with the mill's decision, concluding that "your correspondent believes it will be best for [the workers] in the end." As more and more family members stayed permanently at the mills, they became an identifiable working class. As one report declared, "There seems to be an insurmountable stone wall between the townspeople and the factory hands."[15]

"The Cracker Is the Descendent of the Cavalier"

Despite the fact that the majority of factory families were white, class stratification increasingly designated these workers as the Other whites. The white middle class saw poor whites becoming a class apart, an irony in a region where Jim Crow laws sought to ensure white supremacy and politicians promised white unity. The term *cracker,* used disparagingly to refer to lower-class whites who allegedly shunned work, expressed the social marginalization and racial inferiority that set mill workers apart.

The cracker represented backwoods depravity. Isolated in the hilly farming areas of northern Alabama, Georgia, and Tennessee, he had allegedly grown lazy, ignorant, and morally suspect to the point that he was inferior to "regular" whites. *Cracker* had connotations of racial inferiority because the stereotype included physical and mental deterioration. According to Connecticut's John William De Forest, who worked for the Freedmen's Bureau in 1866, crackers were "ungainly" and "stooping and clumsy in build." Cracker women were "yellow-faced" and "gaunt and ragged."[16] As the Other, crackers became the whites to be hired for low-paying, low-status, wage-labor jobs in the cotton mills. Mill men could advertise that workers were native-born whites while suggesting that these were not the type of people associated with certain privileges.

The whiteness of the southern textile workforce first became an issue as a way of promoting southern development, a potential lure for northern investment. When southern boosters recognized that race could make the cracker an appealing laborer, they stressed his whiteness and capacity for sobriety and industriousness. But New South boosters also had to overcome the image of the cracker as shiftless. Rather than lazy and defective, southern manufacturing interests marketed southern laborers as excellent alternatives to immigrant—and, therefore, supposedly more troublesome—workers. Joseph J. Willett, president of the Alabama Bar Association and big booster of the New South town of Anniston, boasted of the South's labor force when he spoke to New York's Brooklyn Democratic Club: The "wife and daughter of the so-called 'Southern crackers' have proved to be the very best cotton mill help in the world." His hesitation about *cracker* suggested the dilemma of applying a label of racial inferiority to a group touted as a superior workforce.[17]

Criticism of the immigrant workforce in northern factories fueled the promotion of southern workers' whiteness. Northern manufacturers moved South because of the inexpensive labor market but conveniently emphasized the whiteness of southern operatives as a way of criticizing labor in the North, since the mill operators blamed the immigrant workforce for labor problems. In an article announcing the expected arrival of a number of eastern companies, Massachusetts businessman T. Jefferson Coolidge complained that industry was "hampered [in Massachusetts] by trade unions, strikes and legislation, making it more difficult for us to manufacture at a profit and until the legislature of this state, instead of doing all it can to injure manufacturers, turns around and assists them, there will be a further loss of business." In contrast, northern manufacturers argued that southern native-born white workers would be more obedient and trustworthy. The Dwight Company's treasurer, J. Howard Nichols, suggested as much when he stated a preference for the southern "white hands . . . from the mountain districts" because they were "more intelligent than [laborers] in northern mills."[18]

Southern commercial boosters pandered to such sentiments, using race as a trope to overcome stereotypes of the cracker as lazy. The 1892 *Hand-Book of Alabama,* for example, argued that while some northerners considered southern operatives too lazy and ignorant to be good workers, such was not the case. "The *south* knows better," the book reported. "Thousands upon thousands of young children and young women stand anxiously idle for want of *opportunity.*" The *Birmingham Age-Herald* declared, "The cracker is the descendent of the cavalier." "They have strayed from the fold," the piece suggested, "but blood will tell." The new cracker was still the Other white and, therefore, could be treated with less regard, but he was not lazy or physically or mentally inferior. Propaganda made him attractive to employers by discussing "his love of home, his constancy, his devotion . . . his flashes of intelligence in the depth of his ignorance." According to the *Age-Herald,* "shrewd New Englanders" had discovered "what splendid cotton mill hands these crackers would make!" In contrast, "the negro" was too undependable "to run our Southern mills, for he is sleepy and loves to roam. . . . The cracker and his wife and daughter fill the bill exactly." Once "an ugly duckling," the piece concluded, the cracker had become "the swan."[19]

Mill owners tried to take credit for hiring poor whites over blacks even though evidence suggests that if even cheaper labor had been easily available, it would have been used. Justifying resistance to labor regulation, manufacturers' representatives contended at a 1902 congressional hearing that they had been doing southern whites a favor by hiring them and should consequently be left alone. North Carolina manufacturer Lewis Parker argued that "negro labor was feasible . . . and would be cheapest," but "the managements have recognized the fact that the mill life is the only avenue open today to our poor whites, and we have with earnestness and practically without exception kept that avenue open to the white man alone." Evidence suggests otherwise. The Dwight Company's Alabama agent, R. A. Mitchell, eagerly attempted to hire immigrant labor and served on Birmingham Commercial Club's immigration committee.[20] Efforts to recruit immigrant laborers to the southern textile industry were largely unsuccessful, however, and the Dwight Alabama mill never attracted significant numbers of immigrants.

The Dwight Mill and other Alabama mills hired white families almost exclusively for "indoor work" yet employed African Americans for janitorial and "outdoor" jobs and were eager to violate the color line when doing so was convenient. And even though recruitment propaganda encouraged manufacturers to view native white labor as superior, companies did not find southern workers to be superior. Howard Gardner Nichols acknowledged that while "some stress is laid on the quality of the help" in Alabama, he was "not wholey convinced" that "as a rule it is superior to" the quality of northern workers. In fact, he contradicted propaganda when he said, "On the average our northern help will do a larger day's work than the help" in Alabama.[21]

Manufacturers' preference for white labor was self-interested, not altruistic. Mill men protested proposals for a convict farm mill on the basis that it would be "very detrimental to the interests of laboring white help," but these operators were also worried about competition from a state-run mill. More convincing evidence suggests that manufacturers worried that white workers would become militant if African Americans were hired for comparable positions. The proximity of potential black replacements along with the willingness of mill men to hire African Americans for certain jobs led I. A. Newby to argue that white workers ensured that only whites were hired for indoor mill work by engaging in militant protest and manipulation of racial customs. Workers were most likely to protest and find community support when a labor dispute involved threats to hire blacks. White employees forced mill owners to sacrifice the immediate profit of hiring cheaper black workers.[22]

One Alabama incident supports the thesis that introducing black laborers into the indoor work space risked racial conflict and disruptions to mill operations. In the spring of 1903, the state restricted child labor under age twelve, and Lannett Mills consequently dismissed 125 underage children, replacing with "several negro women." Even though the black women worked in a side building, white employees reported that they "thought that the change would interfere with their positions and salaries and decided to walk out on a strike." As a result, the mill owners agreed to release the African Americans.[23]

In addition to threatening wages, the introduction of African American laborers in certain spaces of the mill generated conflict because of the nature of the familial and social relationships among white workers. For mill workers, family was the most important social unit, and work was not separated from family life. Family members often worked together alongside neighbors in the spinning and weaving rooms. Histories based on oral interviews clearly show that mill workers developed close social bonds.[24] In part, white workers were protecting these social and familial bonds when they fought efforts to introduce African American workers into racially segregated work spaces.

Manufacturers utilized racial custom to their advantage, one of many such traditions that mill men learned to manipulate. Mill operators learned to honor custom when doing so cost the mill little and enabled them to take advantage of their workers. For example, operatives worked eleven- to twelve-hour days, but mill men allowed temporary work stoppages for special events such as parades, fairs, or revivals that temporarily threatened production schedules; operators sometimes even permitted workers to leave without prior permission.[25] By honoring such desires, manufactures sacrificed a workday but kept workers' grievances from escalating.

Mill men similarly respected racial custom, including violence, that temporarily disrupted work in exchange for labor at long hours and low wages. In Alabama City, the Dwight Mill "had to shut down for the day" when angry white operatives left to pursue a black man taken prisoner for allegedly assaulting a white woman. According to the *Anniston Hot Blast*, the deputy sheriff and a posse had to rush the man to Anniston to protect him from a mob of mill employees that sought to lynch him. The black man escaped, and the workers returned to their jobs the next day, apparently without being reprimanded for leaving the mill.[26] Race was one aspect of a larger cultural context that mill men and workers negotiated so that the latter had some control over their world. Employers nonetheless ultimately controlled their workforce.

Family Strategies and Child Labor

Most people who worked in Alabama's cotton mills had never had any option other than to put all family members to work to sustain the family. Everyone either worked in the household or worked for wages to support the home. Family labor was an accepted social form, and child labor was seen as intrinsically linked to family autonomy. Child labor put food on the table, and in some cases employers required a certain number of family members to work in the mill before providing low-cost housing.[27]

Child labor also offered men a negotiating tool. A man with multiple children could threaten to take his whole family out of the mill, thereby gaining the leverage needed to obtain leave so that he and some of his family members could farm. A family could sell its labor as a package deal and could threaten to move to another mill if an employer would not hire all of the family members that the head of the family wanted to have work for wages. In this way, children's factory work remained critical to a man's independence and potentially to his identity as a farmer rather than a laborer. For the mills, family labor provided adult workers at a low cost, along with their children, whose labor was even cheaper. Mill men did not think primarily in terms of child labor but rather thought in terms of families that could sustain themselves while mill operators adjusted the number of workers to meet market needs.[28] The trade-off was unequal. With few other options, however, mill families accepted the exchange on terms that allowed them to continue customs while offering new opportunities to socialize and to acquire improved housing and schooling.

A study of why children left school to work found that in 173 southern families with working children, only 20 percent worked out of necessity. Children's wages helped families save money to acquire property or to purchase life insurance. The study also found little evidence of idle fathers; however, fathers, the most expensive labor, were the first to be laid off during slack times.[29]

Children's labor softened the blow of unexpected layoffs of male breadwinners or of illness in the family. Kinship networks formed an important safety net in the age when public relief was nonexistent and charitable relief was inadequate and humiliating. Florence native Patricia Bailey described the importance of family members helping each other out. Her foster grandmother, Florence Kelley, worked in the Ashcraft Mill beginning in the early 1900s. On her mill salary, Kelley took care of her mother, her blind sister, and her infant nephew, whose mother had died. Kelley subsequently married a man who also worked in the mill, and the extended family rented one side of a small clapboard house. The child went to work in the mill as soon as he became old enough. When Kelley's father became ill, he joined the already over-crowded household. Kelley's husband balked and sent his father-in-law to the poor farm. Kelley's father died soon thereafter, and she blamed and divorced her husband: to turn one's back on family was a sin. Kelley continued to work in the mills and raise her nephew.[30]

Children worked primarily in the jobs of sweeping (a necessity in lint-filled rooms), doffing (replacing full bobbins on spinning machines with empty ones), and spinning, a position generally held by girls and single women. All of these jobs required children to be at the mill for long hours but permitted periods of play while on the job. One girl began working in a mill at age nine and remembered her father carrying her into the mill for her first day of work: "I just looked and looked and looked 'till my eyes got tired seeing so many different things." Although the jobs were boring and monotonous, she came to like mill work: "I really enjoyed it, I'll tell you the truth. It was something to do." Further-more, her coworkers—family members and neighbors—were interesting and familiar.[31]

Mill operatives did not necessarily work steadily for the full six-day workweek. Employers complained that workers frequently missed "one or two days during the week," and studies found that male mill workers missed approximately one-fifth of the possible work time each year and that females were absent more than one-quarter of the time. While some of the lost work time resulted from layoffs, workers also took time off to fish, hunt, farm, garden, or take care of chores at home. Flexibility, how-ever, came at the price of lost pay, which kept workers impoverished and ultimately dependent on the mill and child labor.[32]

Mill families valued literacy but saw little value in education as a way to improve their situation, and mill recruiters encouraged this attitude. One recruitment flier declared that "a poor man" could send his child to "common-school," and he or she could become a teacher and make $35 per month during the school term. In contrast, "if he or she should learn to be a good weaver," the mill promised "$40 per month for the year." Parents were most likely to send their children to school when education could be blended with work and household strategies. Chil-dren within families would take turns going to school, with one sibling working while the other attended school. Older children and young adults who had not had previous opportunities for education commonly entered the primary grades to achieve basic literacy, with the result that teenagers and young children often studied in the same classrooms in New South primary schools.[33]

Parents had standards for their children's work in the mill. Even though factory families encouraged the hiring of their children, parents still wanted to retain ultimate control. Letters to South Carolina Governor Coleman Livingston Blease reveal that parents debated the precise age at which children should work. According to one mother, nine was too young, but a thirteen-year-old girl was old enough to work if she was not too small in stature. One mother of a thirteen-year-old reasoned that her daughter "could work in the mill while I kept howse and we could make a good living."[34]

Mill management respected parental authority until it became too expensive. Even parents who sought outside legal aid ultimately had little power to hold the mill accountable for its treatment of their children. One mother at the Dwight Mill in Alabama City "brought a suit against the company for $25,000" after her son fell from the mill steps and was injured. Mill agent R. A. Mitchell reported to the home office that he had convinced Mrs. Rutherford of "the futility of pressing her suit any further." Even though he indicated that she had contacted ex-Congressman William H. Denson, "notorious for unrelentingly pressing just such claims," he expected the mill to get her to settle for "a nominal sum, less than $100.00." Mitchell felt sure that the "Rutherfords and others who are cognizant of this suit" had learned "that it is not an easy thing to get money out of the Dwight Company."[35]

If mill folk were accustomed to putting their children to work and mill men were eager to exploit this custom, manufacturers nevertheless felt the need to hide it from the public. Mills hired eight-, nine-, and ten-year-olds but sought to avoid drawing attention to the practice. After the Dwight Mill opened in Alabama City, mill agent R. A. Mitchell made some effort to keep out the youngest children: he reported, "We are making progress in getting rid of small help along personal lines and have instructed the overseer to take no one under ten if it can be avoided." He further advised that it was "best not to give notices we will not employ any under ten rather than formally call attention to the fact that we are working such small help." Mitchell reported that the mill employed more than 162 children, "very few of ten and under." Data provided by parents in the 1900 census confirm the accuracy of this statement, identifying 19 children aged nine or under employed in the mill.[36]

The Beginnings of Reform

Southern town people generally did not welcome criticism of southern cotton mills. Clare De Graffenried, a Georgia-born woman who had moved to Washington, D.C., and become a U.S. Bureau of Labor investigator, published a controversial article, "The Georgia Cracker in the Cotton Mills," in *Century Magazine* in 1891. Based on interviews with Georgia mill workers, De Graffenried described depressed working conditions and equally deplorable home conditions. The legacy of child labor, she argued, was adult women without the skills to make efficient use of the meager domestic resources available. She drew derogatory portraits of workers to make her case. "Everywhere [mill workers] use snuff and tobacco, and subsist on scanty innutritious diet . . . the butt of ridicule, shiftless and inconsequent, always poor though always working."[37]

While the northern press cited the article as an authoritative statement, southerners, the *Manufacturers' Record,* and, most conspicuously, well-known Georgia reformer and WCTU leader Rebecca Latimer Felton reproached De Graffenried. Felton garnered much publicity by arguing that conditions in the mill were an advancement for poor families—an argument that manufacturers would powerfully repeat in the face of the subsequent anti–child labor campaign. At a United Daughters of the Confederacy meeting, Felton declared her indignation at De Graffenried: "When I recollected through what depths these [mill women] had traveled to reach even the wages of cotton mill existence, my feeling of sympathy was raised to the glowing heat of indignation."[38] Felton's response to De Graffenried showed the difficulty in attacking an industry associated with progress in an extremely poor region.

Dwight representatives opposed the earliest signs of protective legislation as a precursor to the sort of regulation they despised in the North. Moreover, given the high number of children working in the mills in 1900, the firm would have had a serious labor shortage if child labor was curtailed. In 1898 Senator J. A. Hurst, a Populist from Etowah County, which housed the new Dwight Mill, sponsored a bill to limit working hours for women and children. Representative Luther C. Jones, a labor union member from Lee County and president of the Phenix City Trades Council, followed suit. Dwight representatives threw the company's weight against the measures although they received almost no publicity. Mitchell referred to Jones as an "anarchist in embryo" and hired two lobbyists to defeat the measures. After Hurst's bill failed, Mitchell sent the Massachusetts office a clipping from the *Birmingham Age-Herald,* bragging, "This is the bill which I defeated." When two months later, a representative proposed eliminating night work for mill children, Mitchell reassured the home office that he had run "down to Montgomery" and convinced the measure's sponsor not "to press his bill."[39]

It was one thing to know that rural folk had been impoverished before coming to the mill, however, and another to encounter their living conditions. In 1899 the *Florence Herald* uncharacteristically reported, "The terrible epidemic of measles . . . which had the manufacturing district of this city in its grasp, has been an object lesson to many." The article applauded the "kindhearted men and women" who volunteered in East Florence and found "children were dying, . . . new families were being stricken, and the suffering was becoming more widespread." The editorial advocated exactly what manufacturers feared would accompany attention to poor white children: labor organizations. The writer asserted, "The real question, the hardest problem, is . . . how to put the people in a position to help themselves." His solution was a law to prohibit the "employment of children in manufacturing establishments," compulsory education, and the organization of labor so that workers could demand "living wages."[40]

Such endorsements of labor organizing were rare among mainstream New South newspapers during the 1890s, but as townspeople discovered the conditions of the mill areas and as diseases from those areas threatened to bleed across neighborhood boundaries, people began to look more closely at the cotton mills. As a result, dialogues about southern cotton mills began to shift from the New South creed that celebrated commercial development with little attention to ordinary laborers to a more complicated debate about the nature of southern progress.

While most southern textile workers were not union members, organized labor first publicized the workers' plight and raised questions about how cotton mills treated their employees. Competition with southern workers jeopardized the status of northern workers, who were more likely to have ties to labor organizations. As a result, organized labor had an investment in identifying and publicizing just how many of these southern laborers were children.

Sentimentalism, Not Socialism

ORGANIZED LABOR INTERJECTED the first dissonant voice into the warm glow of New South discourse about the coming of the cotton mills but did not do so until several years after their arrival. During the 1886–87 legislative session, two Alabama legislators from Mobile, Senator Daniel Smith and Representative T. G. Bush, had introduced legislation that prohibited women and children under eighteen from working more than eight hours a day and banned child labor under age fourteen. There is no evidence that any sort of reform movement lay behind this measure. The bill passed the legislature with little public comment or controversy and became law in February 1887. In 1888 representatives from Elmore County and Autauga County, home of the new Prattville Cotton Mill, established in 1887, asked for and received exemptions to the law, encountering no resistance. The legislation was repealed for the entire state in December 1894, in response to pressure from representatives from Etowah County acting at the behest of the Dwight Manufacturing Company, which was considering moving its operations there. During the winter of 1894, the repeal prompted no public comment.[1]

Not until more than three years later did organized labor begin paying attention. In March 1898, master machinist James O'Connel, vice president of the state American Federation of Labor (AFL), declared, "What a sad commentary upon our manhood, when little children under the age of fourteen have to support families while the fathers have to tramp the country in search of work." He also called the repeal "one of the most damnable violations of the law of man and of God."

44

According to O'Connel, labor needed to organize to combat the situation.[2]

Organized labor opposed the rise of child labor as part of a larger fight against what the *Birmingham Labor Advocate*'s managing editor, J. M. F. Mosley, called the "love of money"—"the basic evil" behind all of labor's "destruction." Trade unionists recognized how the family labor system depressed wages, arguing that a greedy capitalist class hired children, threatened to enslave working men, and pauperized working people. Unlike the middle class, which celebrated industrial progress, organized labor contended that a rapacious appetite for money had corrupted the "men who pretend to be Christian gentlemen." Trade unionists chastised the commercial classes for failing to save the "helpless children . . . who appeal for deliverance from a child-labor bondage." Child labor inflicted "mental, physical and moral ruin," compounding the "agonies of pain, hunger and other privations entailed by the existing conditions in certain mills and factories in Alabama," declared the *Labor Advocate*.[3]

Organized labor was genuinely enraged, but the timing of the outcry reflected a larger concern lurking behind the sudden attention to child labor: the impact of the South's cheap labor on New England's organized textile workers. By 1898 Samuel Gompers, president of the AFL, focused on child labor in the South because of the larger issue of the impact of cheap southern labor on organized northern workers, an AFL constituency. Textile workers in New Bedford, Massachusetts, struck because employers had slashed wages by 10 percent, blaming southern competition. The AFL took the defensive, warning employers that textile workers would respond with agitation and efforts to organize the South.[4] The *Birmingham Labor Advocate* publicized the AFL's concerns by printing articles about the pain that the southern labor situation was causing at home and in New England.

In 1898 the *Labor Advocate* urged a radical labor politics, alleging that the industry's eagerness to hire the cheap labor of the South's "most ignorant, illiterate and poverty stricken" people lay at the root of the problem. The paper thundered, "Nothing else could more plainly expose the rottenness of the capitalistic system and the necessity for solidarity among the workers of all sections than this latest reduction in wages of the mill workers of New England." The article urged all workers to "unite as a class in their organization and at the Ballot Box and vote for nothing less than the Co-operative commonwealth."[5]

The AFL initiated the South's first anti–child labor campaign in the midst of such labor fervor. By the end of the nineteenth century, Gompers had adopted a practical approach to reform and was uneasy about how to manage local radicalism. He wanted to encourage labor organization without supporting an insurgent labor politics. While the AFL increased support for organized labor's efforts among southern textile workers, he ultimately selected a southern strategy that separated the child labor issue from a larger labor agenda. In short, Gompers chose the route of sentimentalism over socialism.

In 1902 he stood before a conference of the United Textile Workers of America and announced, "in confidence," that the "fight in Alabama has been conducted . . . so that it would appear that the labor movement, as such, was not making the fight, but that the sentimental, the Christian, the noble, the public spirited citizens were making the fight, but we were paying for the fiddler."[6] Gompers was referring to the work of Irene Ashby, an Englishwoman hired to investigate cotton mills in Alabama and to broaden support for child labor restrictions by attracting middle-class men and women's groups.

Gompers focused the fight in Alabama in part to draw attention to Massachusetts. While Alabama was known for its iron and coal and had fewer spindles than did other Piedmont cotton textile states, Massachusetts manufacturers owned many of Alabama's mills. Gompers hoped to put national pressure on the Massachusetts-dominated industry by sending Ashby to expose its practice of moving South to exploit the region's cheap labor.

In 1898, a month before Birmingham's O'Connel spoke out, Gompers published an editorial, "The Crime of '94–95," in the *American Federationist,* the official AFL organ. This piece constituted the first significant denunciation of the repeal of Alabama's 1886 labor law. The AFL president chastised the sponsor of the repeal for saying, "Eastern capital may now be invited South without having the disadvantage of the restriction in the hours of labor of women and children." Gompers called the repeal abominable and urged labor to take an interest in the situation.[7]

Socialist Threat and Southern Exceptionalism

Even though Gompers initially awakened labor to the issue of child workers in the South, he ultimately restrained a radical response because of his desire to avoid the politicization of labor, his interpretation of the South, his gendered view of trade unionism, and his fears that radical labor politics were more likely to ignite a political backlash against the work of trade unionists. Gompers knew that radical labor politics had no chance of success in Alabama. In fact, he saw radicalism on child labor as a potential barrier to enlisting middle-class reformers, whom he felt had a better chance than organized labor did at winning protective legislation for women and children. By the 1890s, the AFL had already joined with reformers to fight for protective legislation for women and children in other parts of the country.[8] Gompers wanted to encourage a more broad based reform effort in Alabama even if it meant muzzling Birmingham's most outspoken labor leaders.

As the situation among Massachusetts textile workers worsened, the crisis threatened to destroy negotiations between the International Union of Textile Workers (IUTW) and the New England–based National Federation of Textile Operatives, which were in the process of forming a national union affiliated with the AFL. Gompers, committed to "pure and simple" trade unionism, opposed an independent labor party and wanted a national textile union affiliated with the AFL. Yet Socialist Daniel De Leon took the New Bedford strike as an opportunity to urge support for the Socialist Labor Party, to declare trade unions inadequate as long as the surplus of labor impeded their bargaining power, and to arouse support for his cause with what one historian called a "virtuoso performance." De Leon's threat to Gompers was serious. In 1897 the *American Federationist* had reported turbulent debate over whether textile workers should affiliate with the Socialists or the AFL.[9]

A pragmatist, Gompers believed that organized labor acting alone had little chance of winning protective legislation, especially in the South. Given white Democrats' political dominance in the southern states and the lack of success of the recent Populist insurgence, he did not want labor to become too invested in a legislative campaign. He needed to show that he was addressing the southern problem and thought the South's "public spirited citizens" would have to be won over to the cause.

As long as women and children dominated the southern workforce, Gompers did not believe that organizing would work because his views were based on a gendered trade unionist model in which a male bread-winner supported his entire family; Gompers thus had no interest in organizing women. When AFL-supported IUTW efforts to organize southern textile workers met with limited success, Gompers concluded that protective legislation was necessary to make trade unionism possible in the southern textile industry, and he hired Ashby to broaden support for child labor reform. Gompers also hoped that publicity about the South's child labor problem from the region's respectable citizens, particularly middle-class women, would increase the chances of passage of a federal uniform-hours law to standardize the length of the industrial workday. The time seemed ripe for a federal law because by 1898, some New England cotton manufacturers hurt by southern competition, including those in the Arkwright Club, a political interest group of the industry's largest companies, were beginning to see such legislation as in their interest. In 1874, large Massachusetts mills had benefited from laws limiting employees to ten hours of work per day, which bigger enterprises could accommodate more easily than could smaller competitors. By the 1890s, however, those large Massachusetts mills faced competition from southern operations, and cotton manufacturers, represented by the Arkwright Club, began to lobby for federally mandated hour limits across the industry as a way to limit one of the South's competitive advantages.[10]

Uniform Hours and the Emergence of the Child Labor Problem

Organized labor in general had a long history of opposing child labor. An early article on child labor in the *American Federationist* had warned that the "kid glove reformer" did not go far enough: "He brings about some few mitigating conditions . . . and this is the statute of his limitations." "The trades unionist," in contrast, "puts his foot down and demands from the politician the abolition of child labor." However, Gompers did not recognize that the child labor issue could generate support for regulation of southern industry until he collaborated with the Arkwright Club in 1898 for a uniform-hours-of-labor law. The federal legislation regarding uniform hours in manufacturing was sponsored by U.S. Representative William C. Lovering, a Republican from Massachusetts whose family had been in the cotton manufacturing business since 1837 and who had served as president and manager of the Whittenton Manufacturing Company and as chair of the Arkwright Club. Lovering couched his stand in moral terms, joining Gompers to argue "the social, the sanitary, and the humanitarian" side of the issue, although uniform hours would also personally benefit Lovering. At stake, the two men argued, was whether the textile industry would degrade workers or aspire to standards established by the better mills in Massachusetts. Lovering and Gompers initially did not even mention child labor.[11]

Testifying before the U.S. House Committee on the Judiciary, James L. Orr, president of the Piedmont Manufacturing Company, inadvertently introduced child labor to the debate over Lovering's bill. Orr began his testimony with a typical southern paternalistic defense of mill practices but ran into trouble when a representative pressed for the ages of Orr's employees. On the defensive, Orr pulled out a standard argument about white unity: employers and employees were one big family characterized by "sympathy between the management of the mills and the employees of the mills" because they were the "same breed and blood." He unintentionally fumbled by concluding that the long hours did not risk the health of workers because "they have worked in those mills since they were children."[12]

Orr's humanitarian defense suddenly took on the face of a child. "How old are the children that are employed?" a committee member asked. Orr answered, "We take them when they are twelve years old for spinners and sweepers." A committee member drove home the point: "I think eleven hours of labor a day is too much to exact of a person twelve years old, whether in the South or in the North, and that no law is humane that exacts sixty-six hours of work per week from a person twelve years old." It became clear that the paternal defense was not an adequate apology for child labor. As a committee member asked, "How are they going to have any time to take advantage of the churches and libraries and gymnasiums that you give them if they work sixty-six hours a week?"[13]

Samuel Ross, secretary of the National Mule Spinners Association, picked up on the child labor theme. He offered himself as proof of the connection between shorter hours and enlightened citizenship. "Take me for a sample," he said. "Ten years ago, when I came to this country, I could not write my own name. . . . I began to utilize my spare time which the laws of Massachusetts gave me; and, in doing so, it was not long until I was able to read the Constitution and write my own name." Yet according to 1890 census data, he warned, "there has been no progress made South with regard to child labor since 1880." Ross was thus introducing a theme of southern backwardness: "I believe there is more child labor in the southern manufacturing establishments than in the North. Those children labor under many disadvantages if they undertake to educate themselves."[14]

The 1898 congressional hearings exposed the potential for the South's white child labor to become a symbol of the southern industry's degrading working conditions. Trade unionism was based on the ideal of the robust, manly wage earner. The white child laborer, often a girl spinner, was the antithesis of the dignified male worker and had the potential to become the righteous image of the enslavement of white wage workers. The emasculation of white male free labor was at stake in the South's fastest growing industry. Furthermore, public-minded citizens were sensitive about the South's image, and the issue of child labor could enable organized labor to send the message that industrial progress could foster social backwardness if children remained illiterate.[15]

Organized labor appeared to have much to gain and nothing to lose from increased publicity regarding child labor in the southern cotton mills. If citizens opposed trade unionism, they nevertheless might be alarmed about the impact of child labor on white southern manhood. If opponents of shorter hours argued that mill owners offered more for operatives than they had been able to provide for themselves, the issue of child labor made it more difficult to defend the industry's beneficence as a substitute for a living wage.

Trade Unionists' Fight to Abolish Child Labor

In 1898, trade unionists were in a position to make the southern cotton mill child the symbol of the enslavement of white southern textile workers. While Gompers did not support an independent labor politics, he followed the historical practices of the U.S. and British trade union movements, believing that organized labor should support legislation to restrict women and children's labor, while men should win shorter hours for themselves. Since women and children were dependent, unskilled workers who moved in and out of paying jobs, Gompers assumed that they were unlikely to achieve shorter hours through unionism. Moreover, Gompers viewed women's labor as dangerous to men by tending to reduce their wages and threaten their manhood.[16]

In 1898, Gompers stepped up the AFL's support of organizing in the South and called on Birmingham's established trade union movement to promote upcoming legislation on the labor of women and children. In May 1899, the *American Federationist* reported that three organizers had been hired for the "herculean yet delicate mission" of organizing in the South. One of these organizers was Prince Greene, of Phenix City, Alabama, who had been elected vice president of the IUTW in 1897 and had helped stave off the movement to join the Socialists. Greene, who shared Gompers's pragmatism, became a key influence on the AFL approach to child labor in the South.[17]

In January 1899, Gompers sent a circular to union members in Alabama: "We have a friend and union member in the Alabama Legislature by the name of Luther C. Jones." Representative Jones, president of the Phenix City Trades Council, supported a bill to limit hours of labor to ten per day in factories, mills, and workshops. Jones, one mill man claimed, had "his pockets stuffed with several different labor papers, was well aware of the crisis among textile workers." Gompers supported Jones and believed that he would help awaken labor organization in the state. "The passage of the laws at this time," Gompers argued, "will simply encourage the workers to more thoroughly organize, and at the next Legislative session a bill to reduce the hours of labor for women and children can be surely passed." Although J. A. Hurst, a Populist, replicated Jones's efforts in the state senate, all labor measures failed.[18]

In the face of failure, organized labor had an interest in portraying the southern textile workforce as helpless. As organizing efforts floundered, organizers constructed an image of a southern textile workforce composed of oppressed young women and forlorn, unhealthy children. The AFL needed such a gendered image to mobilize support from the recently formed and AFL-affiliated national United Textile Workers, whose support Gompers and Greene feared losing in the wake of defeats in Augusta, Georgia, in 1899 and Danville, Virginia, in 1900.[19]

Desperately fearing that organized labor would give up on the South after such glaring defeats, Greene stressed southern workers helplessness as a means of urging outside help. It was easier for organized labor to publicize the plight of women and child workers as pathetic in hopes of provoking support than to expose the mountain of barriers to organizing efforts that might discourage support from national unions. A subsequent AFL investigation of the Danville failure showed that union lists included male carpenters, machinists, saloonkeepers, preachers, lawyers, and doctors who were pushing different agendas, while the "needs

51

and welfare of men, women and children on strike for better conditions were practically lost sight of." Greene had successfully organized women workers in Danville, but rather than stressing the potential for women to organize or the internal conflicts within local unions, it was expedient to blame failure on women and children with the hope that greater support could be generated for those portrayed as unable to help themselves. In an appeal for support, a Danville union leader emphasized, "A large number of our members are women and children who have been compelled to work the long hours at wages that would hardly afford them a bare living, and they are unprepared to meet an emergency of this kind. We therefore appeal to you for assistance." Ignoring the men on Danville's union lists, Greene depicted the workforce as composed virtually entirely of women and "little, pale, pinched-faced children laboring the long hours, with no hopes of ever becoming anything more than tramps or criminals." The image of little children working "all day and both ends of the night" became the symbol of the dependent state of southern textile workers. As the *Labor Advocate* explained, child labor led to illiteracy, and illiteracy led "to dependence and dependence to serfdom." "To come up in ignorance," explained another editorial, meant that "of necessity they must be social slaves, the tools of unscrupulous capitalists." In the *American Federationist*, A. S. Leitch described the "moral hideousness of child labor" that produced the dividends for the "aristocratic stockholders of 'hell's mills' of the South."[20]

This reference to "aristocratic" mill owners suggested that child labor was the new slavery in the New South. One 1899 *Labor Advocate* editorial disparaged Braxton Bragg Comer's Avondale Mills near Birmingham for attracting people "from the country by the promise of fair wages," only to cut wages once the "too-poor-to-move-away mill population" was hired in sufficient numbers. The high rates of child labor demonstrated the poverty and helplessness of the operatives. "The mill people have no organization among themselves and are utterly and completely at the mercy of 'the company,'" argued the paper, urging passage of a child labor law.[21]

Gompers began encouraging the *Birmingham Labor Advocate* and state representative James H. Leath, former president of the Birmingham Trades Council, to narrow the focus of restrictive legislation in Alabama to children under thirteen. In the fall of 1900, Leath introduced a new child labor bill that provided the framework for the 1901 child labor measure around which an anti–child labor campaign began to form in the state. Leath's legislation prohibited children under thirteen in factories, mines, and workshops. The *Labor Advocate*'s editor, J. M. F. Mosley, met with Gompers at the AFL's national headquarters in Washington, D.C., to obtain guidance on how to proceed on the child labor issue.[22]

At the turn of the century, organized labor in Birmingham seemed to be on its way to leading a southern anti–child labor campaign. The city's level of labor organizing activity was unique in the South. The United Mine Workers (with its volatile interracial unionism), the Birmingham Trades Council, and a recent history of organizing by the Knights of Labor and the Greenback-Labor Party made Birmingham a likely southern place at which labor radicalism on child labor could surface. In 1896, a heated political year, Birmingham miners had initiated the idea of an independent labor ticket at a meeting that featured intense debate about child labor and the weakness of Alabama labor laws.[23]

The Birmingham Trades Council, with its organ, the *Labor Advocate*, was the city's central labor organizing body and made organized labor a visible presence with political muscle and labor celebrations. The council sponsored the city's first Labor Day parade on May 1, 1890, and celebrated Eugene V. Debs's 1895 release from jail with a procession led by the Pratt City Band (union musicians). The group had initiated the struggle for child labor legislation in Alabama, holding "lively discussion" about child labor laws as early as 1896, and used its position and its publication to appeal for child labor legislation.[24]

The *Labor Advocate* used several strategies in its campaign against child labor. First, the publication used the cultural cadences of southern Protestantism. When "the Carpenter of Nazareth" proclaimed the "Golden Rule," no one could have imagined that "cotton mills would some day be erected in Alabama, and that somebody's little children would be pressed into service to operate them," declared one article. The paper declared that anyone who had children should stand up for a child labor law, remembering that the "children of the poor are just as dear to them as the children of the rich are dear to their parents." The *Labor Advocate* also incorporated the language of nostalgia for the Old South that characterized so much New South social commentary. A tenet of this nostalgia was to harken back to days of white unity, to recall notions of a white southern family, and to evoke southern pride and patriotism. One editorial reprimanded ministers for not protesting "against the wholesale sacrifice by the textile mill Juggernaut of American children," recalling a former era "when Alabama would not have tolerated" child labor. In bygone days, the "Alabama white man was best," and "down to the last drop of an Alabamian's blood, her children should be protected from wrong."

Furthermore, the *Labor Advocate* made the issue of child labor central to the broader problem of low wages that kept families impoverished, dramatizing the plight of the new white industrial working class: "The truth of the matter is that child labor has done more to lower wages than any other element which has entered into the problem." Organized labor urged support for a child labor law before Birmingham took its place beside "Atlanta and Augusta, which are just now rivaling each other in the horrors of mill squalor."[25]

When the Alabama legislature failed to seriously address child labor legislation in 1898 and 1900, the *Labor Advocate* urged union members to do more. The paper declared that "laboring men should see to it that every member elected to the next legislature pledges himself to not only vote but work for this righteous law." He should vote only for the candidate who will "pledge himself to lend his every effort to the disenthrallment of enslaved children."[26]

Birmingham's anti–child labor campaign was part of a burgeoning labor politics. The Alabama State Federation of Labor, formed in 1901, indicated that state union leaders considered themselves part of a radical labor politics that the AFL saw as potentially risky to the larger trade union cause, both because radicalism drove off potential allies and because politicians could distort labor's agenda. The 1901 Alabama State Federation convention witnessed a movement to stop sending dues to the AFL as a result of federation rules that prohibited elected officials such as labor activist and state representative Leath from being seated. The *Labor Advocate* continued to print articles about Debs, a Socialist who drew crowds during his visits to Birmingham. While not endorsing an independent Socialist Party, the *Labor Advocate,* whose editor, Mosley, was a Republican, encouraged trade unionists to organize politically as well as by craft, declaring, "We all know that the working man is told to stay out of politics or he will be ruined. Of course, this is the advice of all capitalists to the wageworkers. But I notice that the capitalist is all the time in politics."[27]

As trade unionists became politically active regarding the child labor issue, one AFL organizer urged Gompers to adopt such labor politics. G. B. McCracken, a general organizer hired along with Greene, advised Gompers to focus the child labor fight on South Carolina, where the textile industry was well developed and where operatives were beginning to organize. McCracken reported that in one county, operatives had "put up one of their own men, a Textile worker, and elected him to the legislature besides making the other two pledge themselves to the child labor and other measures." The operatives, he felt, would support efforts to restrict child labor and "put a stop to some of the Tyriny that is now being practiced in some of the large Mills." Limited evidence suggests that labor organizers were also making their way into Alabama mills to spread the word about 1898 labor legislation to limit work hours in mines and factories to ten hours per day. R. A. Mitchell, superintendent of the Dwight Manufacturing Company's Alabama City mill, helped to organize large mills against the pending legislation and although the legislation passed the Senate, it was never reported from committee in the House. Despite the ease with which the legislation had been stopped, Mitchell reported to his Massachusetts boss his concern that mill men in the state had seen signs of labor organizers among the mill population.[28]

Toward a More Conservative Southern Strategy

In spite of McCracken's advice and Birmingham's budding labor politics, Gompers chose a conservative southern strategy, taking Greene's counsel over that of McCracken. Greene thought that child labor laws would not succeed in the Carolinas and that legislation was more likely to pass in Alabama or Georgia, where the textile industry was less developed. Greene also believed that McCracken was a Socialist whose tactics hurt chances for trade unionism to take root in the southern textile industry. Greene, like Gompers, thought the "very wild and awful wooly tenets of Socialism" threatened the "substantial rapidity" of the trade union movement in the South. Gompers agreed with Greene that the best interests of trade unionism were not served by politicizing southern workers on the issue of child labor.[29]

Gompers's turn toward a conservative strategy to restrict child labor in the southern cotton mills was indicative of his larger shift away from labor politics and toward a commitment to "pure and simple" trade unionism. In the 1880s, Gompers had invited conservatives and radicals alike into the federation, but he rejected this alliance when socialism, wrought with political factionalism, threatened to put the AFL on a political path that Gompers thought would derail American trade unionism. During the depression of the 1890s, Socialists challenged Gompers's leadership of the AFL. An 1893 program for an independent labor political platform almost turned the AFL toward an independent labor politics. By the late 1890s, Gompers had come to view socialism as a threat to improving trade unionism's ability to win workers' "individual as well as . . . collective independence and liberty." By 1900, the textile workers were reuniting and affiliating with the AFL; Gompers did not want to impede this reunion. Furthermore, the recent demise of the Populists left white Democrats firmly in control of southern politics. Already wary of labor politics, Gompers believed that labor alone had no chance of political success in the South: "Do we not know the obstacles which have stood in the way to secure a reasonable limitation in the hours of labor for the women and children workers of the South, because of former slavery there?" he asked. With Great Britain's trade union movement as his model, Gompers now advocated a trade unionism that focused on winning victories on the shop floor through collective bargaining with employers.[30]

Gompers sought to make the matter of child labor a public issue rather than a labor issue because he believed that the South remained dominated by an aristocratic class especially hostile to labor. Both Greene and Gompers thought that the South's white Democratic power brokers were an aristocratic class that had built the South's cotton mills into "industrial plantations." Greene described owners of one southern mill as "a family of leeches sucking the very life blood out of the working people, they were among the largest black slave owners in the state before that evil was abolished and up until October the fifteenth were among the largest 'white slave owners.'" These sons of slaveholders, known to their communities as "genial Christian gentlemen good to their employees," retained the belief "that working people belong in a sense to the monied class."[31]

Organized labor's failure to win passage of labor laws in the Democrat-controlled South confirmed Gompers's view of the region. Even in Birmingham, where organized labor made a compelling call for child labor legislation, efforts were isolated and ineffective. Gompers thought that

Birmingham's Trades Council risked creating a backlash by becoming more politicized over an issue such as child labor. Alabama's textile industry remained largely unorganized, and mill owners and commercial interests had instituted repressive measures when strikes shook the Piedmont textile industry from 1898 to 1902. Gompers despaired about repeated organizing failures in the South and saw protective legislation as a necessary first step in improving conditions and making trade unionism viable.[32]

Gompers's gendered view of wage earners also contributed to his eagerness to enlist nonunion leadership in the effort to obtain child labor legislation: he did not care who led the fight for shorter hours for children and women. Regardless of who won legislative restrictions on child labor, he thought that doing so would improve the chances for organizing adult textile workers, especially men. At the 1898 congressional hearing on uniform hours of labor, Gompers explained that women and children should be classified as "wards of the nation" because "neither class is empowered to use the elective franchise." In contrast, adult male wage earners with full citizenship rights could work out their "own salvation."[33] Protective legislation was intrinsically tied to the interests of organized labor, but because Gompers saw male labor as so distinct from that of women and children, he had little preference for how regulation of their labor was won or for who headed the campaign.

A Southern Strategy at Odds with Southern Workers

Gompers's gendered view of wage earners was one of the chief reasons that trade unionism failed to appeal to ordinary southern textile workers. The ideal of a male breadwinner was at odds with the way southern textile workers looked on family labor. In fact, labor organizers often misinterpreted as ignorance the rural ways of mill folk. The cultural divide between organized labor and the mostly unorganized textile workers constituted yet another reason that Gompers began to look beyond labor for help to achieve child labor restrictions. He recognized that adult mill workers wedded to a family labor system were less likely to be won over to the trade union cause. As historian I. A. Newby explained, "A cultural chasm separated most folk from union activists. Unions were organizations to join, and their leaders were outsiders who had little understanding of mill folk and their ways. Moreover, the effectiveness of unions depended on paying dues for abstract or threatening purposes . . . at great risk and with no assurance of success."[34]

The trade union ideal was a skilled male worker paid a living wage that enabled him to maintain the American standard of living—a modern definition of independence—and to provide for his wife and children. Organizing around this idea, Gompers and the AFL were struggling to establish the premise that wages should not be set by market forces—price and labor supply—but should be based on what was needed for a man to support his family. Independence for male agriculturists, in contrast, was integrally linked to the labor of their dependents. As Stephanie McCurry put it, "Dependence was the stuff of which independence—and manhood—were made." Male mill workers still identified male independence and the autonomy of the family with collective labor. In the absence of organization, commanding the labor of his children provided a male mill worker with some degree of leverage against his employer. Furthermore, child labor helped provide the funds that allowed some men to continue farming or enabled entire families to return periodically to farming. Trade unionism, in contrast, was built on the idea of a permanent acceptance of industrial capitalism and working for wages. At the turn of the century, many southern textile workers thought of themselves as farmers temporarily working in the mill, not as permanent industrial wage workers.[35]

While trade unionists had an investment in portraying southern workers as helpless and dependent—as symbolized by child labor—unorganized mill workers could only take offense. They saw their lives as a tough struggle that had value in and of itself. They were making lives for themselves and their families and perceived this mission as honorable. They did not see themselves as ignorant, dependent whites. Mill men's acknowledgment of workers' honor facilitated their exploitation and trade unionists' misunderstanding of ordinary workers.[36]

Labor unionizing on the model of a male breadwinner was thus at odds with ordinary workers, but Gompers was less concerned about ordinary workers' resistance to labor organization than about manufacturers' organized power against the AFL's goal of protective legislation. Gompers assumed that organizing would be easier once children and women's labor was curtailed. With organizing efforts under assault elsewhere in the Piedmont, Gompers reasoned that Alabama's less entrenched textile industry might be the best place for child labor legislation to gain a foothold. Furthermore, Gompers was eager to retaliate against the New England–dominated textile industry, which had undermined organized labor's gains by moving South or by cutting wages in response to alleged competition, and several Massachusetts companies operated mills in Alabama.

Gompers initiated the effort to change child labor from a labor issue to a public issue in the fall of 1900, when he hired Irene Ashby, a young, idealistic Englishwoman, to investigate conditions in Alabama mills and to lead efforts to pass restrictions on child labor—the most significant AFL-sponsored action regarding child labor in the southern textile industry. Ashby put the southern child labor problem on the national Progressive map, becoming the first expert on the problem and speaking at famous Progressive venues such as Hull House in Chicago. Ashby, well versed in the rhetoric of trade unionism, paradoxically played a critical role in diminishing organized labor's leadership on the issue of child labor in the South. By the early twentieth century, efforts to restrict child labor in southern cotton mills were no longer closely associated with organized labor and radicalism. As Ashby gained support from members of the middle class, Gompers advised Alabama labor organizations to suspend their efforts and thereby mute labor's profile in the fight, eventually agreeing "to do what he could to restrain [labor] advocacy of a child labor bill" whenever the campaign's emerging leaders asked him to do so.[37]

Alabama's anti–child labor campaign consequently developed within the contours of middle-class Progressivism.[38] The new strategy sacrificed leading voices like the *Labor Advocate*'s hard-edged rhetoric about conflict between capital and labor, the effect of child labor on adult wages, and the need to organize the textile industry. In exchange, Gompers gained national attention and the support of respectable white southerners for protective legislation while shifting the issue away from an independent labor politics that invited socialism and was more likely to drive off allies and even adult mill workers.

Ashby was a prophet of the trade union movement, not a disciple. Experienced in organizing "factory girls" in London, she thought of herself as radical. For an upper-middle-class woman, she was radical, but her radicalism stemmed from her break with gender conventions rather than from a commitment to class struggle. Even though she referred to herself as always "*hungry* to be in the fray" and delighted in referring to herself as the "little crank," she shrank from claiming the credentials of a labor agitator. Gompers initially warned her to be conservative in the South but subsequently became angered by her timidity: "If you want to continue in the work to secure a child labor law, I want you to quit trying to find a way out for the state, for the widows, for the 'worthless or helpless fathers,' or to have your conscience burdened whether the industries of the south or of any other place are going to be hurt or disarranged by the passage of the law." Ashby's radicalism on child labor also must be called into question by the fact that she subsequently hired a twelve-year-old English girl as a maid and saw nothing wrong with having done so.[39]

When Ashby began identifying the problem of child labor in the South, a local middle class was ready to heed her call to action. In southern cities, signs of Progressivism had already surfaced. Populism had introduced opposition thought and provoked Democrats to consider reform. Progressives in the South shared the traits of Progressives elsewhere, which included a preference for reform without the threat of the Populists' radicalism. Rather than advocating the overthrow of industrial capitalism, Progressives generally believed that it merely needed to be reformed when it threatened traditional institutions like the home, which formed the basis of an orderly society and a mature citizenry. To the extent that industrial capitalism disrupted the home, Progressives criticized employment practices. More often, Progressives looked for ways to reform home life and argued that such reforms would ultimately bring greater efficiency to industry. But southern Progressives also bound the spirit of Progressivism to a regional investment in boosterism for industry.[40]

Organized labor assisted Ashby when she arrived in Alabama, but her first public meeting in the state occurred in January 1901 at the Birmingham Commercial Club building, a location that indicated the shift toward broadening support for child labor reform. State Representative Leath, former president of the Birmingham Trades Council, introduced Ashby to the group. After Ashby mapped out a plan of campaigning for the measures, she spoke of ministers such as Episcopal Rector Edgar Gardner Murphy and of doctors who had pledged their support. The new president of the Birmingham Trades Council, F. J. Williams, and President Charles Herbert of the Clerks' Union also came to declare organized labor's support for the pending bills to prohibit labor for children under twelve years of age and to institute compulsory education. J. H. Phillips, Birmingham's superintendent of education and a member of the Commercial Club, also spoke.[41]

Ashby's legislative campaign for child labor reform soon had the support of an array of white middle-class volunteer organizations, including the Alabama Federation of Women's Clubs (AFWC), the Women's Christian Temperance Union, and the Alabama Woman's Press Club. Birmingham's "public spirited" men, however, were the self-appointed leaders of the campaign.[42] While Gompers may have expected that Ashby would ignite organized women such as those involved in child welfare issues in the North, male ministers and educators also initially responded to her appeal.

Ashby called another public meeting at Magnolia Hall in late January, by which time citizens had become eager to hear their suspicions of the significant growth of child labor confirmed. Jerome Jones, an Atlanta trade union leader, introduced Ashby, but speakers were "selected from the different walks of life" with "different reasons for their opinions of unionism." In addition to Ashby and these other speakers, the program featured an orchestra, vocal and violin solos, and a recitation of a sentimental poem about children written by Nora Mitchell, a member of one of the local women's clubs. Local clergy gave prayers and a benediction.[43]

Ashby's main goal in Alabama was the investigation of twenty-four of Alabama's forty-three cotton mills to provide evidence to support reform and human-interest stories to compel support, supplying the first records of the extent of child labor in the mills. From personal observation, she estimated that twelve hundred children under age twelve were already laboring in the state's mills, with that number expected to rise. Ashby presented the problem as one of industrial evolution in the South, urging her audience to learn from the history of manufacturing or risk losing the moral qualities of country life that southerners cherished. "Experimenting with child labor was like the child playing with fire," she said; "it was experimenting with flesh and blood." She assured her audience that none of the mills she had toured would be hurt by the provisions of the bills currently under consideration in the legislature.[44]

By Ashby's second month of organizing, the emerging male leadership had legitimated the issue, while reports of "tearful eyes among the ladies" suggested the subordinate, sentimental place expected of women despite Ashby's public role. In Montgomery, Murphy formed a local executive committee for the state; the committee subsequently became the all-male Alabama Child Labor Committee when the 1901 bills failed to become law. Other speakers at Ashby's meetings included A. B. Curry, pastor of the First Presbyterian church; several educators, including Phillips; and a physician, A. N. Ballad.[45]

Nina Browne DeCottes, editor of the *Montgomery Advertiser*'s society page, became Ashby's closest friend in the state, introducing Ashby to a social world that enhanced her ability to gain broader support. While Ashby found common ground with trade unionists through the rhetoric of capitalist greed, she felt much more comfortable in the social ground of the middle classes. DeCottes aided Ashby's efforts to make child labor a public question in Alabama by blending her reports of Ashby's organizing into the norms of middle-class social life. DeCottes's report on Ashby's visit to Auburn, for example, provided more detail about the hospitality Ashby received than the substance of her meeting, about which DeCottes said only that Ashby had drawn a "large and cultured" audience. The only direct mention of child labor appeared when DeCottes described Ashby's tour of the Auburn campus, and here the subject came up in a way that conflated readers' interest in higher education with the interests of child laborers: DeCottes wrote that the university "grinds" from "the raw material brought to the mills in the form of 'the small boy of America,' . . . hundreds of specimens of the Alabama man of prominence"—that is, boys could be sent either to the factory or to the university. Led by DeCottes in the *Montgomery Advertiser*, Alabama's major newspapers (including the *Birmingham News* and the *Birmingham Age-Herald*) either supported Ashby's call for legislation for child labor and compulsory education laws in 1901 or gave neutral news coverage of the pending bills and reform efforts.[46]

Ashby's ease within the white southern social world made her the ideal agent to enlist broader public support and to encourage organized women's political activism. As she told DeCottes, "Mr. Baldwin told his wife that if only she had known I was so young and pretty and charming and so unlike a labor agitator she would have asked me to come during their [South Carolina's] legislature." DeCottes credited Ashby with creating "a sensation by her exposure of certain conditions." DeCottes felt that it was important to announce that rather than working as a representative of organized labor, which she implied had a narrow agenda,

Ashby transcended "altogether simply the commercial features of the fight and place[d] the whole subject on a plane where it must not only be looked upon, but actually discussed as a great national—a great world problem."[47]

Although she remained in the United States only for a short time, Ashby nevertheless created a career for herself, and she lamented giving it up to join her English husband, Alfred Newth Macfadyen, a captain in the British army. It is unclear how long she officially worked for the AFL, with which she published and collaborated until just a month before her summer 1901 departure from the States. As she returned to England for her wedding, Murphy was already attempting to lure her back to Alabama. She wrote privately in August 1901 that she wanted to move to the United States, and when her husband joined her for her return to the States in the fall of 1901, she was thrilled to be getting her "heart's desire" and her "work too." Murphy helped Ashby-Macfadyen organize what she called a "through-the-South campaign" that she completed before her March 1902 congressional testimony. Her letters indicate that the same social circles that received her in Alabama extended their welcome in other southern states: accompanied by the daughter of a local bishop, for example, Ashby-Macfadyen gained access to mills elsewhere as she initially had in Alabama. Her southern experience gave her the credentials to speak on southern child labor in Chicago, Philadelphia, and New York, but by spring, her husband had taken a job as secretary to the prime minister of Cape Colony, South Africa. After not having heard from him for almost two months, she returned to England in late April 1902. "It was horrible to break away from my beloved America and to have had no word from 'The Man' to whom I am giving career and country," she wrote to DeCottes. But whatever marital friction may have existed, Ashby-Macfadyen joined her husband, took up new reform activities in South Africa, and wrote positively about her new home. One letter written in 1914, when she was still living in South Africa, suggests that she had spoken at a women's suffrage meeting in Johannesburg and that she was engaged in similar activities when she visited Europe. Ashby-Macfadyen's short-term work had a long-term impact because she initiated a nationally recognized southern anti–child labor campaign, and a decade later she was still writing to her Alabama friend about the lasting impact the experience had had on her life.[48]

Although Ashby-Macfadyen and the AFL had failed to achieve a child labor law in Alabama, she had made child labor in southern cotton mills a national issue. Furthermore, she became the national expert on southern child labor and played a key role in alerting leading Progressives to the problem. Ashby-Macfadyen became acquainted with Carrie Chapman Catt, Felix Adler, and leading child welfare reformers such as Jane Addams and Florence Kelley. During the first two months of 1902, she lectured in Chicago and stayed at Hull House, and before one lecture, Addams wrote that the Englishwoman "certainly knows about the children in the southern cotton mills, and if she tells the rest of us, there is no doubt that our emotions will be genuine."[49]

Whereas at the 1898 congressional hearings on uniform hours, Gompers had seen child labor's potential to illuminate the oppressive working conditions in the southern textile industry but had lacked evidence, by 1902 Ashby-Macfadyen's work had made him well prepared to use child labor to make a case for uniform hours in factories. Representative Lovering again sponsored legislation to give Congress the power "to establish uniform hours of labor in manufacturing." Standardizing hours in an industry with fifty-eight- to seventy-two-hour workweeks served the self-interests of large textile companies in his home state, but as markets rebounded, eastern manufacturers as a group became divided on the issue, and Lovering began the hearings in the name of helping the "laboring man." "It is no crime, perhaps, to be rich and to eat the bread of idleness, but it is a crime," he declared, "to eat it at the expense of the lives and blood of others." The stage was set for Gompers and Ashby-Macfadyen to make the case that the lives of children were at stake.[50]

Ashby-Macfadyen and Gompers made child labor conditions their primary reason for demanding federal intervention in the cotton textile industry. Gompers initiated a theme that advocates of a federal child labor law later adopted: just as federal intervention had been needed to end slavery in the Old South, the national government would have to intervene to end child slavery in the New South because the region's hostility to reform was so great. He repeated Ashby's report that a photographer who had taken shots of her with maimed children had been persuaded to destroy the plates. Similarly, a physician who had "amputated fingers and hands of children in mills was influenced to recant." "Where was this?" interrupted the chair of the Judiciary Committee in disbelief. "In the South," replied Gompers. "How old were those children?" another committee member inquired. "Eight, nine, ten years of age," Gompers reported. "As a last resort we come to the Congress of the United States and ask the members to exercise their sovereign power to give us that relief. You can not afford to wait until the consciences of the people of the South have been quickened sufficient to influence the employers of child labor or to influence all the legislatures." Gompers explicitly made the analogy to slavery, saying, "The demand for the abolition of slavery in the Southern States" had its humane as well as its economic reasons; similarly, "economic reasons demand the protection of the women and children of the South, . . . but above all economic considerations is the consideration of their lives and limbs and health."[51]

To prove that both economic considerations and life and limb were at stake, Gompers called Ashby-Macfadyen as the AFL's star witness. Ashby's testimony, which included photographs, represented the climax of the hearings and of her American career. Her images of Alabama children included a photograph of a six-year-old girl as well as one of a nine-year-old girl "who has been working three years and is a broken-down wreck." One mill employed forty-five children under thirteen; one seven-year-old boy had worked for forty straight nights. A Georgia society woman "told me that it was a common sight in the cotton operatives' houses to see children eight and nine stretched out asleep on beds in the daytime dressed just as they came from the mill."[52]

Ashby-Macfadyen argued that mill work "has a terribly stunting effect upon the children" and even caused the death of many children. She testified, "I know of an instance of a child who was not working, but who accompanied her mother into the mill, who lost 20 pounds weight in six months owing to the factory atmosphere." Those who escaped physical mutilation and death were left mentally deprived: "In one city a count was made last year in 8 mills; 567 children under 12 years of age were found working, only 122 of whom could read or write, and those children had entered after their tenth birthday."[53]

Ashby-Macfadyen also argued that the southern textile industry would suffer as a result of overworking its operatives, especially children. She contended that the most successful manufacturing states prohibited the employment of children under age fourteen, while the southern states had no restrictions. Furthermore, the mills needed to develop "all the capacities of the [workers'] Anglo-Saxon race." White southern workers "in one generation, if they are not exploited," could make the South the premiere cotton textile region. "Beautiful" southern mills with "wonderful electric plants" stood ready to make the region wealthy and develop "poor whites"—or to ruin the next generation, leaving the South without the skilled labor to remain competitive. Every one of the South's seven hundred mills had "a batch of children under twelve years of age working from eleven to twelve and a quarter hours a day." There were "babies from six to seven years of age—children who do not know their own age —working all night," she claimed.[54]

Ashby-Macfadyen also appropriated a progressive racial uplift argument that would become a central means for drawing attention to the southern child labor problem, arguing that while white children worked, black children attended school. "I have been told of cases where Negroes are actually giving aid to the children who are suffering from their work in the mills," she alleged. She suggested that white children were becoming the most neglected children in the South: "Suppose these mills were filled with Negro children, you know there would be an outcry through the North of unjust treatment. Is it then nothing to the North that white children—American children—should largely . . . be deprived wholesale of the chance of education and . . . condemned to a thraldom worse than slavery?" Ashby-Macfadyen, who supported the segregation of blacks and whites, also played the race card: "This foreshadows a complication of the color problem . . . a new white illiterate industrial class amid educated Negroes."[55] By praising cotton mills and the South's economic potential and by raising the specter of African American advancement, Ashby-Macfadyen appealed to southerners to view child labor reform as in the region's best interest.

Ashby-Macfadyen concluded that the U.S. Congress needed to intervene because the mill interests were too strong and the costs of inaction too great. The mill owners, she said, cried "labor agitation" and in so doing misrepresented the anti–child labor campaign. Unlike Gompers during the 1898 hearings, Ashby-Macfadyen had proof of widespread public feeling in favor of limiting child labor: she testified that the groups formally supporting the regulation of child labor included the Southern Educational Association, women's organizations, southern governors, religious leaders, and different church congresses. "This is a question for the most patriotic, the most wide-minded thinking people, and throughout the world the protection of children has been championed by the finest people in every nation," she said as she submitted a list of names of "gentlemen who are taking a leading part publicly in promoting this legislation in the South."[56]

Although no legislation was passed as a result of Ashby-Macfadyen's testimony, her performance signaled a new reform strategy built on the twin pillars of efficiency and sentimentalism. It also drew attention to the southern child labor problem, creating a record of evidence that reformers continued to cite. The notion that reforms could bring greater efficiency to industry while easing the potential for violent conflict that had characterized capital-labor struggles in the preceding decade gained credibility in the early twentieth century, while sentimentalism was the cultural tool used to arouse the public opinion required to support reform. Sentimentalism has a long history tied to the development of middle-class culture in the United States, although by 1900 it had become suspect because, as one scholar notes, it had become to middle-class sentiments what religiosity was to religion. Nevertheless, sentimentality suggested the "right feelings" to be held regarding such subjects as children, family, and charity.[57] Progressives used sentimental forms to personalize rising inequalities in society. Reform rhetoric urged members of the public to envision their children in the shoes of working children.

Between the 1898 public hearing and its 1902 sequel, the AFL had failed to achieve passage of a single child labor law in the South; however, the labor activists had broadened the issue of child labor in the southern cotton mills from a labor issue to a public issue. Child labor would be on the legislative agenda of every southern textile state every year after 1901.

Edgar Gardner Murphy and the Alabama Child Labor Committee

A Progressive Era anti–child labor movement began to build on Ashby-Macfadyen's pioneering investigations and to elaborate on her basic arguments. Episcopal Rector Edgar Gardner Murphy was the most significant new leader of the Alabama movement, forming the Alabama Child Labor Committee (ACLC) after the 1901 bill failed to become law. Under Murphy's leadership, the ACLC produced the most substantial body of reform pamphlets in the state, distributing more than twenty-eight

thousand copies by May 1903.[58] The ACLC recast the child labor problem, removing organized labor's concerns about exploitation, wages,
and rights for workers and replacing them with issues of racial order,
white literacy, and the sanctity of the home. Murphy made the child labor issue a major middle-class reform concern in Alabama and throughout the South by interpreting the child labor problem within the context
of larger problems that concerned the white middle class. As the ideologue of the Alabama movement, Murphy shifted the debate between
mill men and reformers from the immobilizing war between capital and
labor to the contested terrain of middle-class public culture and standards of social progress.

Because Murphy and the ACLC wanted to disassociate reform from
organized labor, they turned to middle-class women. Clubwomen had intimate knowledge of the child labor problem and seemed like good candidates to push for strong protective legislation in response to Ashby's
appeal. Ashby had addressed the AFWC in 1901, the first time the group
had concerned itself with the issue of child labor, and she identified
women's clubs, the Women's Christian Temperance Union, the Jewish
Women's Council, the Mothers' Union, the Women's Press Association,
the Alabama Education Association, the Jefferson County Teachers Institute, and several individual women as endorsers of the 1901 child labor
and compulsory education bills. Kate Morrissette, head of the AFWC
education committee, taught "domestic science" to a group of "factory
girls" on Saturdays. Montgomery's Ionian Club was "making every effort
in our power to elevate and educate the children at West End in our
city," where the cotton mill was located. Club members took "charge of
classes of these poor children one evening and one afternoon of each
week." Bessie Booth Sloan, teacher at the West End School in Montgomery, told the AFWC delegates about the "bareness and discomfort
of the school house" and the "worth," "need," and "the charm of the
factory child."[59] In the absence of organized labor, women emerged as
the most organized group dealing with the welfare needs of the children
and the most likely group to join the ACLC's effort to win a child labor
law. Furthermore, the *Montgomery Advertiser,* which endorsed child labor
regulation, encouraged women's involvement.

Because Murphy and the ACLC felt close association with organized
labor in the South would hurt more than help the cause, he turned to
organized women. Women's groups had been some of the first to iden-

tify with the child labor movement, and women reformers in other areas of the country were in the vanguard of child labor reform. But in Alabama, men had broadened and legitimated links between the impact of the home and child development on the public sphere. The all-male ACLC put children and their well-being at the heart of the solutions to the South's social problems. Even though Murphy assumed that men were intellectual and political leaders, he and the ACLC paved the way for Alabama's women to domesticate the public sphere.[60]

Working on behalf of children put women squarely in the midst of the politics of the child labor movement. Yet although concern for children was strong, Gompers and Ashby underestimated these reformers' ties to mill men as well as the women's hesitancy to push for legislation that these men fought. Because women believed that the power of women's humanitarian work stemmed from its separate nature based on their roles as mothers, some eschewed male-dominated politics. One of the women who opposed taking a side against mill owners warned, "We all know what we are to expect when politics takes charge of humanitarian enterprises." The AFWC denounced child labor, but its support of a law faltered in the face of mill opposition. AFWC President Lillian Milner Orr, the daughter of a major stockholder in the Avondale Mills near Birmingham, argued that mill men's benevolence under the watchful eye of women could do a better job of curbing abuses than could the state: Orr urged AFWC women to trust in the goodness of the manufacturers, whom the women knew personally—to "help our husbands, fathers and sweethearts, and if we see them taking the wrong path, edge them into the right one. . . . If we carry on the issue as Mr. Murphy has begun it, these are the men whom we are to antagonize," Orr warned.[61]

Antagonizing men of their own class or their own families not only was personally threatening but also could jeopardize Alabama women's other child-centered reforms. In Florence, cotton mill owners opposed child labor regulation but funded the free kindergarten supported by children's author Maud Lindsay and by Lulie Jones, a local member of the AFWC. The president of the town's largest cotton mill also served as a trustee of the Lauderdale County Education Association. Moreover, "the crowning work of the women's clubs," in which they took "their chief glory," was the "Industrial School and Farm for Wayward Boys." In 1898, the Birmingham Commercial Club had helped the AFWC secure the necessary land for their premier philanthropic endeavor. Braxton

Bragg Comer, head of the Avondale Mills and later a Progressive Alabama governor, had helped organize the Commercial Club, and Orr was reluctant to support legislation that he opposed: "The directors of [Avondale] are some of the best men in our community. The very men to whom we women must go for advice and assistance in any humanitarian enterprise—child-lovers every one of them." Women preferred to support the industrial school, which provided an opportunity for reform that was consistent with the state's commercial interests. In 1903, the AFWC did not want to jeopardize winning a larger appropriation for the boys' industrial school by supporting a child labor law that major commercial interests opposed.[62]

The few Alabama women who supported the 1903 ACLC-backed child labor bill lacked family ties that conflicted with child labor regulation. These women were rare among Alabama clubwomen in 1903, finding sources of political identification other than the AFWC. In a public exchange, Priscilla C. Goodwyn, the wife of a Republican state senator with Populist sympathies who ran for governor in 1896, disagreed with Orr, arguing that women "are agitators indeed when the subject is one that touches the vital welfare of the laboring children of Alabama." Priscilla Goodwyn, a delegate to the March 1902 National Mothers' Congress conference in Washington, D.C., and founder of the Mothers' Union in Montgomery, believed that a law was absolutely necessary. When the AFWC was slow to mobilize in support of the child labor law, she created a special child labor committee within the Montgomery Mothers' Union and distributed ACLC pamphlets. Another strong supporter of the law was Lura Harris Craighead (the wife of Erwin Craighead, the editor of the *Mobile Register*), who wrote a pamphlet in support of child labor legislation and who tried to rally AFWC members to support the pending child labor measure.[63]

Women in Alabama's anti–child labor movement followed a slightly different trajectory in becoming leaders and policy makers than did Progressive Era female reformers in other contexts. While reformers like those at Hull House in Chicago were already establishing a "female dominion" on child welfare issues, Alabama's organized women were active but not yet activists in the name of a gendered politics. Women in five prominent literary clubs had formed the Alabama Federation of Women's Clubs in 1895. Even this act was considered so controversial that club news constantly reiterated that club activities were not detrimental to women's work in the home. Their consensus of concern for children broke down along class lines and around regional and local relationships when it came to policy solutions. Scholars of northern women's policy-making leadership have shown the importance of institutions such as Hull House and the U.S. Children's Bureau in incubating female reform culture and activism. In Alabama, such an incubator was still missing. In fact, only when the state's women developed ties to this established female reform culture in its institutionalized form were individual Alabama reformers able to shift their organizations' goals into line with those of leading women Progressives elsewhere.[64]

Ironically, Ashby, whom Gompers at one point had chastised for being an accommodationist, recognized a cost to turning over the fight, writing to DeCottes, "I was disappointed at the Alabama women's action. . . . Women are so easily duped by these capitalists." Gompers muzzled Birmingham's organized labor on the issue of child labor and turned the campaign over to the middle classes in a region begging for capital and worshipful of manufacturers. Murphy realized the problem that reformers faced: "To alienate 'prosperity' has seemed almost like apostasy." Reformers needed to identify a villain without vilifying southern mill men. This conundrum remained a continuing challenge for the southern anti–child labor movement.[65]

Ashby's work and the nascent Alabama movement under Murphy's new leadership, however, kept alive the issue of reform of southern child labor. Murphy helped to found the National Child Labor Committee, and national figures such as Jane Addams began to speak about the "southern problem." Northern and southern Progressives began to collaborate in search of national standards. In 1898 organized labor had ignited a protest and made the child laborer the quintessential symbol of the degraded conditions of the southern cotton textile industry. While initially it looked like labor would use child labor to talk about low wages, class conflict, and the enslavement of a new working class, within four years Gompers and Ashby had enlisted Alabama's white middle classes, which had their own agenda. These Progressives would make Alabama's cotton mill child into a touchstone for debate about the social status of poor whites in the New South and the future of the South's common man.

CHAPTER FOUR

Inventing the "Forgotten Child"

WHEN SAMUEL GOMPERS TOLD THE United Textile Workers that "the sentimental, the Christian, the noble, the public spirited citizens" were taking up the fight for child labor regulation in Alabama, he was relieved. He assumed that the clubwomen who had entertained Irene Ashby and the male physicians, educators, and ministers who had turned out to hear her talk would press for protective legislation and win what labor alone could not accomplish. On one hand, he was right. A southern, white, middle-class reform movement coalesced during a push for a child labor law in 1903 in Alabama and won the first southern child labor law of the twentieth century. On the other hand, he failed to appreciate how the fight would change from one about exploitation of the region's poor, capitalist greed, a living wage, and class conflict to one about white middle-class concerns for social order.

The issue of child labor reform in Alabama confirms that southern women's reform efforts lagged behind those of northern women.[1] Gompers and Ashby-Macfadyen had drawn attention to the southern child labor problem among women reformers at Hull House, the famous Chicago settlement, where Florence Kelley and Jane Addams were becoming leaders on child labor reform and child welfare issues. However, in 1903 there were no ties between these leading advocates for protective legislation and Alabama's conservative white middle-class women. While female reform culture was emerging in Alabama with vibrant, determined women at its helm, the movement remained in a provincial phase, taking its cues from conditions within the state.

Instead of women leading the way, an all-male Alabama Child Labor Committee (ACLC) emerged and spearheaded early reform efforts. This white middle-class committee had a social agenda based on its members' ideas about social order and progress, with little understanding of laborers' perspectives and no commitment to organized labor's larger issue of a living wage. When Gompers worked with Addams and Kelley, he was working with kindred spirits who shared the goal of a living wage. The ACLC men did not represent the same brand of middle-class Progressive. These new southern middle-class reformers hesitated to criticize manufacturers, eagerly blamed poor families for their condition, and determined that closing the mill doors and opening the school doors for white children would create a truly New South.

Episcopal Rector Edgar Gardner Murphy was the most significant new leader of the Alabama movement. Murphy and the ACLC captured public attention in a way that Birmingham's *Labor Advocate* could not. Murphy made the child labor problem in the southern textile industry part of a larger Progressive debate about standards of social progress in the South and the nation as a whole. His work was critical to inviting interregional cooperation among state reformers and leading national groups like the National Child Labor Committee. Founded as an all-male body, the ACLC nevertheless played a critical role in transforming women's reform culture in Alabama.[2]

The ACLC gained support and publicity by talking about white child labor in terms of racial order and social and economic progress. But Murphy and the ACLC's very regional response floundered on the regional realities of extreme rural poverty, inadequate public education, a lack of a rural tradition of regular schooling, and an absence of compulsory education laws. Mill men's paternalistic defense played well under such conditions. Reformers had trouble pressing for child labor regulation in the face of the state's apparent inability to provide adequate schooling and of the mill men's obvious ability to build or help fund local schools.

Murphy and the ACLC reflected the intellectual roots of a certain brand of southern Progressivism. They shared a cluster of ideas about race, social order, and democracy, believing that whites were superior because of their Anglo-Saxon blood but that all races could advance. These reformers held that the advancement of the white race was seen in character and institutions. Whites of character were the most fit for governing in a democracy. While not simpleminded believers in the Lost Cause, these southern Progressives shared a nostalgia for the Old South as a place and time of white refinement and leadership. In their view, the "better sort" of white man had had more influence in an antebellum world where poor whites and blacks knew their place, and poor whites and blacks now had opportunities to better their place but lacked the leadership to ensure that they did so in an orderly, respectable way. These reformers saw themselves as offering leadership on racial progress for whites and blacks while reinforcing a brand of white supremacy. Indeed, Murphy considered himself an advocate of Booker T. Washington and after an illness wrote that "letters from negroes like . . . Mr. Booker Washington have touched me most."[3]

These southern Progressives championed democracy and the coming of the white man but distrusted him in his common form. In fact, they blamed the region's ongoing racial violence on his ignorance, lack of character and self-control, and economic vulnerability. Above all, they viewed education of whites as the key to unlocking their region from its tortured past of slavery, Reconstruction, and racial conflict and political corruption. These men were not simply tenderhearted sentimentalists whose earnest judgments were misdirected in the public sphere. They were "manly" men, valorizing self-control, character, and independence over the raw, unrefined, masculine traits of strength and competitiveness. The core of the ACLC came from the Ministers' Union of Montgomery, a group that spoke out in favor of moral order. The ministers condemned the rowdiness of street fairs, encouraged the formation of church-affiliated men's clubs to spawn new moral leadership, sponsored charitable work (holiday dinners, night schools, libraries) among mill populations, and supported the 1901 child labor bill. They considered their work absolutely serious, not sentimental.[4]

The charge of sentimentalism was gendered, situating emotionalism in the female-centered private sphere. Sentimentalism was associated with the familial world of the middle classes, and by the early twentieth century, the middle classes used rhetorical conventions to express the affection of the bonds of the private sphere. Opponents of child labor reform sought to discredit humanitarian public concerns regarding children by calling the reformers "sickly sentimentalists," a reference to the conventions of middle-class private expressions of affection. According to Murphy, cotton manufacturers' attempted to discredit the reformers as "agitators" or "sentimentalists."[5]

Faced with such charges, Murphy and the ACLC avoided overdrawn pictures of forlorn children and pathos. Murphy and other ACLC members were professional men who were not leaders of political parties but were earning credentials as arbiters of public culture. For Murphy, legislative achievements had to be accompanied by changes in public attitudes about the norms for poor children in a more democratic South. These men placed great emphasis on the productive power of discourse and on their ability to win acceptance of their interpretations.[6]

These male activists interjected political and social significance into middle-class notions of home, family, and childhood at the same time that white middle-class women's literary clubs had moved from reading Shakespeare to studying recent literature on the educational needs of children and on the kindergarten movement. In addition, women had formed mothers' clubs around their interests in child and family issues. Middle-class women, furthermore, were close to the child labor problem through their charity work and thus represented likely constituents for a reform movement.[7]

Alabama's male reformers helped to create an ideological passageway between the private and public spheres. Although women addressed child matters, women's marginal position in the polity limited their concerns' impact on public culture. Murphy and the ACLC added social and political urgency to organized women's growing interest in children's studies, carving out a place in public culture for Alabama women's heretofore private concerns. In so doing, these men distanced concerns about children and family from the emotional but politically vacuous middle-class sentimental culture. The 1903 campaign for an Alabama child labor law fostered the growth of male and female Progressive cultures.

Roots of a Reformer

Education had transformed Edgar Gardner Murphy, and he believed that it could transform his home region. Murphy was born in 1869 in Fort Smith, Arkansas, and was raised in San Antonio, Texas. After graduating from the University of the South at Sewanee, Tennessee, and the

New York General Theological Seminary, Murphy became a rector at St. John's Episcopal Church in Montgomery, Alabama. A disciple of William Porcher DuBose, who taught a practical Christianity, Murphy saw his role as a priest as engaging the world and transforming it by getting other people to want to change. Education helped people to see choices. Murphy believed that reform depended on changing the customs, traditions, and habits of opinion about child labor and progress in the South. More than any other citizen in the first half-decade of the twentieth century, he politicized the problem of child labor within middle-class concerns while remaining sensitive to regionalism. His analysis stemmed from his personal experiences and the philosophies of the men who joined the ACLC.

Murphy's life contributed to his great faith in education as the tool to the personal fulfillment and worldly improvements that Christianity as he understood it promised. He saw education as the key to becoming a person of character who could understand "the success which comes from your power to know the better things." When Murphy was a child, his mother was deserted by her husband and supported her family by running a boardinghouse. Episcopal Rector Walter Richardson of St. Mark's Episcopal Church, a regular visitor at the boardinghouse, urged Murphy to become involved in the parish, eventually leading to Murphy's scholarship at Sewanee at the age of sixteen.[8]

Attending college freed Murphy from the struggling lower middle class and resulted in his view of education as a peaceful means to shrink the social inequalities at the root of industrialized society's conflicts. A 1911 letter to his son, Gardner, a boarding student in Massachusetts, illuminates the character development, self-control, work ethic, and liberating potential that Murphy and his peers expected from education: "You have 'made good' . . . not in any cheap . . . sense but by the good true work. I also know that it has meant . . . the choosing of work rather than loafing, and a preference for *real* pleasure rather than pleasures of the other kind. All the marks in the world are of less importance than this power over one's own choices, the capacity for *selections . . .* that is education."[9] Faith in education became the cornerstone of his reform philosophy.

Education and Christian living went hand in hand for Murphy, who became a practitioner of the social gospel in parishes in Laredo, Texas; Chillicothe, Ohio; and Kingston, New York; before accepting the position in Montgomery in 1895. In both northern parishes, his commitment expanded as he aided African American groups in founding parishes, provided dinners for poor children, started men's clubs, and began publishing articles in periodicals that supported an activist Christianity, including the *Outlook,* the *North American Review,* and the *Churchman.*[10]

Murphy viewed the social gospel as a harmonious alternative to Edward Bellamy's nationalism and labor agitation. During the social unrest unleashed by the Panic of 1893, Murphy warned, "Times of commercial disaster or of political unrest are rich times for the people who have 'theories.'" He referred to Bellamy and Henry George as "prophets of calamity." By 1898 Murphy was proclaiming that the "Christianizing of aid [represented] the only rescue of mankind."[11]

Murphy's faith in deliverance through education and Christianity was intensified by his anger regarding white acceptance of racial violence. In 1893, while serving as a rector at Christ Church in Laredo, Murphy was baptized in the viciousness at the heart of white supremacy. Thousands in nearby Paris, Texas, watched relatives of a murdered child torture the accused abductor, African American Henry Smith, applying hot irons to the bound Smith before burning him alive. Murphy, in what he later called his "first public act," called a meeting in Laredo to condemn the Paris lynching. Although heated debate broke out, few citizens signed Murphy's resolution condemning the "orgy of torture and . . . festival of agony."[12]

The Paris lynching and the lack of moral leadership in Laredo became a touchstone for Murphy's interpretation of southern moral and social chaos. When he returned to the region in 1898, he looked for ways that education and the social gospel could rescue the South. Murphy believed that the death of slavery and the transition to modernization had led to increased democracy, but he grieved for what he saw as a loss of virtuous leadership. Although he stated with satisfaction, "The *real* thing, in the unfolding of the later South is the arrival of the common man," Murphy liked the common man better in theory than in practice, and he feared that as long as vulgar leadership prevailed, lynching would continue. But lynchings were only the most brutal examples of a broad spectrum of violence and lawlessness. He saw education as the key to ordered liberty, precisely what was lacking in a region where "the mob" with "its barbarities burn to-day the guilty and set aflame the hates and humors which to-morrow burn the innocent."[13]

Murphy believed that racial antagonism was increasing because politicians manipulated the "apprehensions" of the "ignorant white man concerning the negro." He argued that there had been "no friction" between the "negro and planter class," but "between the negro of any class and the representative of the 'plain people,'—between the new negro and the new white man, there is likely to be enmity." Murphy thought that whites had to be educated to broaden their racial outlook before racial progress could occur.[14]

Murphy read and admired eighteenth-century Tory political philosopher Edmund Burke and espoused a Burkian conservatism that stemmed from his belief that the common man needed to be tutored by enlightened peers. Reconstruction, in his view, left "power in the hands of the young and the irresponsible." Like many of his southern intellectual contemporaries, Murphy believed that despite the indefensible institution of slavery, the slaveholding class represented the "nobler traditions of the South." Reflecting a typical New South nostalgia, Murphy lamented the passing of leaders who knew the "true basis of an enduring peace between the sections and between the races." In the absence of cultural leadership, "the neglected masses of the white population," he explained, "exhibited the traits of the 'white world,'" such as being "vigorous, confident, [and] assertive," but lacked character, self-restraint, and virtue. Lawlessness, racial violence, and ignorance were the products of the neglect of common white men.[15]

The core of the manly man's self-definition, in contrast, was self-control. Based on an older Victorian gender ideal, "gentlemen" controlled their passions and earned a reputation for character and standards. Manliness had a "moral dimension." Murphy's masculine ideal was noble, large-minded, and independent, and "manliness" was "a standard to live up to."[16] This past of virtuous manliness had never in reality dominated the South, where both common and elite white men had a record of rowdiness, but Murphy invented this history to press for standards for masculinity other than physical strength, aggressiveness, and competitiveness. With those attributes as the criteria, any man could be masculine, regardless of character, a situation that disturbed Murphy.

In Murphy's mind, the Democratic Party had become a masculine arena of power-hungry men who seemed to have little regard for character or the broad-mindedness that would take into account the public good. The common white man was no better. He asserted his masculinity through high jinks, excessive consumption of alcohol, and gambling. He was ruled by passions and was easily manipulated by power brokers who tapped into those passions. Murphy believed that the untamed masculinity of the common white man led to the horrendous violence of lynching, which he abhorred. Murphy was a racial paternalist, viewing manliness as white men's ability to act benevolently toward inferior races. If Murphy was repulsed by vulgar exertion of powerful masculinity, he embraced an ideal of the common white man and believed in his potential: racial inheritance meant that all white men were capable of becoming respectable. As was typical of educated Victorian men, Murphy conflated culture and biology.[17]

Murphy assumed that certain cultural developments flowed from race. White men had the potential to evolve toward the highest forms of civilization and culture because white men had created the apex of civilization. Racially primitive men could also evolve, but their potential was limited to the cultural tiers below Anglo-Saxon civilization. With race and culture conflated, Murphy claimed that "it may be quite true that some negroes are better than some white men; but no rational man, cognizant of the facts, believes that the average negro is the equal, still less the superior, of the average white man."[18] Culture and race went hand in hand in Murphy's worldview, and this perceived relationship explains why he was so interested in the culture of the common white man as a key to improving southern civilization.

The Manly Men of the Alabama Child Labor Committee

Murphy was involved in the Ministers' Union, the Southern Society (a group of twenty-four prominent white Montgomery men committed to studying and writing on the "race problem"), and the Southern Education Board (SEB), organizations that he envisioned filling the vacuum of enlightened masculine leadership. All of these groups focused on whites first. While the SEB supported vocational education for blacks, the organization believed that whites needed education that not only would prepare them to be productive but also would enlighten them. From these groups, Murphy recruited ACLC members, with the goal of improving the common white man by saving his children. The men who joined the ACLC were involved in a constellation of southern social problems and interpreted the problem of child labor within the broader context of issues about humanity and social order in the South. While Murphy and a handful of others did the bulk of the work, a total of sixteen men gave their names to the cause.[19]

Active ACLC members included Murphy, who served as ACLC chair; Neal L. Anderson of Montgomery's First Presbyterian Church, who served as president of the Ministers' Union and as a spokesperson for the ACLC; J. H. Phillips; and Erwin Craighead. Like Murphy, Anderson had become involved in reform efforts that increasingly took him beyond the church. One admirer remembered him for his work "for the betterment of the conditions of the negroes of the Southern States" and his work with "Mr. Murphy of St. John's." Father O'Brien, John G. Murray, and Rabbi Morris Neufeldt also participated in the group; although little is known about O'Brien and Murray, Neufeldt later served on the advisory board of the Birmingham juvenile court and helped to organize the Birmingham social workers' association. Phillips served as Birmingham's school superintendent and had made his reputation as an education reformer, and *Mobile Register* editor Erwin Craighead, whose wife, Lura Harris Craighead, had urged the AFWC to support the ACLC-backed child labor legislation, was a recognized reformer when he joined the ACLC.[20]

Murphy, Anderson, and ACLC members Thomas G. Jones, a former governor; Judge J. B. Gaston; and B. J. Baldwin, a physician, Tuskegee trustee, and promoter of public education, also participated in the Southern Society, which sponsored "A Southern Conference for the Study of Race Problems in Relation to the Welfare of the South" in Montgomery in 1900. The conference program shows that the all-white society promoted a more conservative version of what had become Booker T. Washington's philosophy, renouncing northern intervention in the South's race problems and focusing on industrial and educational progress while sacrificing political equality for ordinary whites and blacks, thereby supplementing rather than opposing the New South creed for industrial progress and white supremacy. The Southern Society believed that when whites had more education, economic leverage would follow, and the race problem would fix itself. This simple solution assumed that society was stratified by race even in the face of growing divisions and conflict among whites and was based on the premise that black progress would not threaten whites when they felt secure about their future.[21]

Through the Southern Society, Murphy became friends with leading national education reformers, who convinced him to resign from St. John's and become executive secretary of the SEB in 1901. The SEB, a propaganda organization that supported public education for whites first, comprised both northerners and southerners and complemented the Southern Society. The broad aim of the SEB, Murphy declared, was to begin with the "plain people," by whom he meant illiterate or poorly educated whites. While Murphy later lamented that a focus on white education contributed to declining opportunities for blacks, he promoted the SEB by arguing that the "exclusive interest in the Negro [was] a mistake."[22]

Since 1898 northern philanthropists and education leaders and southern education leaders had met annually under the auspices of the Conference for Education in the South. The conference's first two presidents, J. L. M. Curry and Robert C. Ogden, both significantly influenced Murphy. Ogden, a philanthropist and manager of John Wanamaker's New York department store, and George Foster Peabody, a Wall Street banker, served as trustees of Negro industrial schools. Although the conference evinced an early interest in African American education, it lacked a commitment to African American civil rights, and the SEB reflected a shift in focus exclusively toward white education. Members of the SEB, like Murphy, did not see their emphasis on whites' education as a disavowal of African Americans' problems. Rather, these reformers decided that the root of racial friction, which thwarted progress for blacks, lay in ignorance and economic strife among plain whites.[23]

Child Labor, Race, and Illiteracy

A 1915 letter written by Kate Gordon, president of the Southern States Woman Suffrage Conference, expressed middle-class fear of white vigilante groups. "It is said the Ku Klux Klan are forming," she wrote. "I hope it is not true. But the temper of the negro papers I subscribe to, is alarming." She wrote that she had never "realized the menace that is ever present in the sections where [the Ku Klux Klan] predominate" until she "started off the half mile through a corn and sugar field [and] suddenly came across one and positively I was almost paralyzed with fear." Murphy and the ACLC understood these fears and viewed advocacy of education as an effort to create a South where the conditions that gave rise to these groups were eliminated, shifting the child labor debate into categories of analysis already engaging concerned members of the white middle classes. Murphy, for example, linked white illiteracy and racial violence when he declared that the South had "one of the greatest race problems of history" and that the only hope for solving it was "control of our white population," which was impossible "if the children of this state are kept, by the operation of our factory conditions, from the schooling, which our negroes are eagerly seeking."[24]

The only language in the South more powerful than that of industrial progress was the rhetoric of white supremacy, which pervaded the movement for education reform. By focusing on the problem of child labor as a problem of illiteracy, Murphy shifted the issue from the immobilizing war between capital and labor and from the disempowering charge of sentimentalism into powerful rhetoric of racial politics. Child labor was a "policy of compulsory ignorance," which Murphy maintained was at the root of racial friction that would eventually stand in the way of industrial and social progress.[25]

As a leader in the emerging southern public education movement, Murphy was among the first to sound the alarm about white illiteracy rates. "Of the native white population of our whole country, ten years of age and over," he said in a 1903 address to the National Education Association, "the South has 24 per cent; but of the native white illiteracy of our country, the South has 64 per cent." Even as "educational enthusiasm" was producing public schools that could teach "the masses" "the great realities of order, liberty, and culture," the growth of child labor threatened to undermine this progress. "The isolated family," he maintained, was "redeemed . . . only that its helplessness may bring profit to the instrument of its redemption." In one of the first ACLC pamphlets, *Pictures from Life,* which included the first published series of photographs of southern mill children, Murphy pointed out that "everyone of the children . . . was in easy reach of a public school. Yet almost all are growing up in total illiteracy."[26]

The ACLC sought to win public support for child labor reform within the public education awakening: if education of the white masses was right, child labor was wrong. In towns such as Florence and cities such as Birmingham and Montgomery, education rallies symbolized the growing enthusiasm for public education. After one southern education conference, J. B. Phillips declared that "the enthusiasm was like that of a great religious revival," adding that people were recognizing that "other things [in addition to skin color] differentiate [the black man] from the white man, and . . . that the education of the white masses of the South along the highest and best lines is for the true good not only of this section, but of the nation."[27]

Concern about white illiteracy had the potential to mobilize public opinion in support of child labor reform but also diverted attention from regulating capital. In fact, the new focus on education gave mill men a way to deflect attention from their labor practices. Charged with abuse of young children, mill operators argued that they were already addressing the educational needs of mill children better than the state could, given the absence of compulsory education and the brevity of the school year. While urban schools were expanding to a nine-month school year, the annual public school term in Alabama was fewer than eighty days. In rural school districts, low attendance rates and short terms were the norm. The *Anniston Hot Blast*'s report that "only about 15 percent of the [town's] school population attends" spoke to the public's sense of the enormity of the problem. Many concerned citizens agreed with the *Florence Herald* that "to say as a rule rural school houses of Alabama are old shacks, could be a truism."[28] Public education was a shambles.

Florence's mill men typified the way southern mill operators stood out as some of the men most concerned about education in the context of a truly deplorable education system. By 1903, John Ashcraft, owner of Florence's largest cotton mill, served as a trustee of the Lauderdale County Education Association, which aided in building, equipping, and repairing public schools. He was a leader at local education rallies and eventually donated land for a mill district public school, which the town named in honor of his family. His brother, Lee Ashcraft, served as president of the Florence Free Kindergarten Association. Although the Kindergarten Association had a budget of only $389.97 in 1903, the other cotton mill in town, owned by N. F. Cherry, was the association's largest donor. Maud Lindsay, the leader of Florence's kindergarten movement and later a nationally recognized children's author, filed reports with Ashcraft that demonstrated her belief that the mill school improved the lives of the children, countering their families' ignorant, unrefined ruralism. "We find that children from the same house from which we formerly had pupils are much neater and orderly than the brothers and sisters who preceded them," Lindsay reported. "We find great refinement in the tastes of these children. We find it easier every year to help them."[29]

An editorial in the *Florence Herald* suggested that operators' education work had enhanced the mills' image as agents of social improvement. The president of the Lauderdale County Education Association wrote about the social benefits of the development of manufacturing, which not only brought increased revenues and material conditions for the workers "but include[d] in its wider aim the development of stronger, healthier and better men and women." Manufacturers, he argued, sought "to open the eyes of ignorance and inspire the poor and oppressed with ambition that will enable them to see and strive for the sphere of usefulness."[30]

While mill men had a public relations incentive to exaggerate social uplift in mill villages beyond any semblance of reality, in the absence of good schooling alternatives it was not hard for manufacturers to contend that workers were better off than would otherwise be the case. In an attempt to prove that industrial progress was aiding rather than hampering literacy, the *Manufacturers' Record* argued that "as a matter of fact, the census of 1900 showed . . . there has been a reduction . . . in the total illiteracy among whites." Reformers claimed that the public school movement had caused this decrease; mill men countered that it was a sign that industrial progress meant social progress when government let capital alone. The *Manufacturers' Record* tried to discredit the SEB and child labor reformers' warnings about white illiteracy by characterizing the board as an organization of "cranks," child labor reformers, radicals, and "Negrophiles." Manufacturers argued that the attention to white illiteracy was a cover for rekindling support for federal aid for education, which would mean more money for black schools. One editorial argued, "How easy to draw pictures—harrowing pictures of poor little tots being worked into premature ages by hard-hearted service, and how easy to make statements in general terms in pathetic appeals to our lawmakers. Yet how seldom can these statements be backed up by 'specific information.'"[31]

"To Alienate 'Prosperity' Has Seemed Almost Like Apostasy"

When Murphy indicted mill men for opposing regulation, he had to balance this criticism with respect for public esteem for manufacturers. "To alienate 'prosperity' has seemed almost like apostasy," Murphy cautioned. He tried to avoid interfering with the political, economic, and social status of mill men in the South, recognizing a "peculiar appreciation upon those practical and material forces which have wrought the rehabilitation of the land."[32]

The ACLC pamphlet *Pictures from Life* acknowledged improved material conditions in mill towns as well as the mill men's good intentions. "In going into the mills," Murphy wrote, "I have been impressed by the growing feeling among the mill men in favor of improved conditions for the children." In contrast, his view of the parents was harsh: "The blame for our child labor conditions largely rests upon the parents," he declared. Murphy then subtly made the case that the ultimate responsibility lay with the mills, which, by uniting against regulation, "have thus aided the continuance of a low standard of parental duty." The pamphlet showed "a little girl six years old, barefoot, happy looking, . . . who can't read or write, [while] her father, an able-bodied man, draws her pay and the pay of two other children, but he has done no work in two years." Elsewhere, Murphy wrote, "Every close observer of our factory conditions [knows] of dozens of grown men who pass their days and nights in idleness and dissipation, while they live upon the wages of their tender children." The ACLC did not contend either that these men were lazy or that they had been robbed of their jobs by mills that preferred the cheap labor of children; rather, the group argued that child labor destroyed the home and proper family roles—independence for men and dependence for children. Murphy focused on what child labor did to the standard of parenthood, the home, and white southern manhood. Drawing on powerful middle-class notions about gender hierarchy and the sanctity of the home, he explained that "women and children all find places in the factories, but the men are left with nothing to do but to care for the little kitchen garden and carry the lunch pail to the family at the mill at noontime." The child labor system fostered a "temptation to the father to shift" the burden of breadwinning "entirely to the woman and the children."[33]

The system's corruption of traditional gender arrangements jeopardized southern civilization, he argued. "Prosperity," he maintained, should be based "not on the labor of the immature, but on the fertility of [the South's] fields, the advantages of her climate . . . above all . . . upon the character and the capacities of her manhood." He called on potential reformers to see their job as calling on the state to prevent this lowering of the "standard of parental duty" and the quality of manhood. Murphy justified intervention by presenting fathers of mill children as emasculated and incapable of using the "wholesome forces of legal ex-action and social expectation" to protect themselves.[34] Portraying male mill workers as emasculated painted protective legislation as benefiting both children and their fathers. Murphy begged the public to hate white child labor for what it did to white southern men.

Childhood in a Rural Society

In this first phase of reform, Murphy and the ACLC faced the cultural task of defining how the factory differed from the farm, another effort that was confounded by the attempt to avoid attacking mill men. Murphy came closest to identifying mill men as the problem in a pamphlet where he declared that a farmer would never be permitted to hire a workforce in which "30 percent of his labor were child laborers," citing the 1900 U.S. census for the information that 30 percent of Alabama's cotton mill operatives were under sixteen. "No man would be permitted to op-erate his farm with that labor for ten days," he argued. More commonly, Murphy avoided addressing employers' hiring practices and focused in-stead on what became a powerful reform trope: the healthy rural out-doors versus the unsanitary indoors of a factory. He contrasted photos of child factory workers with photographs that showed a pasture with a grazing cow, "where the children *might* have been." The child labor movement effectively identified factory labor as more pernicious and ex-ploitative than farm labor. Alabama newspapers began reporting factory accidents with an alarm that was absent in reports of children's inju-ries or deaths on farms or under parental supervision. For example, whereas the *Florence Herald* reported nothing extraordinary about the tragic death of a four-year-old "left to tend roasting potatoes" while his mother was picking cotton, the *Montgomery Advertiser* used a headline— "The Baby's Lost Fingers"—to announce eight-year-old mill worker Corea Talley's accident, in which two of her fingers were severed while she was working at the Merrimack Mills in Huntsville, where she was appren-ticed to qualify for a spinning job at nine cents a day. "Perhaps the poor little mite of a worker," wrote Nina Browne DeCottes, "will be through her suffering, the cause of good to her kind," leading to "increased interest . . . in the campaign that is on foot against child labor in the factories."[35]

Mill owners responded to criticism by arguing that they tried to avoid hiring children under twelve. To match Murphy's clergy credentials, they had a clergyman from Lanette, Alabama, report that mill families in his congregation were distressed and even in tears at the possibility of a law restricting child labor. Mill managers even claimed to carry at a loss young children brought in by their parents. The solution to getting the youngest children out of the mill, they argued, would come with "awakening a sense of parental responsibility" and "the enactment of a compulsory education law."[36]

Murphy and the ACLC responded not by talking about mill men's interest in cheap labor but by stressing the effect of premature labor on children's health: "There is no disposition on the part of the mills to treat the children badly," Murphy wrote, "yet the chief injury of the factory to the child lies in the unnaturally long hours and in the monotony of the work—dulling the senses and really retarding mental development." To the mill owners' insistence that parents sought work for their children, Murphy responded, "The father and mother do not easily perceive the difference between factory labor and farm labor." He suggested that parents were misled by the work being "lighter than the work brought to the child upon the farm." Without referring to such actual farm tasks as the backbreaking work of picking cotton, he called on potential reformers to recognize that the "benumbing monotony" of factory work had a "reactive effect upon the mind" that caused "dullness, apathy, a mechanical and stolid spirit, without vivacity or hope."[37]

Murphy also began to form an argument about racial degeneracy, citing 1900 census data to argue that if child labor laws were not instituted, southern mill workers under sixteen might "constitute an army of 100,000 souls" by 1906. The current generation of parents might be "ignorant," he suggested, but "our plain people are not a degenerate stock." But any natural racial superiority would be undermined by long hours at monotonous jobs. However, "if we will give the children a chance," Murphy wrote, the plain people will show themselves to be "a sturdy and resourceful folk, ready in wit and in power." The accompanying photograph showed a six-year-old boy sitting in front of a spinning machine, where the text reported he worked for twelve hours straight with only a forty-minute break at noon.[38]

Victims of Northern Capital

Murphy and the ACLC blamed mill men most directly by arguing that the villains were not "representative southern men" but were northern mill men who took advantage of conditions in the South to work children who would have been protected in the companies' home states. "In the history of this movement in Alabama the most aggressive opposition to the proposed measure came from the representative of New England investments," charged Murphy. Murphy debated J. Howard Nichols, the treasurer of the Dwight Manufacturing Company, in a series of letters to the editor of the *Boston Evening Transcript*. Nichols defended the company's Alabama City mill, declaring that the people of New England and of the South had nothing to be ashamed of in the mill, with its orderly, civilized village of 2,300, its school, its library, and its church. Murphy acknowledged Nichols's benevolence while insisting that it was no substitute for a law to protect children under twelve. "Advertisements of a unique establishment," he argued, "are used to cloak the wretched lot of the average factory [and] men are taught to ignore the essential cruelty of the whole miserable system."[39] Nichols did, however, force Murphy to concede that mills could be positive influences on mill families.

Horace S. Sears, Boston treasurer of the West Point Manufacturing Company, which owned a mill in Langdale, Alabama, joined the debate at this juncture to argue that Dwight was not unusual. Rather, all of the northern-owned mills and the majority of all mills in Alabama provided more of the "civilizing" influences of church and school than families experienced in isolated homes. He painted a picture of a "peaceful, happy mill settlement at Langdale with its pretty church filled to the doors on Sundays with an attentive, God-fearing congregation, . . . with its fine school and kindergarten department, with its well-selected library of over 1,000 volumes, with its pleasant reading room . . . and with the mill agent and his beloved wife going in and out among the homes of the people, participating in all their joys and sorrows." Because Murphy had appealed for child labor regulation not in the language of the rights of working families but in the language about uplift, the ACLC became caught in a debate over what atmosphere provided more uplift. Mill owners met calls for a child labor law with demands for a compulsory education law. Sears began arguing that compulsory education should be in place before a child labor law was enacted. Moreover, he and other Alabama mill owners declared their willingness to follow Georgia's lead and regulate child labor through "voluntary agreements" among mill owners. In a position where criticism of mill owners was constrained by the southern public's esteem for the cotton textile industry and where he feared provoking the charge that he sought "class legislation," Murphy had trouble finding words to clarify the necessity of state intervention. He resorted to an analogy between white child labor and African American slavery. Only a generation earlier, slaveholders had defended the peculiar institution on the grounds that "there were good plantations upon which the slaves were treated well." Just as the civilized world had declared slavery repugnant to a republic, he declared that the "very idea of enforced labor for the child under twelve is monstrous both from a moral and an economic stand point." As historian David Brion Davis has pointed out, however, the force of rhetoric about slavery diminishes when it is applied to a labor situation that represents a different type of oppression.[40]

Alabama's 1903 Child Labor Legislation

In 1903 the Alabama Legislature passed an ACLC-backed child labor bill. A compromise measure, it represented reformers' conservative attempt to legitimate the idea of regulation as well as the mill owners' attempt to take the wind out of the sails of the anti–child labor movement by cooperating with the passage of an ineffectual law. The measure prohibited child labor under the age of twelve but offered various exceptions and lacked an enforcement mechanism. A manufacturer could not employ children under age fourteen for more than sixty-six hours in one week but could require children to work more than eleven hours per day as long as the weekly limit was not exceeded. The age limit for night work was lowered from fourteen to thirteen, and parents were required to file affidavits stating their children's ages. If a mill was found to have hired an underage child, it could be fined up to $250, but the parental affidavit offered legal protection to the employer.[41]

The president of the Alabama Federation of Women's Clubs (AFWC), Lillian Milner Orr, facilitated the compromise between the mill men and the ACLC that led to the enactment of the law. Because women's groups both supported reform and had ties to the mill men in the communities, women were positioned to bridge the gap between the anti–child labor advocates and the mill operators. Delegates applauded when Orr declared in her opening address to the 1903 AFWC convention, "We cannot afford to be partisans . . . where woman is not the peacemaker, she is the mischief maker." Priscilla C. Goodwyn, who supported stronger legislation, apparently refrained from arguing on its behalf for fear of alienating women's support for even the compromise measure. "We who are fortunate are banded together to give to the unfortunate, the ignorant, the guilty . . . but because love constraineth us," she declared. Murphy and S. B. Marks, the only banker on the ACLC, an SEB supporter, and husband of an AFWC delegate, joined the meeting to urge the women to support the compromise bill.[42]

The press praised the weak law both for what it accomplished and for what it avoided. The *Montgomery Advertiser* gave the AFWC accolades for its support of the bill: "By your federation, every masculine lip is silent, and every masculine voice is dumb. For twelve thousand children amidst the noisy looms of the cotton mills are lifting up their puny hands to you in gratitude that you have given them their inheritance." In Gadsden, where the Dwight Manufacturing Company's mill was the largest employer, the *Times-News* reported with relief, "We are glad that this matter has reached an amicable adjustment, for there were some outsiders who were agitating measures that would be hurtful to manufacturing interests. The spirit manifested in this compromise is to be commended."[43]

In framing the issue of child labor in such a way that it captured widespread interest and by equivocating on the issue of responsibility for child labor, the ACLC had misjudged the possible responses to such a strategy. More attention to child labor could translate into restrictions on child labor without inspections, greater support for public education, greater expectations for mill-sponsored welfare, or support for vagrancy laws and other punitive measures aimed at the parents of working children rather than at manufacturers. Even though Murphy and the ACLC defined the problem of child labor in terms that politicized the sentimentalized realm of family, they were not prepared for how much they would ultimately need women's groups as allies. Murphy, who looked first to male-dominated associations to lead the child labor movement, underestimated the degree to which changing public opinion would involve substantial changes in women's participation in public culture. In 1903, Murphy and the ACLC failed to achieve much in law. But through a focus on white child labor, regional reformers were beginning to formulate a mobilizing symbol for greater attention to the children of "plain" whites. Murphy named this child the "forgotten child of the people" and took the mill child as his symbol. After 1903, the issue of southern child labor was increasingly evaluated in terms of race, citizenship, education, and the South's relationship to the rest of the nation. White southern Progressives turned their social reform lens toward the development of white children. Murphy explained, "The culture of the South will find the occasions of its supreme and immediate interest, not in the issues presented by the negro, but in the problems presented by the undeveloped forces of the stronger race." "The presence of child labor" had initiated a "strong and wholesome protest" that the "industrial system" alone was not training and educating the "undeveloped" whites.[44]

Whiteness of Reform

CHILD LABOR REFORM WAS saturated with the rhetoric of Anglo-Saxon superiority and peppered with comparisons of African Americans and whites. Before a national group of reformers, Alabama Child Labor Committee (ACLC) member Neal Anderson pointedly declared that "our dear Southern land" held "the largest undeveloped pure stock of Anglo-Saxon people." "The significance of the danger overhanging the South," he argued, was the "greed of the capitalist who dares lay his hand upon those children, with all their splendid possibilities of this noble though undeveloped people." Anderson added that "the negro boy is provided with the opportunities for an education, while the white boy is given the opportunity—not for growing into an intelligent and useful citizen, which should be his by right of inheritance—but to wear away his young life in the close confinement of factory and mill."[1]

At first glance such rhetoric appears to be vulgar opportunism. Yet Progressives such as Anderson and Edgar Gardner Murphy were unlikely candidates to manipulate fears of African American advancement because Murphy had a history of denouncing the scare tactic of "negro domination," calling it the "merest bogy."[2] Early supporters of Negro industrial education, Murphy and Anderson were not worried about African American progress: they were trying to establish a new fear of white racial degeneration.

The Anglo-Saxon mantra of the southern anti–child labor movement seems cruel and crude when the dearth of African American opportunity is considered. Little was being done to help African Americans acquire education for their children, yet white Progressives knew southern blacks valued education as a lever of freedom and felt that they were taking advantage of any opportunity while poor whites were not. These white Progressives, unlike many other whites, supported education for blacks, yet in the quest to boost opportunities for whites, Anderson, Murphy, and their allies fueled the idea that "plain" whites should be helped before blacks, supporting the concept of white privilege and emphasizing that race should matter the most, "by right of inheritance."[3] In Alabama in particular, the passage of the 1901 state constitution linked literacy and voting rights, leading to competition for education funding and helping to explain the racialization of child labor and compulsory education laws. The southern white Progressive reform movement ultimately helped to divert northern philanthropic efforts from some African American schools to efforts to help white children. Despite this culpability, these white Progressives cannot simply be dismissed as run-of-the-mill southern racists. Their attitudes, rhetoric, and reform strategies reveal multiple racial attitudes, different brands of white supremacy, and barriers to reform that contributed to making forward-looking reformers appear backward on the subject of race.

If Anderson and Murphy's race-based rhetoric seems insincere because their inflammatory declarations resembled threats of "negro domination," which they denounced, their project was genuine. Reformers extended "racial meaning" to the issue of southern child labor because of the racial context, the power of racial idioms, and a belief that northern philanthropy had been focused on helping African Americans while desperate need among plain whites had not yet been recognized by any larger reform movement. Southern child laborers were white, and reformers sought to assign meaning to this whiteness by contextualizing these workers as racialized subjects, in part by categorizing them using familiar, powerful ideologies about Anglo-Saxon superiority.[4]

Ideas about Anglo-Saxonism formed a basis for claims about white supremacy. In the early twentieth century, educated citizens retained nineteenth-century biological theories that assumed that human races considered biologically superior were also culturally superior. These dominant ideas about race drew on Darwinian notions to declare Anglo-Saxons the most highly evolved race, and their "civilization" was considered a "natural" result of their race and a sign of their racial superiority.[5]

But these were not the only racial classifications through which social

93

interpretations of white southern child laborers could be filtered. It was not a given that white southern cotton mill children would be looked on as Anglo-Saxons in all their glory. Southern mill children could also be categorized as *poor whites, mountain whites,* or *low whites,* terms that suggested economic and social marginalization and that stressed that these were the Other whites. In the more extreme categories, the Other whites were "crackers," a label undergoing a transformation in meaning from merely a reference to a backwoods or corn farmer who cracked corn to a racially inferior white. In the postbellum South, the term *cracker* increasingly became a synonym for *white trash.*

One reason that reformers sought to establish white southern mill children as Anglo-Saxons was part of an ideological struggle to extract these child laborers from racial classifications that had made it easier to justify their exploitation. At the same time, reformers had an investment in exaggerating the image of the degraded cracker because doing so helped to underscore the need for reform. The less white a person was in the turn-of-the-century United States, the more vulnerable he or she was to degrading labor conditions and inferior citizenship status. To be racialized as "the 'trash' of whiteness" was to be relegated to the rank of justifiably impoverished. While the South's Jim Crow system encouraged a privileged racial identity of whiteness and an inferior one of blackness, historians of this period stress how racial meaning was in flux in the late nineteenth and early twentieth centuries. The rise of segregation was raising the stakes of who was classified as white, and labels such as *cracker* threatened the meaning of whiteness. Even though manufacturers touted the superiority of native-born white workers over immigrant workers, there is evidence that cotton textile interests had an investment in the concept of the cracker, which helped to support southern manufacturers' arguments that employment was advancement. So although manufacturers advertised the whiteness of southern mill workers to make them seem like a stable workforce and respected the whiteness of the workforce as a way of honoring the independence of white working men, mill men also supported the idea that these poor whites were inferior, thereby justifying low wages and impoverished conditions. The "piney-woods cracker, with a house full of scant-clad ignorant children, living in a pine-pole cabin or a mountain dugout," declared the *Manufacturers' Record,* was better off in "the factory town, filling the factory school and church," than left to his own devices.[6]

Middle-class reformers chose Anglo-Saxonism as a basis for arousing public opinion about the exploitation of cotton mill children, linking these children to a widely held belief about racial superiority that stressed potential and likeness to the white middle classes and was critical to the reformers' idea of racial and social order. Emphasizing that mill children were Anglo-Saxons rather than inferior whites had the benefit of disassociating reform from a rhetoric about the rights of labor. But the language was more than mere strategy: reformers such as Murphy really believed that these children had a known potential. Reformers' choice of language reveals the racialized nature of their concept of social order as well as why forward-looking reformers would refashion common racial rhetoric to press for a more democratic and more humane New South.[7]

The racialization of the southern child labor problem was a strategy to put manufacturers on the defensive, appeal to popular notions of racial superiority, and disassociate the issue as a labor problem, but it also sprang from reformers' interpretations of race as an "organizing principle" of society.[8] Murphy, head of the ACLC and a founder of the National Child Labor Committee (NCLC), identified race as the "basis" of southern "ascendancy" in his popularly acclaimed 1909 book by that title. When he talked about the "double basis of our race security," he declared that each race had to improve its "self-respect." Before the "negro" could advance, Murphy argued, the "stronger group" had to rid itself of its "vicious elements," "its own forces of irresponsibility."[9]

In other words, it had to eliminate the cracker. Murphy, a racial paternalist, assumed that if all whites saw themselves as relatively politically, economically, and socially superior to blacks, if caste were a single bold line between whites and blacks, then the "stronger" race not only would advance but also would encourage rather than fear the development of the "weaker race." Without such a sense of superiority, inferior whites would provoke racial violence. Ignoring the extent to which elite white southerners were involved in racial violence, Murphy blamed lynchings on competition between poor whites and blacks.[10]

Murphy also feared that poor whites would begin to feel so alienated from others of their race that they would become sexually involved with African Americans. Murphy referred to miscegenation as the "tragic fusion of white and black," partly because he shared popular views that civilizations advanced as races evolved. Contamination of Anglo-Saxon blood could only hurt the New South's social and democratic development. He believed that a sign of Anglo-Saxon achievement was its success at republican forms of government. Better forms of government would result as the master race evolved. Blacks, whom he thought had a barbarous past to overcome, might be included gradually in a white-dominated democratic order.[11]

"Anglo-Saxon men," Murphy wrote, "became civilized republican men of virtue, devoting their lives to hard work, frugality, sobriety, and the mastery of both their passions and their lives." The problem of the New South was that a number of white men who had been denied full participation in the planter-dominated Old South had become sudden participants in politics before their Anglo-Saxon attributes matured. He was certain that with the right opportunity, the children of these men would assume what he believed was their natural leadership position and would become benevolent rather than brutal toward inferior races.[12]

Murphy's racial interpretations of the South's social and political problems shaped the emerging national child labor reform movement as northern reformers capitulated to this rhetoric. Frustrated by manufacturers' opposition to reform and legislators' and clubwomen's acquiescence to Alabama's mill operators, Murphy looked for assistance from veteran reformers. At the May 1903 National Conference of Charities and Correction, held in Atlanta, Murphy's speech, "Child Labor as a National Problem," followed Jane Addams's remarks about the South. The NCLC was founded in April 1904 by Murphy; Felix Adler, founder of the free kindergarten movement; and Florence Kelley, general secretary of the National Consumers' League. The committee ensured an emphasis on the whiteness of southern mill children by hiring as a regional director North Carolina's Alexander J. McKelway, who shared many of Murphy's views.[13] In his first call for a federal child labor law, Progressive Republican Senator Albert J. Beveridge nationalized the issue of the racial integrity of southern mill children, and Elizabeth Van Vorst's *The Cry of the Children: A Study of Child-Labor* popularized the anti–child labor movement's invention of the whiteness of southern child labor.

White Supremacy or White Trash?

The president of the Alabama Federation of Women's Clubs (AFWC), Lillian Milner Orr, declared that "to go barefooted and wear one garment only is the blessed privilege of the cracker child, and in no sense a degradation," when she thought that the ACLC was becoming too critical of southern cotton mills. Although Orr supported reform, her statement reveals one of the biggest barriers to the effort to substantially improve the lives of textile families: many middle-class southerners assumed that mill work represented a step up for poor whites. Mill men counted on this public opinion that a mill wage, a sturdier house, and the civilizing influences of church and school were enough to improve the cracker. They argued that mill work offered the rural white, who had "largely drifted into a . . . a kind of drone life" in the hills, a chance to become industrious. Reformers understood that such attitudes made it difficult to win southern support for child labor laws. W. H. Swift argued that this perspective explained why white southerners "have been perfectly willing for [children] to lose their chance in life and for them to be premature wage-earners."[14]

Once a child labor reform movement emerged, the propaganda of the *Manufacturers' Record* created an image of the mill as a healthy alternative to the cracker lifestyle. "Employers witnessed with pleasure the emaciated, pale-faced children gaining the appearance of robust health and changing their tattered garments for comely ones," reported the editor of the *Manufacturers' Record*. Even reformers were affected by such attitudes. "We need to remember," one suggested, "that to most of these unfortunate people, factory life is a distinct improvement over the log-cabin, salt pork and peach brandy, white-trash and Georgia-cracker type of life from which many of them were sifted out when the mills came."[15] Reformers came up against the idea that cotton mill employment already improved the crackers' marginal claims to whiteness, an idea reinforced by the segregation in the mills, where white families had exclusive claim to certain types of jobs, relegating blacks to even less desirable positions.

To overcome attitudes such as Orr's, reformers searched for a scientific basis to support their contention that mill work damaged white children, finding the necessary evidence in the eugenics movement. Reformers drew on the "science" of eugenics to suggest a racial crisis for mill children. The racial concepts of the eugenics studies provided the premise for reformers' warnings of racial deterioration. For example, McKelway warned that "already the signs of degeneracy are becoming apparent, even in one generation of a naturally vigorous stock." Other investigators concurred, with Elbert Hubbard observing that once a child labored in a southern mill, "he is defective from that time on." "Observation shows that even these few years of manufacturing development of the South have brought deterioration to many of the white children," reported Mrs. A. O. Granger in the *Annals of the American Academy of Political and Social Science.*[16] Although eugenics studies supported assumptions of the defectiveness of poor whites, reformers focused instead on the narratives' greater promise that intervention could prevent further racial deterioration.

By the early twentieth century, periodicals such as the *Proceedings of the Conference of Charities and Correction* and the *Survey* had published eugenic studies that "scientifically" demonstrated that something was amiss with "backwoods" families. These studies traced the genealogy of families, usually to some noble ancestor of English extraction, and then focused on documenting pollution and "devolution." Bad blood and/or bad character could infect a family, with lasting consequences, as occurred in one large family referred to as the "Tribe of Ishmael." Oscar C. McCulloch traced relatives of this degenerate family to Kentucky, where he discovered that they were "well-regarded." The study identified Ishmael as the source of the corruption of this family line because he introduced nonwhite blood when he married a "half-breed woman." The "wandering blood from the half-breed mother," explained McCulloch, who became president of the National Conference of Charities and Correction in 1891, unleashed "in the second generation the poison and the passion that probably came with her." Ishmael's family was ruined, "so intermarried with others as to form a pauper ganglion." In such extreme cases, when families were past redemption—a "festering mass," likely to "sink back" regardless of attempts to save them—McCulloch and other eugenicists sometimes encouraged repressive measures such as sterilization.[17]

The drama of eugenic narratives revolved around the theme of discovering how the normal became perverted. Eugenicists referred to families with good genes who had become degenerated as "cacogenic." The "degenerate family" preserved "from its *normal ancestor* strong and attractive personal characteristics" but acquired its "low mental and moral endowment from the *subnormal side.*"[18]

Reformers were familiar with these studies but subverted them to inject urgency into arguments for protecting mill children, relying on popular recognition of the possibility that good genes could become contaminated to urge middle-class intervention to prevent it. To make this case, reformers had to establish that mill children were unadulterated Anglo-Saxon stock and then identify threats to this racial purity. Opponents of child labor borrowed the eugenicists' warnings that "we must get hold of the children."[19] Despite the eugenicist argument about racial deterioration, their studies ultimately sought to encourage reform. The larger agenda of eugenicists in the field of social work was to alter the nature of charity and benevolence, which they thought contributed to deterioration manifested as laziness and lack of ambition. Eugenicists believed that such deterioration occurred in stages and that early intervention could save children who had the right Anglo-Saxon blood.

Reformers, however, feared that bad work environments could be the first step toward irreversible contamination. In degrading conditions approximating those of nonwhite workers, anti–child labor activists believed that white mill workers might lose their race pride. At a 1903 conference on child labor in the South, southern speakers warned that the "ignorant and under-vitalized white man" would eventually succumb to "promiscuous association with his better developed black neighbor." "Can a hereditary racial antipathy alone," the report implored, "be counted upon always, under such circumstances, to check the awful evils of miscegenation?"[20]

Early-twentieth-century reformers commonly mixed advocacy of intervention, which indicated faith in the impact of social environment, with biologically based racial theories. These reformers stood at the crossroads of nineteenth-century biological classifications of race and twentieth-century social science, inventing a hybrid social theory that combined assumptions about innate racial attributes with the new social science emphasis on environmental factors. Reformers used racialized rhetoric to reconcile what seemed like an inherent contradiction—a call for reform to reshape human behavior and an insistence on innate Anglo-Saxon racial superiority. Despite the innate racial differences, Anglo-Saxons too were vulnerable to adaptations and deterioration.

McKelway and other reformers had an investment in classifying southern mill children as unadulterated whites because doing so supported the argument that these children had all of the potential of Anglo-Saxons. But McKelway also had an investment in eugenic narratives about the degeneration of whites, which provided evidence that Anglo-Saxon genetic potential had to be protected from ruin before it was too late. With early intervention through schooling, mill children could use their natural inclination for economic and social success to fulfill their hereditary potential. Premature factory work, conversely, could impair the "vital stamina of the rising generation."[21]

One argument that McKelway used was to warn that the employment of young girls jeopardized the "future mothers of the race," claiming that the drain of standing on their feet all day posed a "grave peril" to their childbearing capabilities. Furthermore, "numerous cases of bigamy" were cause for concern about the mill girls who went to work as children and married too young. McKelway believed that child workers tended to "remain children" mentally and emotionally, condemning them to membership in a "class apart."[22]

In Alabama, which had a negligible number of foreign immigrants, reformers saw the possibility for crackers to become immigrants in their own land. Despite textile manufacturers' claims that native-born whites were better workers than were immigrants, mill operatives were socially segregated and exploited in the same way as allegedly racially inferior immigrant groups elsewhere, threatening to erase the whiteness of these laborers. Weeks before the Alabama legislature debated the 1903 child labor bill, Raleigh W. Greene, a minister in Eufaula, Alabama, wrote a letter to the *Montgomery Advertiser* expressing concern about the exclusion of "mill people" from dominant white society: "It is very plain that the division between [mill people] and other people is widening all the time," he warned. "It is no wonder that they do not feel at home among other circles," he explained, "when those of other circles are treating them with such little regard and . . . permitting things to continue that unfit them more and more for better service in life." Missionary E. O. Watson suggested that mill villages "practically form a ghetto," a term associated with nonwhite immigrant living quarters.[23]

Although mill workers were still considered white in a southern society where most social divisions lay between blacks and whites, reformers understood that as poor whites began to live more like immigrant and black groups, claims to the privileges of whiteness diminished. The mill workers would become a permanent second-class group of whites. By 1901, the *Birmingham News* had recognized the potential for gradations of white citizenship when it published a northerner's view that not all immigrants should be awarded equal citizenship rights: "We have got to get rid of that idea that all men are equal and that every man has an equal right to a vote, and equal right to a place in society and an equal right to stand where everybody else does," declared Dr. Lyman Abbott of Brooklyn, New York. He added that people needed to stop being "discouraged when we have not been able to turn the mongrel into a well bred collie in one generation."[24]

In a highly racialized context where difference and otherness were racially categorized to justify subordinate social, political, and economic status, reformers sought to create a positive racial identity for cotton mill children. By the second decade of the twentieth century, these rhetorical efforts had largely succeeded, and references to the southern child laborer as the "cracker child" virtually disappeared from print. Reformers elevated the Anglo-Saxonism of mill children beyond manufacturers' promotions of a reliable workforce. Opponents of child labor argued that these white children deserved better, referring to them as "our pure Anglo-Saxon stock," "noble though undeveloped people of the mountains and hills," "white native Americans, descendants of those who fought under Washington and of those who followed Lee," related to "the most prominent men of the state," and "the white non-participants of the older civilization." These children were not incapable but were simply "the unstarted," the "neglected masses of the white population," "our humbler white people," "real Americans," and "the best we have."[25] Although the Anglo-Saxon rhetoric was not new, reformers had a new goal of making it hard to say that factory work was acceptable for white children in the South.

"The Qualifying Principle of the White Race Is Character"

Reformers sought to reclassify mill children as Anglo-Saxons rather than crackers in an attempt to claim rights for southern mill children. However, the southern reformers also tended to be racial paternalists who assumed that rights came with responsibilities. And the reformers denigrated adult mill workers as part of the process of establishing that mill children had potential that their parents were squandering.

Murphy's interest in reforming the character of poor whites included a willingness to disfranchise them. He opposed the "grandfather clause" in Alabama's 1901 constitution, which granted permanent voting rights to all Confederate soldiers and their descendants who registered before January 1903 and paid their poll taxes before each election. Murphy believed that the grandfather clause was dangerous: "Who is to determine whether the descendant is a descendant or a degenerate?" he implored.[26]

He expressed fear of a mass democracy of degenerates in *Problems of the Present South* (1904), a book that won wide contemporary acclaim as a "wise" interpretation of the "South's growth" from "aristocracy to democracy." Murphy argued that nonslaveholding white men had been "non-participants" in the Old South. They may have voted, but they certainly were led by an educated aristocracy and were poorly prepared to realize the sudden potential for participation. Murphy not only distrusted the way that Reconstruction governments, oligarchic Redeemer governments, and demagogues manipulated illiterate whites' votes but also recoiled at the idea of ordinary men forming political organizations, cautioning that where the "common people have ruthlessly assumed the reins of power," chaos had ensued.[27]

These assumptions informed Murphy's interpretation of the politics of the Populist insurgency in the 1890s and ongoing struggles between Redeemers, who represented commercial and planter interests, and ordinary white Democrats. He interpreted what historian Albert D. Kirwan has labeled the "Revolt of the Rednecks" in the Democratic Party as menaces to the "particular form of public order" that the South needed. In Murphy's eyes, the "non-participants" had become participants merely through a superficial understanding of race. He opposed the idea that simply having white skin qualified a man to vote. Murphy's fear of popular democracy grew in part from his disdain for the South's legendary electoral fraud and racial violence, especially lynchings. Alabama's gubernatorial campaigns of the 1890s were distinguished by corruption and physical attacks, and the state constitution provided no legal means for contesting elections.[28]

With his faith in the superiority of the Anglo-Saxon race and his belief in the myth of a nobler white southern tradition of political and social leadership, Murphy interpreted this violent political landscape as the result of a low standard for white citizenship. Murphy contended that the "poorer classes of the white population" were "determined in enmity." "It is between this class and the mass of the Negroes that race antipathies are most violent," he explained. He believed that the only solution was to educate the white population because "training upon the one [black] side, and general culture upon the other [white side had] always brought peace." The grandfather clause, he held, betrayed whites' responsibility to uphold "culture," a concept that he understood as racially based. If too many illiterate whites voted, he assumed that the civilized opinions of enlightened whites would be overshadowed. "I am wholly against the proposals which are calculated to kill my vote . . . with the ballot of the penniless illiterate who would vote a patent medicine advertisement as quickly as a ballot, if the right man 'fixed it,'" he declared.[29]

As much as they asserted the superiority of Anglo-Saxons, reformers such as Murphy believed in the transformative power of education too much to think that a biological predisposition was enough. Murphy wanted a social commitment to educating whites, and on those grounds he opposed the grandfather clause for eliminating an education incentive for white men. While he pandered to racist fears by suggesting that African Americans were "ambitious" and eager for education, he was not suggesting that the dominance of the white race was up for debate. Murphy reassured the white public that education for African Americans was not a threat, yet he saw a danger in any African Americans "passing" any of "our white people in any respect," a situation that would create competition between the races and thus fuel violence. In his estimation, black education was a threat only if whites were not more highly educated. And he feared that the grandfather clause would cause ambitious African Americans to seek education to qualify to vote, while the lack of a literacy requirement eliminated the motivation for white men to become educated. "Do our white people not need the incentive of a slight educational test?" he demanded of delegates at the state constitutional convention.[30]

Murphy had support among middle-class Progressives who believed that poor whites needed prodding to send their children to school. The *Montgomery Advertiser* argued that white illiteracy was "not all due to lack of opportunity to learn, but rather to disinclination on the part of those whose duty it was to send their children to school." During debates over the grandfather clause, the *Birmingham News* complained that "illiteracy was on the rise in the voting population. . . . Yet the suffrage committee [plans] to offer an incentive for Negroes to educate, but to offer none to whites." Like Murphy, the editorial warned that "unlettered negroes . . . are already proportionally outstripping the ignorant whites in acquiring education." Concern was great enough to motivate the Alabama State Supervisor of Rural Schools, N. R. Baker, to launch an "investigation as to causes of non enrollment" in Talladega County, the home of two cotton mills. This study confirmed reformers' perceptions of white apathy toward education by reporting that "a much larger percentage of negro pupils are enrolled than white pupils." "The most significant figures," Baker declared, "are those placed opposite the excuse 'Do not Desire Education.'" Of the 797 white pupils not enrolled in a county with 2,734 white school-age children, 375 indicated that they did not attend school because they did not desire it, whereas only 18 cited poverty as the reason for foregoing school. Among the 435 black children not enrolled out of the 2,955 identified as school age, only 79 listed lack of desire for education as their reason for not attending, and 87 identified poverty as the main barrier to regular attendance.[31]

While popular opinion was growing regarding the apathy of poor whites, a few advocates of white education suggested that such numbers reflected the stigma that whites felt about admissions of poverty. J. T. Hefflin, a delegate to the constitutional convention who opposed the grandfather clause, suggested as much with a dire warning about future racial conflict: "[Negroes] are being educated very rapidly. Why, they will attend school with but few garments to wear and with but little to eat, when the child of the white man would be kept at home because he hasn't good clothes to put on and good victuals to send with him to school as his neighbor has. . . . Some day the clash will come and the survival of the fittest."[32] Such comments suggested the degree to which dominant white society had made poor whites feel marginalized because of their inability to afford to appear respectable.

After its incorporation into the 1901 state constitution, the grandfather clause became a touchstone for the race-based rhetoric of Alabama's child labor reform movement. For example, in support of a 1907 child labor law, the *Alabama Baptist* warned, "The new constitution of Alabama makes an educational qualification for the negroes to vote; but under the 'grandfather clause' no such qualification is required of the whites. A stimulus is thus given to the negro to improve himself mentally . . . but a premium is put upon ignorance among the whites." Furthermore, the paper complained, it was "notorious that the negroes are sending their children to school," making it "next to impossible to hire a negro child to nurse the baby in any home." Equally disturbing were the "many white parents" who were "careless about the schooling of their

children." The ACLC's Anderson exploited the idea that literacy requirements for suffrage disfranchised the next white generation when
he argued in 1905 that the "newly adopted constitution" placed a "premium" on the "education for the negro." He suggested that "largely
through the efforts of the philanthropic North," African American boys
were more likely to become educated citizens than were poor white boys.[33]

Other southern reformers echoed the concerns expressed by Murphy
and his fellow Alabamians. The NCLC's McKelway contended that North
Carolina's literacy requirements for suffrage meant that employers were
dooming poor white boys "to a rank beneath citizenship" by keeping
them at work instead of in school, where they could acquire the education needed to pass literacy tests. Walter Hines Page, former editor of
the *Raleigh (North Carolina) State Chronicle* and a nationally known jour-
nalist, popularized the cause of the educational uplift of "plain whites"
with the phrase the "forgotten man," the title of a speech he delivered
in June 1897 at the State Normal and Industrial School for Women in
Greensboro, North Carolina. The forgotten man resembled Murphy's
nonparticipant in that both were identified as men marginalized by the
slave South's white aristocracy. Using literacy rates, Page estimated that
"one in every four [southern white men] was wholly forgotten" and had
become "the sorry Southern white man," "a dead weight" on southern
progress. But Page chose to invent the forgotten man not to disgrace
him but to compel reforms to improve his social status. The forgotten
man, Page argued, had never been given the opportunity to develop
himself, and the forgotten woman had been too overworked and under-
nourished to provide a moral force among the ranks of common white
people. The goal for white female teachers, he declared, was to provide
education to "these people," who were "capable of development, capable
of unlimited growth and elevation," but had been neglected until they
had become unfit to help themselves.[34]

Murphy responded to Page and echoed his call, urging reformers to
help the "children of the forgotten people." Education of the children
of the forgotten man was the means to reconstruct white southern manhood and womanhood, and a more orderly and noble New South would
follow. Page articulated reformers' preoccupation with the next generation as the key to change in the New South when he concluded, "The
most sacred thing in the Commonwealth and to the Commonwealth is

the child, whether it be your child or the child of the dull-faced mother of the hovel. The child of the dull-faced mother may, for all you know be the most capable child in the State."[35]

Reformers increasingly found the forgotten child and his or her family in the cotton mill. While the concept of the forgotten man referred to rural whites in general, the mill child became the most accessible figure through which reformers could evaluate the status of white rural families, and reformers determined that the child laborer represented the ultimate breakdown of the forgotten man's home. "Is not the home, the American home, destroyed" when "the duties of wifehood and motherhood are complicated with the unending task of winning bread?" asked McKelway.[36]

Reformers judged mill families as in disarray because degenerate women were assumed to be incapable of performing their duties as mothers and wives and because child labor emasculated the forgotten man. The counterpart to the factory child was the "idle father," whom reformers described as the family member who carried the "dinner-pail at noon, perhaps working a little on odd days when he gets tired of loafing." He did the woman's work of serving food while the women and children won the bread.[37]

Such analyses did not adequately assess mill families. Many men worked in the cotton mills, most men had some kind of work, and married women did not often hold full-time jobs outside their homes. Reformers' analyses reflected more about their assumptions about respectable male citizenship's relationship to specific gender arrangements than about the actual pattern of family wage labor. Reformers thought that respectable, white southern manhood depended on educated, moral womanhood and on good homes. When gender arrangements fell outside the prescribed boundaries, southern manhood and womanhood, the gendered identifiers of whiteness, were threatened. Regional reformers raised concerns that "in most of the southern states the illiterate females outnumber the illiterate males" and argued that "an illiterate mother does not augur well for the child of tomorrow."[38]

The child labor movement became bound up in southern reformers' greater concern for educating white children. One reason references to literacy qualifications for suffrage remained an issue that shaped the racialized rhetoric of reform was because competition for education funds was tight and reformers could use the idea that African Americans might surpass whites (no matter how far removed that suggestion was from reality) to bolster their case for greater funding for white education. Researching black education in Alabama during the 1930s, African American scholar Horace Mann Bond remarked on the impetus the new constitution gave to education for whites: "The suffrage provisions of the [1901] Constitution . . . focused attention on the necessity of education of white children." Bond's work illuminates the intense competition for education funding "between the two separate systems."[39]

At first glance, for example, it appears that Murphy made too much of the impact of Alabama's grandfather clause on perpetuating white ignorance. Future generations of illiterate whites were not grandfathered into the franchise. Although illiterate whites might still qualify to vote under the discretion of a white registrar whose literacy standards could be lowered at convenient times, future generations of whites would have precarious claims to the right to vote without proof of literacy. "Care was taken," Murphy explained, "that all the rising generations and all future generations of white voters should be constrained to accept the suffrage test, a test applicable, therefore, after a brief fixed period, to white and black alike." White males not registered by January 1903 faced a literacy test. Murphy's claims regarding the harm caused by the grandfather clause may have been disingenuous, reflecting purely his desire to keep any illiterate person—black or white—from voting. He was pleased that future generations would be held to a higher standard and stressed this fact to urge that apathy among whites would have to be addressed. Child labor reformers warned that the new constitution provided incentive for blacks to educate their children but not for whites to do so while at the same time arguing that white boys had to be educated to qualify to vote. If those white children were to be citizens of character and if they were to pass a future literacy test to qualify to vote, they had to be educated. Reformers exploited the new literacy qualifications for suffrage in contradictory ways, but their goal was consistent: greater support for white education.[40]

Alabama's 1901 constitution had increased state funding for education, one reason that some Progressives had supported the document's ratification. However, education reformers were frustrated by the constitution's prohibition on local taxation for education. In 1904, according to Murphy, Alabama spent $4.41 a year per pupil—"less than five cents a day for only about one hundred days in the year"—compared to $8.82

in Louisiana and $17.59 in Kansas. Beyond providing needed revenue, reformers believed that local taxation would inspire the commitment to public schools that was absent from a society in which persisted a strong suspicion of the masses as "ignorant and unpatriotic."[41]

There was never any doubt that whites would get more of Alabama's education funds than African Americans would: an 1890 school funds appropriation law that was essentially incorporated into the 1901 constitution had opened the way for local officials to distribute funds in a way that favored white students. White politicians from the Black Belt consequently lost interest in pushing for local taxation to fund education, since their counties' shares of school funds had to be divided among fewer whites, resulting in higher per-student expenditure rates. Predominantly white counties thus lacked Black Belt political allies in the fight for local taxation. As a result, white reformers argued that the counties with the highest percentage of whites were the most in need of school funding, focusing on the fact that six of the eight counties where white illiteracy surpassed 20 percent were in the northern, predominantly white, half of the state. These counties received less funding per white student.[42]

The racialized nature of the child labor reform movement was part of a larger racialized politics over education funding. The intensity of efforts to win greater support for white education can be seen in white southern Progressives' criticism of northern philanthropy directed toward Negro industrial education. Groups such as the AFWC began criticizing the Peabody and Slater Funds and the General Education Board, among other northern philanthropic organizations, for aiding blacks and neglecting whites. Alabama clubwomen chastised northern philanthropist Robert Ogden for supporting the Tuskegee Institute but not the white girls' school. The women complained, "No one came to know or see that the white girl in Alabama has no library or reading room, that she does not possess one room industrially fitted up as is should be for her instruction. . . . Compare these long flights of stairs with the smooth running elevators and cushioned stools of Booker Washington's school. . . . Who is caring for or coming to view the poor white girl in the South as she is?" Competition for education funding for whites was intense, and white reformers pressured northern philanthropists to begin paying more attention to whites. The AFWC and other local groups exaggerated northern aid for blacks in an effort to increase attention on the enormous problem of white illiteracy. In 1913, the Alabama Business Men's League literally rerouted a group of northern philanthropists from a visit to the Tuskegee Institute to a league meeting in Montgomery. John H. Movements Jr., commissioner of the Alabama Department of Game and Fish, told the philanthropists that "the most imperative requirement . . . is the education of the mountain children of this country," who represented the majority of the nation's "pure blooded Americans." "These little mountain children," were "being drawn on to recruit the forces of the cotton-mill employees of this country," resulting in the exploitation of "their little bodies, their brains, their brawn." He urged the northern philanthropists to redirect their interest and support for education to these mountain children.[43] A tidal shift among reformers occurred as the increasing whiteness of child labor reform left education for African Americans with little legacy from earlier reform efforts.

Nationalization of the Whiteness of Reform

U.S. Senator Albert J. Beveridge, a Progressive Republican from Indiana, became the impassioned champion of a "national method" for stopping child labor and expanded throughout the country the growing emphasis on whiteness in child labor reform. After helping to enact a federal meat inspection law in 1906, Beveridge became an advocate of congressional power to regulate industry to stop such abuses as child labor. He publicized the problem as a "national evil" in 1907 in the first attempt to win a federal prohibition on child labor. His speech, heralded by Albert Shaw of the *American Monthly Review of Reviews* as "very strong" and by other Progressives as a great boost to the reform movement, was peppered with race-based rhetoric about the South's child labor problem. Before making the speech, Beveridge had written to Jane Addams that "public opinion is our only hope."[44] He apparently believed that emphasizing the whiteness of mill children would rally public support.

Using Irene Ashby-Macfadyen's data on Alabama mills, Beveridge took special aim at the South. "I come to a section of the country where this evil is greatest and most shameful and where it is practiced *upon the purest American strain that still exists in this country*—the children in the southern cotton mills," Beveridge said on the floor of the U.S. Senate. Echoing arguments made by NCLC reformers, Beveridge declared the great potential of the Anglo-Saxon children of the South: "Every sociological investigator testifies that those southern children of this origin are capable of infinite development." But they were being wasted, just as England had wasted its best "country people" to the point that it lacked fit soldiers, he argued. Drawing on the arguments of Ashby-Macfadyen, Murphy, Anderson, and McKelway, Beveridge stated that the "children who are working in the South's cotton mills are from the white working class" yet were doomed to an inferior status because while they worked, "Negro children" were "going to school."[45]

Beveridge and his supporters did not expect the bill to become law but were encouraged by how much public support his speech generated. Supporters of a federal law vowed to continue the fight, growing increasingly critical of opposition from the South. Southern Democrats united in opposition to the bill, and Beveridge charged that "three-fourths of the cotton factories of the Southern States" worked to defeat his bill.[46]

Beveridge understood that southern opposition would be strong, but he probably did not expect Murphy to turn reformers against the measure. Murphy resigned from the NCLC over the group's initial support of the Beveridge bill, provoking the committee to withdraw its support and sowing seeds of dissension among its members. General secretary of the National Consumers' League and NCLC member Florence Kelley wrote to her son about her embarrassment and anger: "I do not see how I can self-respectingly remain in the committee and I hate to resign from it. Whatever its faults, the bill embodies the first attempt to deal justly with *all* the children and all the employers. And rescinding an endorsement of a federal bill, by a so-called national body is the most serious injury which can be inflicted upon a pending bill."[47] As the national reform committee splintered, a more virulent emphasis on the whiteness of the South's textile child laborers became a crude effort to maintain a common ground and to urge a national interest in reform.

Murphy's opposition reflected more than deep-seated fear of federal interference in the South but rather was consistent with his belief that cultural and democratic advances went hand in hand. He felt that legislation would not work without the support of public opinion. He believed that federal legislation in the face of southern opposition would lower the "sense of local responsibility." "The local processes of social education are arrested, the cause of the children is set backward and the interests of the Nation are defeated rather than advanced," he contended. Rather than seeing the matter as involving "state's rights," he declared that he "preferred to conceive it as a question of duties." Child labor could not be abolished in the South until it had been eliminated from the "hearts of our people."[48]

Some northern reformers, however, did not want to wait for the hearts of southerners to change before achieving better standards at home. Kelley wrote to her son, "Too long have the states exerted their alleged right to do nothing, to refrain from doing necessary things, to let harm come to the whole Republic, their sins of omission." She was adamant that the Beveridge bill was a step toward ensuring that a "child in Georgia" have the "same human need and claim upon the Republic as a child in Illinois or Oregon." NCLC member Samuel McCune Lindsay, the director of New York's School of Philanthropy, wrote to Beveridge, "I am sorry to say that practically the whole bunch of people at the National Committee seem to be reactionaries." Lindsay exempted from his criticism Kelley, who was fighting to establish a standard for an eight-hour-law for children under sixteen by winning such legislation in Massachusetts.[49]

Murphy's racialization of the South's child labor problem had been tied to his specific ideas of white southern culture and social order, but after he became increasingly isolated on the national scene, reform gave way to a racialized rhetoric that lampooned southern culture. After Beveridge's bill failed, he endorsed one of the most sensational pieces of racialized reform rhetoric when he wrote an introduction to Elizabeth Van Vorst's *The Cry of the Children: A Study of Child-Labor* (1908). In a 1906 *Saturday Evening Post* article, Van Vorst had reported on her investigations of Alabama mills, a muckraking effort she and her sister had begun in 1903 when they worked undercover as factory operatives, but when she republished this article along with others in a book after the Beveridge bill failed, she made the whiteness of southern mill children central to her story. Van Vorst argued in lurid detail that the purest white Americans were imprisoned by the lint, dirt, filth, and lewdness of life in mill villages. At first glance, she argued, it was hard to see the virtues of the mill people, buried as they were under "old tin cans, decayed vegetables, pieces of dirty paper, rags, and chicken feathers." In vignette after vignette, however, Van Vorst washed away the layers of dirt to reveal the truest white native-born Americans, down to phenotypical descriptions of their "fine and delicate features," "deep eyes," "high-arched nose," and "slender lips."[50]

Like eugenics studies that described authors' perceptions of inherited deficiencies among backwoods families, Van Vorst relied on animal imagery and insinuations about sexual depravity to draw sordid pictures of mill families. She described an almost inhuman mother who not only let her child play with rats but who let the rodents "make the tour of her bodice, wriggling, burrowing, crawling." The adults and children were dirty with ubiquitous tobacco grime. A boy recently in a knife fight "drawled his words; they seemed to dribble slowly, without intelligence, from his mouth, like the tobacco juice which spilled over his lips when he spoke."[51]

Yet Van Vorst sought to show that beneath the unsavory appearances of the mill workers were signs of Anglo-Saxon civilized traits. In an 1891 *Century Magazine* article, "The Georgia Cracker in the Cotton Mills," Clare De Graffenried had used similar derogatory descriptions of mill workers to urge reform but had been attacked by white southerners as if she were criticizing the character of the people. Van Vorst sought to deflect criticism and urge white southern support through a subplot of the great potential of mill families based on their underlying whiteness. After describing the woman with the rats, for example, Van Vorst revealed that the woman was friendly, offering to help the disguised author find work at the mill. The slow-speaking boy turned out to have engaged in the fight in defense of his sister's virtue, demonstrating his "chivalrous desire to protect his sisters," an "instinctive respect for his father's will," a "fine fiber of loyalty," and a "demand for justice." The "poverty-stricken people of the South—the poor white trash," she argued, were like discarded cherished possessions whose "faded elegance" invokes memories of a simpler "more noble past." Her investigations led her to conclude, "This stuff is worth saving. There is the making in these children of first-class citizens."[52] Van Vorst sought to popularize the myth of Anglo-Saxon character as a basis for reform.

The whiteness of reform, while pervasive, was not ideologically consistent. It was a fiction through which reformers such as Murphy and his ACLC colleagues liked to view the South, imagining themselves as architects of its new racial and social order. The whiteness of reform questioned whether a mill job was good enough for white children, raising questions about the meaning of southern progress. It offered a convenient camouflage to overcome white class conflict and sectional disparities. In the hands of Van Vorst, it was caricature. In the early twentieth century, many northerners and southerners could agree that whiteness was worth saving. The whiteness of reform had different meanings for different white reformers, but they all understood the language. Focusing on whiteness ensured the southern child labor problem's centrality in the national reform debate.

CHAPTER SIX

Transregional Progressivism

ELIZABETH VAN VORST ALSO criticized the role of Alabama's women in the anti–child labor movement. The "several ladies" who had been "active in passing the only laws" in the state were, according to Van Vorst, tranquilized by aristocratic pretension: "My chief informant was a pretty woman of the graceful, languid type we designate in a word as 'Southern.' It was a shock to hear her affirm in her soft musical voice, with its drawling intonation: 'Why, child-labor in Alabama is a necessary evil.'" With such overdrawn portraits, Van Vorst declared that southern ladies were not new women. This southern lady, a mill stockholder (perhaps based on Lillian Milner Orr's role in the 1903 compromise), was so reactionary that she dismissed poor white workers as "just like animals."[1]

Van Vorst's stereotype of the southern lady was as exaggerated as her images of mill workers (see chap. 5), but it expressed her belief that many southern women did not measure up to Progressive standards. Van Vorst's insulting picture of southern ladies was inaccurate but nevertheless raised serious questions. What was the nature of southern women's reform? What was the influence of the image of the southern lady? While Van Vorst's fact-based but sensationalized account was trivial, her questions were ones that scholars have seriously investigated in such works as Anne Firor Scott's pioneering *The Southern Lady: From Pedestal to Politics, 1830–1930* and particularly since historians began questioning the "New Englandization" of women's history.[2]

Recent scholarship on southern women documents the activities of many new women in the Progressive Era with an eye to what made their

114

work uniquely southern. A study of Texas women found that southern women led the region's men in demanding social reform, a finding that suggests a flaw in comparing southern and northern women. After the Galveston hurricane of 1900, organized women stepped into the vacuum created by the government's lack of infrastructure to address the many health problems exposed by the crisis. Anastatia Sims examined white organized women in North Carolina, showing that the image of the lady had real power over women's actions but instead of prohibiting reform was reaffirmed and reconfigured to endorse women's Progressivism. She found many examples of women talking about being "efficient and sweet and womanly" and "Progressive yet sane, cultured yet unassuming, [possessing] that sweet graciousness of manner which is characteristic of southern womanhood."[3]

Women's reform in the Alabama anti–child labor campaign illuminates why it is difficult to compare southern women's Progressivism to northern women's reform. What qualifies as new public activity for Alabama women in the name of helping children, families, and communities is not always the same as political activism judged by those who have a stake in the political outcome of women's reform. Alabama's organized, white middle-class women were more and more active in efforts to help the state's poor children. Yet, simply put, southern women were more conservative than their northern counterparts, and female activism in the region was in step with movements to address compulsory education before child labor regulation. Their Progressivism was provincial.

Southern women's activism became a concern for reformers elsewhere, however. In the wake of Senator Albert J. Beveridge's 1907 attempt to win federal legislation to restrict child labor, the national movement seemed to be stalled by the South. A 1910 U.S. Bureau of Labor report, *Woman and Child Wage-Earners in the United States,* confirmed reformers' worst suspicions about bad conditions in southern mills and flagrant violations of weak laws, raising the stakes for Alabama's women reformers.

The nationalization of the whiteness of southern child labor triggered the growth of southern women's leadership in reform by hooking a significant minority of Alabama women into a network of leading Progressives. A race-based ideological foundation dampened southern suspicions of outsiders. While reformers could talk about whiteness and mean different things, an emphasis on saving "forgotten" white southern children facilitated interregional reconciliation. The whiteness of reform was critical for legitimating white southern reformers' relationships with northern reformers, distancing northern reform from older concerns about African American education. The whiteness of reform validated the worth of poor white southerners and made them popular reform subjects. Focusing on the whiteness of mill children rather than overtly discussing the South's "race problem" facilitated a burgeoning national conversation about the South's child labor problem in a way that politicized Alabama women's work for poor white children.

Southern women's leadership emerged partly because ambitious women took advantage of the new political conditions created by the whiteness of southern child labor reform as well as because northern groups called on white southern women to do more. In 1916 the trustees of the National Child Labor Committee (NCLC) wrote, "We must 'nag' the South a little more."[4] Sectional disparities among child labor laws led national organizations to pressure southern women to become more involved. Racialized rhetoric helped make these calls easier for white southern women to heed. Northern reformers reached out to white southern women and offered them new credentials and new standards for judging their reform efforts.

As a result of interregional reconciliation in the name of reform for white children, a transregional Progressive culture emerged as Alabama women embraced new images of themselves and their work and found support for demanding more of their region than their local movements had imagined. A new, alluring ideal of white middle-class womanhood lay at the heart of this transregional Progressivism. Not all Alabama women active in the name of poor children adopted this new model, but a minority became leading Progressive activists as a result of it. Leading northern Progressive groups sought to pull the southern lady from her pedestal, only to find that some southern women were all too ready to leap down.

The national child labor movement played a key role in changing women's reform in Alabama and fostered the rise of a transregional Progressive culture that valued the advice of experts, supported a standard of new womanhood, and was interested in setting national goals with local women helping to overcome local hurdles and to take into account unique local conditions. The racialized national child labor movement pressured southern women to do more, created fictional images that honored southern women who dared to stand up to local evils, and linked local women to leading Progressive women in the U.S. Children's Bureau, National Consumers' League (NCL), and the NCLC. In 1907 Alabama women's work for a new state child labor law remained isolated and provincial; four years later, however, the NCLC held its annual conference in Birmingham. The meeting became a celebration of inter-regional reconciliation and gave birth to a transregional Progressivism that judged the South by its own cosmopolitan standards, including a standard for new women of the New South.

By 1915, the campaign for a new child labor law in Alabama was the product of a transregional Progressive culture and featured truly new women at the helm. In contrast to earlier southern reform, this women-led campaign demanded that Alabama conform to the standards of the proposed federal child labor legislation supported by the NCLC. Sig-nificantly, this transregional Progressivism also began demanding work-hour limitation for women and child laborers. Alabama's women reform-ers had become closely aligned with the NCLC and the U.S. Children's Bureau and possessed a professionalism and confidence that came from being part of something larger than their local movement. These new Alabama women were insiders, not just in their local club networks but in a larger reform world. Like Progressive Era new women elsewhere, Ala-bama's women became experts on child welfare and imposed their ideas on their state.[5] They looked first to national Progressive organizations for standards, goals, and personal professional aspirations and in turn offered national organizations expertise regarding local peculiarities.

Provincial Progressives

White Alabama women thought of themselves as some of the only friends of the state's poor white children and would have been insulted by Van Vorst's aloof southern lady accepting the necessary evils southern men created. Organized Alabama women saw themselves as responding in an unprecedented manner to the needs of the state's poor white chil-dren. Elizabeth Johnston, a leading member of the Alabama Federation of Women's Clubs (AFWC), recognized the broadening of the federation's goals from caring not only for the "orphans and bad boys, but all the factory and school children."[6]

Although Alabama's female reformers talked about the public responsibilities of "holy Motherhood" and about their work in terms of the "redemption of the race," they did not leave long accounts explaining their ideas about racial order in the South, as Edgar Gardner Murphy did. The whiteness of child labor reform had increasingly validated their public activism, however, and by 1907 they had overcome their initial hesitancy and supported Murphy and his Alabama Child Labor Committee (ACLC) in a successful campaign for a new child labor law. The new measure was stronger than previous Alabama legislation: even though it still barred child labor only under the age of twelve and covered only mills and factories, it required eight weeks of compulsory education for all child workers in manufacturing under the age of sixteen and prohibited night work for children under sixteen. Parents were required to submit to employers affidavits certifying the ages of any employed children under eighteen. The inspector of jails and almshouses, charged with monitoring all factories where children worked, checked the ages on the affidavits, which employers filed with the office of the judge of probate.[7]

Alabama's reform efforts remained provincial in that they responded more to regional concerns regarding compulsory education than to issues of regulation of manufacturing. The state handled the child labor problem by pursuing a compulsory education law, an alternative touted by mill interests. Local reform in Alabama remained bound up in unique regional relationships with manufacturers and ideas about local conditions, but women had reason to believe that calling for reform was forcing manufacturers to do more for mill children.

Rather than antagonizing manufacturers so that they would turn their backs on humanitarian initiatives, the Alabama child labor campaign had generated a middle-class consensus in support of public education for all white children. Whereas women reformers previously had worried that support for child labor regulation risked alienating the same manufacturers who supported some of their educational causes, by 1906 they had found a comfortable consensus by approaching child labor in terms of compulsory education. Cotton manufacturers could play to this demand for education because it really did not affect their labor supply. Braxton Bragg Comer owned the Avondale Mills near Birmingham and was a 1906 gubernatorial candidate. During his campaign, Comer, an advocate of local industry who wanted to attract the reform wing of the Democratic Party on the issue of railroad rate reform, found that charges of violations of the child labor law were the "most serious" against him. Forced to show his concern for Alabama's poor white children, he publicized his support for compulsory education, winning approval from local women's clubs, which already knew him to endorse their premier reform effort, an industrial school for white boys and girls. He also announced his support of a local taxation option for school funding, a long-term goal of education reformers.[8]

After winning election, Governor Comer asked for reformers' support for a compulsory education law. "The militant childhood nurseries," he argued, were not the factories but the "homes of the farmers." The solution to protecting the state's children was not regulating manufacturers, he argued, but making school compulsory. Local women reformers saw themselves as helping more children by winning more support for education, and southern manufacturers were much more willing to provide schools than to support labor restrictions. More than half of the southern mills investigated by the U.S. Bureau of Labor in 1910 supported a day or night school, while New England mills had "practically nothing to do with the educational affairs of their localities." In Alabama, for example, the Anniston mills provided a free kindergarten and contributed to the public schools that abutted the village. Larger establishments, including the Merrimack Mills in Huntsville and the Dwight Mill in Alabama City, maintained day and night schools.[9]

Manufacturers muted criticism from reformers in Alabama at the same time that reformers elsewhere were becoming angrier at the South. Progress in Alabama could still look like backwardness to supporters of a national standard of regulation of child labor under fourteen rather than twelve and of an eight-hour day. And even as Alabama's white organized women remained active, helping poor white children in various ways, the Alabama child labor reform movement virtually dissolved once the weak 1907 child labor act became law and interest shifted to compulsory education as the preferred goal. The prison and almshouse inspector, Dr. Charles F. Bush, complained of a "lack of real interest on the part of many who agitate." Bush found numerous violations of the law based on inaccurate or absent paperwork showing age and school attendance. Given the lack of vital statistics to verify ages (the Department of Vital Statistics was not organized until 1908) and the relationship between manufacturers and mill schools, merely checking papers was inadequate to determine the extent to which the law was violated.[10] Without volunteers or a paid staff to help him, the investigator was little more than a token regulatory agent. With women reformers focused more on education issues and in the wake of the decline of the ACLC after Murphy and Neal Anderson moved away from the state, the Alabama anti–child labor movement appeared to be dead.

Perpetuation of Child Labor

Paradoxically, the Alabama child labor movement's achievement of the 1907 law with its meager eight-week education requirement tightened mill men's control over their workers by uniting employers and employees against a common enemy, reformers. Workers despised meddling middle-class reformers and changes that interfered with family independence and economic strategies. Reformers were doing what they felt was right for children, but manufacturers had some understanding of how their workers thought in terms of family strategy. Charles H. Moody of the Dwight Mills later showed not only his own self-interest but that of the workers when he suggested a compulsory education law that allowed children to attend school half a day and work the other half: "In this way," he said, "they will be able to attend school longer without the hardships which they claim they are put to now." As David L. Carlton pointed out in his history of South Carolina's mill populations, mill workers frequently supported up-country politicians who opposed both child labor legislation and compulsory education on the grounds of standing up for workers' independence. Employers' control over their employees and collusion between workers and manufacturers in breaking the child labor law meant an entrenched child labor problem.[11]

Alabama workers earned much less than their counterparts in Massachusetts but still preferred the mill to their other limited options. Alabama's operatives compared their situation not to Massachusetts but to their bleak choices as farmers: with mill work, children's wages raised a family's overall income. Workers thus viewed child labor laws as a threat to economic security and could not relate to reformers' interest in downplaying the number of "poor widows" and "disabled fathers." Even if the number of destitute adults who needed their children's wages was low, workers could easily imagine themselves in situations in which children's wages were all that would stand between their parents and a poor farm, considered disgraceful and hazardous.[12] Child labor brought a degree of security to a family's precarious economic life, in which illness or lay-offs could be devastating.

Alienated by reformers' arguments, workers turned to employers as accomplices in violating the law. Even though factory inspection reports showed that employers and workers violated the 1907 law with impunity, its education feature, which went into effect in 1909, affected every family, thereby reinforcing bonds between workers and their employers. Six of the required eight weeks of school attendance had to be consecutive, and every child under the age of sixteen had to comply.[13] This was the only statewide law to compel education.

The factory inspector reported that as soon as the education feature became effective, "protests, objections, suggestions etc. . . . began pouring into the Department" from "both operators and operatives." "Every subterfuge they can devise has been tried to dodge the educational requirement of the law. Likewise the children are apathetic, indifferent, and negligent, and on every occasion try to evade the school."[14] As the education requirement made beating the law more important, a manufacturer's self-serving willingness to permit violations or offer a mill school with flexible hours became a way of showing respect for workers' family autonomy.

Factory inspection reports testify to the collaboration between mill men and their employees. The inspector found that mills permitted children to return to work even after the inspector found them in violation of the education requirement. In Alabama City, where the Dwight Manufacturing Company was publicly applauded for its day and night schools, 118 of the 331 children under sixteen had worked at the mill at some time during the year without school certificates. Mill families could support education for their children when it did not cost them wages, but they resisted compulsory education.[15]

Commissioned in 1907 as a concession to supporters of the failed Beveridge bill, the U.S. Bureau of Labor's *Woman and Child Wage-Earners in the United States* documented the ongoing problems of child labor in the southern cotton mills. In 1910, the first three volumes appeared— a report on the cotton textile industry, a report on children leaving school to go to work, and a comparative study of child labor legislation. The study blamed southern manufacturers and sought to discredit their support of education as a defense of their labor practices. The study underscored mill men's power over their workers and demonstrated the control employers accrued by providing housing, schools, and other community needs. The document did not hesitate to blame manufacturers and led to rumors that in Alabama's Merrimack Mills, a Massachusetts-owned company in Huntsville, the mill men arranged "that the school session shall begin at six in the morning and end at 12: this is done that the children may spend the other half of the day working in their mill!" While the southern textile states prohibited child labor only under the age of twelve, only two of thirty-two investigating agents failed to find violations of the law, and Alabama had the highest number of working children ages twelve and thirteen. Furthermore, the report exposed the inadequacies of mill schools: of 114 Alabama mill children between the ages of fourteen and fifteen surveyed, 46.5 percent were unable to read and write.[16]

The report also sought to discredit notions that employers treated children kindly, illuminating children's grievances against their employers. While acknowledging children's "desire" to leave school for work, the report exposed their resistance to mill discipline. Doffer boys, fined for "playing" in forbidden parts of the mills or not "sweeping the floors between doffs," retaliated by throwing bobbins into the privies. The *Woman and Child Wage-Earners* report provided new ammunition for propaganda about the South's "social infamy" and increased the urgency for the NCLC to reinvolve itself in the southern child labor problem.[17]

The Southern Problem and Southern Women

Reformers used the report as ammunition for an attack on the South as a drag on the whole nation's child labor problem. According to reform propaganda sanctioned by members of the NCLC, "New England has its evils, but it is in the South, the real center of the cotton industry, that the essence of this social infamy is found." The southern cotton mills shut out the "odor of the magnolia" and the sound of the "mocking bird" and shut in a "gaunt goblin army of children." Publication of the report rekindled interest in the South and added pressure on the NCLC to get the South on board with national reform goals. Until southern textile states adopted what leading reformers defined as the minimal standards for child labor, opponents of child labor felt that efforts to improve conditions in northern manufacturing states were futile. As Progressive Florence Kelley had explained to Senator Beveridge, "A reduction to the ten hour day in Massachusetts for women and children was impossible as long as manufacturers felt the pressure of southern competition."[18]

The desire to force the South to enact more meaningful reform encouraged the continuation of the focus on the whiteness of southern children. Although Kelley personally helped a variety of immigrant groups through her settlement house work and criticized southern race relations, she adopted a language that valued whiteness when she felt that doing so would attract more attention to the southern problem. She argued that the "native American white children" in the southern cotton mills were becoming "third class" citizens behind the "first class" "fortunate boys and girls who live on the Pacific Coast and in the northeastern states, where every child receives a generous education," and the "second class" immigrant children, who were "getting a degree of education" unheard of "twenty years ago."[19] Kelley knew that such terminology suggested that the privileges of whiteness were at stake.

As the national study of child labor in the textile industry and faltering reform efforts elsewhere heightened attention on the "southern problem," a number of forces were coming together to encourage and support white southern women as leaders of reform. Northern Progressives measured the South's social structure with a gendered yardstick, often arguing that the fate of the southern white mill children hinged on the southern lady reformer. This approach sought to encourage well-to-do southern women to play a greater role in awakening their backward region to the evils of child labor, using the southern lady as a figure who transcended regional boundaries because of her gender and moral fiber.

Reform fiction appeared in such periodicals as the *Saturday Evening Post* and the *Child Labor Bulletin* as well as in larger works such as Mary Fenollosa's *Red Horse Hill* (1909, published under the pseudonym Sidney McCall). Van Vorst's sensationalized reporting in *Cry of the Children* also drew on the familiar characteristics of reform fiction to identify heroes and villains. These writings tended to be sentimental, made southern mill children lovable and admirable, and featured well-to-do women as either heroines or villains. Such works also cast white southern women as agents of interregional reconciliation. In *Red Horse Hill*, for example, a young northern college graduate awakens her southern sister-in-law's social consciousness. The relationship between the northern Ruth and southern Maris is initially fraught with tension because the "practical" Ruth fails to appreciate her sister-in-law's southern belle social graces. Maris, in turn, thinks Ruth has lost all sense of romance by spending too much time with her "female professors."[20] When Ruth, determined to investigate her brother's mills, enlists a doctor to help her establish mill work's harmful effects on children, it appears that the southern Maris has been ignoring the child horror in her own backyard. A reunion story unfolds after Ruth discovers a deathly ill eight-year-old mill girl who turns out to be Maris's daughter, from whom she had been tragically separated. The work urged white southerners to view mill children as part of a larger white southern family. The story concludes with Maris and Ruth uniting to do the right thing by the children. Interregional reconciliation achieved, Maris not only saves the mill child but begins working to transform her husband, the northern manufacturer. She becomes the agent who opens his eyes to the child labor problem in his mills and to the true potential of the white children. In this sentimental way, reform fiction encouraged readers to look to the quality of southern womanhood as a measure of continuity or change in the New South.

Festival of Interregional Reconciliation

Even though the NCLC publicized findings of regional disparities, thereby fueling negative propaganda about the South in reform fiction, the group's 1911 meeting in Birmingham was designed to promote reconciliation. Through the language of race and a growing middle-class acceptance of women's activism in the name of children, the NCLC conference became a festival of interregional reconciliation. A transregional middle-class culture emerged as the conference publicized national standards and leading reformers bestowed new credentials and connections on local women reformers.

Former president Theodore Roosevelt, who stopped at the Birmingham conference as part of a larger southern tour, encouraged the spirit of reconciliation with the whiteness of southern child labor as his currency. To a cheering crowd, he declared, "I believe intensely in the New South. I believe in what it is doing; but I want it to be sure to keep the spirit of the old South in it. . . . We have reached a condition, we have reached a state of mind that all good men in whatever part of the union they live can feel the same pride in the great deeds done alike by the men who work the blue and the men who work the gray." Roosevelt spoke in an interregional language of Anglo-Saxon superiority to urge southerners to get in step with the nation: "You are asked to protect children of native Americans. . . . You are asked to see that your stock does not go down as the stock in the parent country [England] has gone down." He also told an enormous crowd, "You know my views on the baby question. I like all your crops, but I like the children crop most."[21]

At the conference, Owen Lovejoy, the NCLC general secretary, who had been known for vitriolic remarks about the South, muted his criticism and fostered a spirit of reunion: "You are still behind in the matter of child labor and children are permitted to work here at an age and under conditions that would not be tolerated in the North." But, he continued, "I believe that education will take but a brief time in this section and that the South will make strides . . . that will be astonishing for their rapidity and effectiveness." Alabama's white educated classes turned out in testimony to their membership in the nation's concerned middle classes. One way Alabamians signaled their place among the nation's mainstream was to announce the role of the state's Progressive women. Giving the lie to Van Vorst's propaganda about the southern "ladies" who dismissed child labor as a "necessary evil," Alabama women hosted a special luncheon for leading Progressives Florence Kelley and Jane Addams. While one observer later had to retract her statement that "nine-tenths" "of the interest shown" came from women because so many men turned out, local commentators believed that it was important to publicize Alabama women's ardent support of the conference. The *Birmingham News,* for example, declared that the "good women who are striving to do for Birmingham what [Addams] is striving to do for [Chicago] will give her a warm welcome." The same piece also hinted at southern sensitivity to criticism by wondering whether Addams, the American "saint," thought "bad Birmingham" needed her help.[22]

Nellie Kimball Murdoch, a veteran of several women's organizations, including the Women's Christian Temperance Union, was one of the Alabama women who helped forge links between leading national reformers and Alabama's female advocates for change. At the 1910 National Conference of Charities, Murdoch had first heard Kelley and other leading reformers from the NCLC, NCL, and other Progressive organizations discuss the findings of the federal report on women and child wage earners. Murdoch was so impressed by what she heard that she encouraged the NCLC to hold its next annual conference in Birmingham.[23]

By bringing the NCLC to Birmingham, Murdoch facilitated the rise of the transregional Progressive culture, which would embrace her personal ambitions and support her local work. She acknowledged that reform fiction profoundly affected her when she claimed that after reading "A Box of Christmas Candy" (a story "written especially to show the labor of children at the holiday season"), she developed an interest in child labor.[24] For Murdoch, who would reorganize the ACLC in the wake of the 1911 conference, and for others like her, stopping child labor in the South was becoming a point of virtue and even a validation of womanliness.

The new transregional Progressive culture provided reformers with an audience tolerant of criticism of manufacturers. Despite the tone of regional reconciliation at the 1911 conference, NCLC agent Alexander McKelway directly challenged manufacturers and publicized the federal report, peppering his controversial speech, "The Herod among Industries," with references to the study. He focused on the high illiteracy rates among mill children and on comparisons between the North and South. McKelway offered a hard-hitting indictment of an industry that asked for protective tariffs because it was an "infant industry" while conducting a "slaughter of the innocents" by hiring young children.[25]

Child Labor Reform and Women's Suffrage

The 1911 NCLC meeting in Birmingham was a turning point for Murdoch and for Alabama women's reform culture. Addams and Kelley were greeted as celebrities. Murdoch referred to Addams as a "woman whose life has meant so much; whose days have been filled to the utmost with active work, and yet who gives you the impression of perfect repose." "To have met and talked with her is like having a beautiful dream come true," Murdoch confessed. Likewise, she referred to Kelley as a "remarkable woman" who as the "head of the National Consumers' League . . . has accomplished more than I can tell you."[26]

Addams and Kelley asserted that women had to do something about child labor and needed the vote to do it. A number of women at the

Birmingham meeting shared Murdoch's admiration of Kelley and Addams and were attracted to women's suffrage as a means to promote child welfare reform. Frances Nimmo Greene wrote that the conference provided an "opportunity for the hundreds of bright, studious and sincerely progressive women of Birmingham to broaden their education by the study of a subject which, more than any other, contributes to the general culture." She argued that Alabama women needed to learn from leading reformers how to "handle the overwhelmingly great sociological problems which confront us here." The meeting stimulated the formation of the state's first women's suffrage leagues and initiated an ongoing relationship between Kelley and Murdoch, who became an expert on Alabama conditions and turned to Kelley for advice and explanations about the politics of reform. Murdoch also named Kelley as the sustaining force in the Alabama woman's work for child labor regulation.[27]

Born in Boston, Murdoch grew up in Atlanta, returning briefly to Massachusetts to attend Bradford Academy in Haverhill. In 1891, she married William Lincoln Murdoch and moved to Birmingham, where her husband ran the W. L. Murdoch Brokerage Company but was not involved in politics or reform. She soon started the Amaranth Club, a study group devoted to examining art, politics, and history. Like many Progressive women, her experience in the Women's Christian Temperance Union in the late 1890s was a "baptism of power and liberty." Within a body of organized Christian women, she found the strength to make public stands. In 1898, the *Labor Advocate* praised her for "keeping the saloons closed on Sunday."[28]

Through the Women's Christian Temperance Union, Murdoch in 1896 helped to found the Mercy Home, a refuge for up to sixty white women and children that represented Birmingham's best-supported welfare agency as prominent women and a large advisory board of men raised donations and secured city and county subsidies. Around 1905, she began serving as probation officer for the city's Boys' Club, a job that later led her into work to establish a state juvenile court system. The Boys' Club, run by an all-female board, in 1911 helped start a Children's Aid Society, a private agency that would provide the organizational skeleton for the state's first Child Welfare Department in 1919. Sometime during the first decade of the twentieth century, Murdoch became active in the AFWC, although the precise nature of her role is unclear prior to around 1914, when she became the group's leader on child labor and

child welfare. Her leadership in the state's illiteracy commission beginning in 1915, however, suggests that she had probably been involved in
the AFWC's education work.[29] All of these reform experiences shaped
Murdoch's view that women and children were especially vulnerable in
an industrializing southern city surrounded by acres of rural poverty.

In direct response to the 1911 NCLC meeting, Murdoch and a handful
of other women, most notably Pattie Ruffner Jacobs, founded the Birmingham Equal Suffrage Association (BESA). By 1912, the BESA had
joined with white women in Selma who had founded the state's only
other suffrage association to form the Alabama Equal Suffrage Association (AESA). The suffrage leagues eventually led to a consumer league
modeled after Kelley's NCL, tying the Alabama women to a transregional
Progressivism committed to abolishing child labor and to gaining greater
political rights for women in support of humanitarian political goals.
Kelley also stimulated the development of an interregional women's reform culture by hiring Jean Gordon, a Louisiana factory inspector and
reformer, to strengthen the NCL's role in the South.[30]

An NCLC member and general secretary of the NCL, Kelley dressed
her politics in the conventional gendered forms of the day but was not
bound by them. She believed that labor organization was the ultimate
solution to the plight of the southern textile workers and envisioned
women's support of child labor laws as aiding the larger cause of labor
organizing. In 1898, she forged links between gender and labor politics
when she formed the NCL, a group of upper-middle-class women who
aided the Women's Trade Union League in a fight against sweatshop
conditions.[31]

By 1911, the NCL garnered support for child labor laws by illuminating female consumers' direct responsibility for child labor: "It is we who
are the real employers of the children, we who buy the product of their
labor."[32] The NCL provided a model for women's leadership on the child
labor issue that Murdoch embraced for increasing women's activism in
Alabama.

At AESA meetings, Murdoch spoke about the need to regulate child
labor, and the association's resolutions reflected the influence of Kelley's
gender politics and the possibility that they could serve as a surrogate
for labor politics. In 1914, the AESA declared its support for an "adequate compulsory education law for Alabama," "for equal work for equal
pay," and for the "abolition of child labor." More to the point, the AESA

declared that the "simple right to organize trade unions is essential to democracy." This request was clearly a product of the group's connections to national reform groups and of Alabama women feeling part of a larger Progressive culture. The AESA protested conditions of women's and children's work conditions in sweatshops and factories and endorsed "all efforts for an eight hour day and minimum wage for women."[33]

The AESA's agenda was the most advanced among Alabama's middle-class reformers, having used the support of a larger reform network to broaden its goals. The AESA focused on the impact of industrialization (not agriculture, the main user of child labor) and echoed what organized labor for so long had demanded. Murdoch recognized that she and the AESA were promoting a program that some of the state's women reformers felt was too controversial.[34]

The suffrage league radicalized women's commitment to child labor reform by supporting the idea that women had a right to be involved in politics, especially in support of a reform agenda. The AESA contended that women, however different from men, had an equal right to promote social reform. Murdoch acted on this right by resurrecting the formerly all-male ACLC, recruiting women from the suffrage leagues, including Lura Harris Craighead, an AFWC member and longtime supporter of child labor reform, and Amelia Worthington, a young suffragist.[35]

Even though men continued to serve on the ACLC, Murdoch's leadership departed from the group's male-dominated tradition. Earlier ACLC members, such as J. H. Phillips, had encouraged women's auxiliary support but balked at women's political assertiveness. Phillips, for example, tried to curtail Worthington's distribution of suffrage literature by dismissing her from a teacher training course.[36] Murdoch's ACLC also differed from earlier women's organizations, refusing to defer to male reform leaders or to compromise with manufacturers.

Murdoch's ACLC also reflected the influence of the U.S. Children's Bureau, a federal agency. After the failure of the 1907 federal child labor bill, the NCL and NCLC had lobbied for the creation of the bureau, which Kelley conceived as dedicated to the protection of the "right to childhood." Created in 1912 and headed by women, the Children's Bureau reflected Progressivism's emphasis on the relationship between child welfare and democracy. The bureau had the power to investigate and report on "all matters pertaining to the welfare of children and child life," and its philosophy was rooted in middle-class notions of childhood and family and concern with democracy and social order. The bureau stood for reformers' arguments that child labor and illiteracy endangered the quality of citizenship and thus the quality of American democracy. Murdoch linked her resurrection of the ACLC to the bureau's efforts to gather information to support a national standard on child labor and to educate poor families about child welfare. ACLC members began talking to the mothers of child workers, investigating conditions, and visiting homes to "carry on a campaign of education." Murdoch reported to the NCLC that the Alabama group had "put twenty-four newsboys in Birmingham back in school by personal visits to their homes." And Murdoch reported to Children's Bureau chief Julia Lathrop, "I'm hard in the fight for a child labor bill in the coming session of our legislature. . . . We are finding some interesting things."[37]

Transregional Progressivism for a National Standard

The 1915 campaign for a new law united local reformers with the NCLC and expressed the standards of a transregional Progressive culture with new women at the helm. These groups joined forces in support of an Alabama law that would conform to the uniform child labor legislation endorsed by the NCLC and the American Bar Association: prohibition of child labor under age fourteen (up from the current state minimum of eleven) and an eight-hour-a-day limit for older children in all occupations except agriculture and domestic service. The 1908 state law had capped at sixty the number of hours children under fourteen could work per week but did not limit the number of hours per day.

The NCLC and NCL sought a victory in a southern state on hour limitations in hopes of improving the chances for passage of a federal law to limit child labor under fourteen and to restrict older children's labor to eight hours a day. Even some middle-class southern reformers had begun to argue that southern textile workers needed to organize and would be enabled by the creation of an eight-hour limit on child labor. Wiley H. Swift, an NCLC special agent in North Carolina, expressed such attitudes at the 1913 NCLC annual conference, held in Jacksonville, Florida. Swift told his colleagues that southern reformers had made "a very serious mistake" when they talked to mill men but not to the mill operatives. If reformers had taken the time to "sit down with pencil and paper" with the workers and had shown the "absolute loss which comes from working children," Swift believed that a "terrible row" would have erupted. He encouraged reformers to align with textile operatives organizing to end child labor. In fact, Swift told his audience, only "labor agitation" could truly abolish child labor.[38]

Alabama's factory inspector had previously complained about a lack of help from reformers, but the regenerated movement worked closely with factory inspector W. C. Oates. A physician, he helped reformers sustain the race argument by supplying scientific data about racial deterioration. "The trained eye of the Inspector is often times unable to tell whether the age of a weazend, dried up, anaemic specimen of the genus homo is twelve or eighteen," he reported. He concluded that the mill children were becoming a "race within a race." Oates helped the ACLC expose the ineptness of the current law, reporting that although it was violated, juries had been unwilling to convict anyone for doing so. Murdoch and Oates helped to forge strong ties between the NCLC and the ACLC, attending the 1913 NCLC meeting, along with representatives of all other southern textile states, to report on the Alabama situation. In 1913, Murdoch invited the NCLC to help local reformers educate the public about children working in fish canneries. She believed that the public would support stronger child labor legislation if working conditions were better known, and she wanted the NCLC to help: "We simply must wake the people out of their indifference," she said at the 1913 NCLC meeting. Southern representatives such as Murdoch realized that they needed help in gaining support for stronger legislation. As the representative from Georgia put it, "It just seems to me that I want to say to this National Child Labor Committee, one and all, as the Macedonians did, 'Come over and help us.'" The NCLC responded by sending Herschel Jones and Lewis Hine to support the 1915 Alabama legislative campaign. Murdoch believed that the national attention to the child labor problem and the ACLC's local efforts to publicize it were winning support for stronger legislation. In 1913 she wrote that "articles on the evils of premature labor for children are no longer confined to the *Survey* and kindred magazines, but *Life,* the *Saturday Evening Post* and many others are revealing conditions so shocking that the reading public has awakened from its lethargy. . . . Even the grossly exaggerated and rather silly articles in *Life* have served a purpose in Alabama, for inquiries have come from all over the state."[39]

The state factory inspector reported in 1912 that 1,802 cotton mill laborers were between twelve and fourteen years of age, and 1,086 were between the ages of fourteen and sixteen. Hine reported that the Merrimack Mills in Huntsville employed an eleven-year-old boy, two ten-year-old girls, a nine-year-old, and an eight-year-old, along with eight other children under the age of twelve. Hine also found that eleven-hour days were the norm in the state, but one mill used fourteen-hour days several times each week. By talking with children and their families, he found violations of the current law at every mill he visited. By 1915 the NCLC and ACLC had reached a consensus on the need to tighten the compulsory education requirement, which had been easily violated, by getting the school superintendent involved in verifying attendance.[40]

Both Jones and Hine worked in accordance with the ACLC's new approach, expanding the scope of reform beyond the cotton mills while pointing out that that industry remained the state's largest employer of children. Jones's study featured on its cover Hine's photo of children shelling oysters and included images of a messenger boy, a newspaper boy, a theater usher, a waiter, and a "cash girl." Only one photograph showed a girl spinner running home for lunch. Jones made a point of saying that the "investigation covered not only cotton mills," listing a string of other jobs.[41] Reformers thus hardened their stance on the need for stiffer regulation of southern child labor while broadening their target beyond the well-organized textile manufacturers.

Murdoch took charge of the 1915 campaign, with the AFWC women doing the bulk of the lobbying. Unlike the previous state campaigns, in which Murphy's manly men had made the arguments, this time middle-class womanly women, armed with the NCLC's study and Hine's photographs, made the case for a new law. Murdoch, Oates, and Jones drafted a bill modeled on the NCLC's proposals for a federal child labor law, and Murdoch and AFWC head Lura Harris Craighead testified before the legislative committee considering the measure. After the bill was introduced, mill men refused to compromise on the limitation on hours, despite the ACLC's effort to publicize child labor in the street trades (newspaper stands and peddlers), theater, and department stores. Murdoch told mill men that the ACLC was not specifically targeting them but had investigated the conditions among messenger boys and found that a stronger law was warranted. Nevertheless, manufacturers remained the only organized opponents of the legislation, arguing that if child laborers were limited to working forty-eight hours a week, limits for all em-

ployees would have to follow. Alabama cotton manufacturers, represented by Colonel H. S. D. Mallory of Selma, Scott Roberts of Anniston,
T. H. Rennie of Pell City, and W. L. Harris of Lanette and with the full
support of former governor Braxton Bragg Comer, hoped to curb public
criticism by giving in on the age limit while refusing to budge on the
issue of hours. Murdoch appealed for a white middle-class consensus
that parents were at fault, that children's earnings were not essential,
and that the state had an interest in curbing child labor in the interest
of improving standards of white citizenship. As the debate heated up,
Murdoch sought to bypass the mill men's opposition by focusing on children employed elsewhere—a bright eight-year-old girl whose mother had
removed her from school to work in a soap factory, an eight-year-old
"cash girl" in Mobile, a thirteen-year-old who preferred working in a
beauty parlor and earning three dollars in spending money to going to
school, and an eleven-year-old "fellow" in Birmingham who worked at a
soft drink stand while his nine-year-old brother worked in a department
store.[42]

Murdoch, as chair of the ACLC, and Craighead, former president of
the AFWC and current chair of the group's legislative committee, prepared women to be effective lobbyists, arguing, "If the men think that
the women are thinking, they are more likely to pay attention to them."
She advised women to have answers to all arguments against the bill and
turned to the NCL, NCLC, and U.S. Children's Bureau for ammunition.
The legislation's chances improved after the newly elected governor,
Democrat Charles Henderson, endorsed the child labor bill. Reflecting
women's high profile in the effort, the *Montgomery Advertiser* warned lawmakers "to beware or the 'women'll ketch 'em' if they don't watch out,
for every women's club . . . in the whole State, [is] working heart and
soul" for the child labor bill. Murdoch stressed the righteousness of the
cause based on what women knew not only as mothers but as professionals on the subject. The *Advertiser* remarked on Murdoch's "world of
information on the subject." Jones felt that the women were so well prepared that they could answer any question. Recalling the charge formerly leveled against reformers, he suggested that with their superior
knowledge of the subject, women could charge that "their opposition is
'mere sentimentalism.'"[43] Alabama's ladies had become Progressive new
women.

As in earlier legislative sessions, the AFWC had multiple bills to support, but this time Murdoch organized women into separate lobbying committees and urged them to concentrate on one bill at a time. She made it clear that "it's the child labor bill in which we are primarily interested." She warned women to talk about only one bill to each legislator to prevent him from saying, "My, there's that woman again."[44] Murdoch wanted the legislation—not the woman—remembered. Murdoch's efforts prevailed in some respects, resulting in a law that raised the minimum age for employment to fourteen for all occupations other than agriculture and domestic service. However, the campaign failed to win the more significant demand for an eight-hour day for laborers under age sixteen.

The NCLC-ACLC alliance could not overpower mill owners' opposition to hour reductions. Transregional middle-class Progressivism had come closer to supporting labor's goals of a shorter workday for women and children yet had blunted the mill men's charge that the labor movement was using child labor reform as an entering wedge, even though the labor movement was trying to do just that.[45] Reformers had made child labor reform about the rights of children, not about laborers.

Disappointed at their failure to win hour reductions and strong enforcement mechanisms, local reformers nevertheless saw 1915 as the legislature's first acknowledgment of Progressivism's modern standard of child welfare. In addition to prohibiting child labor under the age of fourteen, laws passed during that year compelled school attendance and permitted the creation of juvenile courts. These measures were the product of women reformers working in conjunction with men and women from the NCLC and the U.S. Children's Bureau and of a transregional rather than purely southern Progressivism.

Alabama's female reformers had recognized that they had to look beyond their state for help winning meaningful Progressive policy. The Mercy Home president's complaint about lack of support for women's welfare work summed up a problem women faced: "The men of our city and state are indifferent to the care of the dependent and defective; and most of them seem to consider all effort for this class a kind of woman's 'fad' instead of an important social obligation." In his history of welfare services in Birmingham, Edward Shannon LaMonte found that women organized and remained active in welfare agencies, but men served on advisory boards "active only in promoting annual operating fund drives or special building-fund efforts." Women had learned how to get men behind welfare policy. Murdoch reported to the NCLC annual convention held in May 1915 that "with the vigorous education campaign which is being carried on with the help of the newspapers we hope to come to the annual meeting in 1916 and report that Alabama has come up to standard at last."[46]

Laws that acknowledged a new standard did not translate into enforcement of that standard, however. In the absence of an adequate bureaucracy and financial support, the laws simply provided blueprints for protecting the state's children. The 1915 child labor law, for example, increased the state factory and prison inspector's duties without expanding the bureaucracy devoted to enforcing the law. Another problem was education about the expanded law: no agency was in charge of educating workers, employers, or school officials about their roles and responsibilities. Most people only had a "vague idea" about a child labor law "applying to cotton mills." In areas without cotton mills, school superintendents, charged for the first time with verifying school attendance, did not realize that they were responsible for issuing employment certificates to children leaving school for work, with the result that in other industries, children continued to work without employment certificates. Problems also arose in cotton mills: those with their own schools often handled work permits through teachers or principals hired by the mills, which meant that in forty-four out of ninety-five cases, work permits were handled by mill schools.[47]

The new compulsory education law, the state's first, required eighty days of school attendance through the age of fifteen, with exemptions for cases of extreme poverty. This loophole was interpreted as permitting even children under fourteen to work, in violation of the child labor law. Many schools could not handle more children, and the legislature did not appropriate funds for truancy officers.[48] And although the 1915 juvenile court law permitted the creation of such courts, monitored by advisory boards, to evaluate the needs of delinquent or neglected children, the measure provided no means or money to stimulate creation of the courts.

The weakness of the 1915 laws strengthened the emerging transregional Progressivism. In the absence of a strong state, reformers revved for action became an unofficial child welfare bureaucracy. Between 1915 and 1919, with the help of the NCLC, the AFWC and the ACLC initiated statewide investigations of child welfare needs to help arouse public support and to generate pressure on the state legislature to do more for Alabama's children. Interregional reconciliation was under way even in the face of ongoing sectional disparity in conditions. The new women of Alabama had found a calling, new credentials, and national support for their local work in urging their state toward a more modern child welfare model.

CHAPTER SEVEN

New Women and Child Welfare

CHILD LABOR PERSISTED IN THE Alabama textile industry. During the 1920s, researcher Katharine Du Pre Lumpkin interviewed a number of Alabama mill families and found that although children left school for work at a later age, they remained a critical part of the textile labor force. In one family, parents who had begun work at ages twelve and eight managed to keep their children out of the mills until their teens. All who were old enough to work in the cotton mill, however, did so, "the oldest beginning at fourteen, the next two at fifteen and sixteen." Each time an older child married, a younger child would leave school to help the family. Another family put all eight children to work, beginning at the legal age of fourteen. The family's youngest daughter wanted to be a nurse, but wage cuts and the lost wages of an older son who married meant that she too joined the mill workforce.[1] The story of family labor in the New South featured more continuity than change even as the law gradually raised the age at which children began working for wages. The persistence of southern poverty is an old tale constantly retold. Edgar Gardner Murphy's "forgotten" children of the first decade of the twentieth century were rediscovered thirty years later by James Agee and Walker Evans in *Let Us Now Praise Famous Men*. The biggest result of the southern anti–child labor movement was the creation of a transregional Progressive culture that kept the vision of a better life for Alabama children alive in the face of persistent poverty and child labor. Some people remembered the needs of Alabama's poor families, especially its poor white families.

Progressives accommodated and manipulated the politics of white supremacy, valued and validated the activism of new women, set standards based on the advice of experts, and turned for support to such national organizations as the National Child Labor Committee (NCLC), U.S. Children's Bureau, and National Consumers' League (NCL). The transregional Progressive culture created a vision for the direction in which the state should grow, redefined the child labor problem as a larger child welfare issue, and linked southern citizenship to privileges of whiteness. The new culture kept states like Alabama in a larger national discussion about public welfare from the Progressive Era to the New Deal Era. Despite overwhelming need and woefully underfunded state programs, a minority of reformers—primarily women—persevered.

Alabama's anti–child labor campaign culminated in the 1919 creation of the Alabama Child Welfare Department, the state's first public welfare agency. The new department institutionalized reformers' vision for a better life for Alabama's children. By 1922 Alabama Governor Thomas E. Kilby, whose own formal education included only public grammar school in Atlanta, turned to members of the transregional Progressive culture to institute the child welfare department. He placed a leading Alabama woman reformer, Loraine Bedsole Bush, at the head of the department. Overlooked in most histories, she was recognized at the time as the "author of most of the 'children's laws'" in Alabama and was well known by national groups such as the NCLC. Kilby acknowledged the authority of a larger Progressive network when he privately wrote to the NCLC's Owen Lovejoy, who had previously hired Bush, that federal regulation, which had just been overturned by the U.S. Supreme Court, was necessary to prevent the "exploitation of America's child life which is a national disgrace."[2]

Between 1915, when Nellie Kimball Murdoch led the campaign for a new Alabama child labor law, and 1919, when the Alabama Child Welfare Department was created, transregional Progressivism matured. Murdoch and Bush played pivotal roles in persuading local reformers and national reform organizations to begin to create plans for instituting the organizational structure for a child welfare program in Alabama. Reformers had almost no state tools to address the needs of poor working children and instead had to turn for support to local women's organizations, the University of Alabama, and a national network of reform organizations. The timing was right. Mill demand for child labor decreased at the same time that reformers' demands for stricter laws increased. Once mill opposition dissipated, reformers could use the mill child to raise public awareness about child welfare needs. Opponents of child labor had to make it a public issue and remained bound to white supremacy in their publicity. Finally, World War I generated new public concern about social conditions in the state by exposing the illiteracy and poor health of the state's young men. The door to the state was cracked open, and the new women of Alabama, supported by leading Progressive organizations, widened the space with the establishment of Alabama's Child Welfare Department.

Pioneers of a Child Welfare System

Copying a trend learned from national NCLC meetings, Murdoch used the 1915 juvenile court law to begin establishing "advisory boards" that served essentially as county welfare boards. Murdoch, U.S. Children's Bureau agent Evelina Beldon, and Alabama Child Labor Committee (ACLC) member Judge Samuel D. Murphy imagined that the boards would organize citizens and charitable organizations interested in child welfare so that judges could turn to a single advisory board rather than multiple local groups for aid when faced with a "neglected" or "delinquent" child. Beldon also envisioned the boards organizing health campaigns in villages and reporting violations of the child labor and compulsory education laws. The 1915 law defined juvenile wards so that courts could have jurisdiction over "any child under sixteen years of age" who violated a law; "knowingly associated with thieves"; or simply was idle, used profanity, wandered railroad tracks, or possessed an "indecent" picture. Such a broad definition meant that almost any poor, unsupervised child could be brought before an advisory board.[3]

The composition of advisory boards reflected their child welfare responsibilities. For example, when Beldon established an advisory board for Lee County, the home of cotton mill villages in Opelika and Phenix City, the members included the superintendent of the Opelika schools, the president of the Mothers' Club of Opelika, the town's mayor, the president of the Women's Christian Temperance Union, a veteran volunteer at the mill village, a physician, and two teachers.[4]

The advisory boards reflected a grand vision of centralizing local help, evaluating local child welfare needs, and hiring trained social workers as probation and school attendance officers. Judge Murphy hoped that the advisory boards would undertake "all the social work for the community." Reformers envisioned the boards as a "charity organization . . . protective society and a leader of recreation . . . and anything else that the community needed." Murdoch told Julia Lathrop, the U.S. Children's Bureau chief, that the advisory boards could be a "piece of genuine construction work" that would "be epoch making for the South." "*So much* depends upon getting the people interested," Murdoch believed.[5] The reality of child welfare work in Alabama was tedious and tenuous— a constant uphill battle—given the lack of state support and public interest.

When efforts to obtain advisory boards floundered, Murdoch, her local supporters, and the NCLC and U.S. Children's Bureau realized that more state support and public interest were necessary. Key local reformers and representatives from the NCLC were responsible for the legislative achievements of 1919 that led to a nascent child welfare system. Murdoch was pivotal because she strengthened the relationship between the ACLC and the NCLC. In 1918, the NCLC worked with the ACLC and the University of Alabama to produce a publication titled *Child Welfare in Alabama* that urged support for a state child welfare agenda. The university became a vital resource for Progressivism in Alabama—three of the nine articles in the volume were written by university personnel. Bush and Murdoch worked closely with the larger organizations to make the "study as thorough and complete as possible," and it concluded unsurprisingly that child welfare action in Alabama to this point had been "remedial rather than preventative" and had occurred in response to "isolated impulses and agitations." With NCLC assistance, Murdoch and the ACLC "set about the task of planning a definite program for social legislation and administrative agencies to submit to the 1919 legislature."[6]

A "Broader Plan"

The ACLC and NCLC deliberately sought stronger child labor regulation by laying "a broader plan, viz—a thorough investigation of child welfare conditions" that would arouse public support for effective child welfare legislation. *Child Welfare in Alabama* resulted from significant collaboration between local reformers and their allies in a larger Progressive network. The publication advocated a new child labor law enforced through a newly created agency, such as a department of labor or a state board of social welfare with a child welfare division. As the report's director, Edward Clopper, wrote, "We all agree that children unfortunate by reason of orphanage, defectiveness, environment, poverty, disease, or neglect must have the fostering care that their peculiar circumstances require." The NCLC hoped that a broader child welfare approach would "arouse enough public interest to" win substantial child welfare legislation.[7]

Both Bush and Murdoch believed that their relationships with national Progressive groups uniquely qualified them to lead their state toward its first child welfare department. They were well positioned to mediate between their state's political peculiarities and more nationally oriented Progressive standards. Bush, the widow of factory inspector Charles F. Bush, who had complained that reformers abandoned him when he most needed them, had worked as a deputy factory inspector, had worked for the U.S. Children's Bureau, and had served briefly at the NCLC headquarters in New York. Bush also was involved with the Children's Aid Society, an organization that in 1916 launched a statewide program to find homes for destitute children. Her work with this private group positioned her to broaden the child labor reform movement into a child welfare campaign and provided her with experience in an organization that utilized social workers. Although her role in the society remains unknown, she may have made her impression on the NCLC through her work there, and she would have known Murdoch through the group, which was headquartered in Birmingham's Juvenile Court Building. The Children's Aid Society placed ninety-one children in permanent or foster homes between October 1, 1917, and May 31, 1918, and *Child Welfare in Alabama* applauded the society's "modern" and "business-like" organization. It was the only group that conducted "carefully-recorded social investigations": a social worker regularly visited placed children.[8]

Bush felt that the NCLC's *Child Welfare in Alabama* was critical for generating public alarm at the "number of our children out of school and in various kinds of labors." She explained, "The facts brought out in the child welfare study had cut too deep. Leading minds took a stand for a better child life in Alabama. Aided and abetted by the NCLC, a bill relating solely to the care of children was carefully prepared. . . . The state treasury balked but a National Child Labor Committee field agent, . . . the state child labor committee, the federation of clubs and others were busily showing the Governor and legislature why and how the work could be undertaken at this time." Murdoch and Bush inched their state closer toward the standards and goals of the national Progressive groups that supported and encouraged the Alabama efforts. After working at the NCLC headquarters, Bush wrote that having seen "what is being done in other states, I grow eager and impatient to preach the gospel to every man and woman in Alabama—the gospel of a fairer chance for every unfortunate child."[9]

Murdoch and Bush recognized themselves as part of a larger Progressive reform culture with a mission to win acceptance for a state role in child welfare. A 1949 biographical sketch of Bush acknowledged that she "became a social worker in the days when such activities were not so well appreciated as they are today, and did not command such wide cooperation from the public and from departments and functionaries of the government." Alabama reformers engaged with leading child welfare voluntary associations to raise awareness and turned to allies beyond their state for support. Birmingham reformer Mollie Dowd complained to Florence Kelley that because the legislature met only every four years, sustaining interest was difficult, adding, "And this part of the country seems so hard to realize any way the importance of this work."[10]

In 1919, with the help of the NCLC's publication of *Child Welfare in Alabama,* Alabama's reformers won a strengthened compulsory education law, the creation of the Child Welfare Department (CWD), and a stronger child labor law. The school and child welfare laws did more than had ever previously been done to create bureaucratic support for the measures' enforcement. The new child labor law prohibited all employment of children under fourteen except in agriculture and domestic service and limited children under sixteen to "no more than forty-eight hours in any one week or more than eight hours in any one day." Beginning in 1921, the new child labor law also required completion of fourth grade or 120 consecutive days of school attendance before older children could receive employment certificates. The compulsory education law, furthermore, required attendance for the full school term, to be set by the county or city board of education for "not less than one hundred days," for all children between the ages of eight and sixteen.[11]

Leaders of the Alabama reform movement recognized their state's political limitations but found themselves in the position of advocating increased changes in Alabama while explaining to outsiders why even more reform was not possible. "The Department of Child Welfare was a compromise measure, brought about because it was impossible to get a State Board of Public Welfare," Bush told a national meeting of reformers. She explained that a "department of child welfare" had "distinct advantages," such as a popular name. "Work for children makes a direct appeal to many people whom other forms of social work do not interest," she continued. Furthermore, "a child welfare department can always count on the solid support of the women of the state and the woman's vote is now a factor to be reckoned with." Bush also acknowledged that Alabama fell short of Progressive goals when she added that she hoped that with time, the new department would foster a sense of "public responsibility for the care of the state's unfortunate" that would allow for "the creation of a strong Board of Public Welfare." Murdoch later wrote to Elizabeth Davidson, a scholar of child labor reform in the South, that Alabama's women continued to honor their ties to manufacturers and remained sensitive to criticism of the cotton textile industry, a position Murdoch understood. Governor Kilby acknowledged that the establishment of the CWD generated criticism from "social workers, educators, and other prominent men and women in quite a number of the states of the Union."[12] But he and Alabama's other reformers knew that support did not exist for anything bigger. Alabama's reformers fashioned plans inspired by leading Progressive groups but tailored to the state's conservatism.

As part of a transregional Progressive culture in Alabama, Bush and Murdoch mediated between provincialism that honored a creed of industrial progress and the Progressivism of a larger band of emerging child welfare experts. While Murdoch liked to send glowing reports to the U.S. Children's Bureau about progress being made, she also reminded the agency of restrictive realities. In one letter she reported that the "serious thing is going to be lack of schools—Alabama is a state with no money and the situation grows more acute—we hope something will shortly be done." Although Murdoch and Bush broadened their agenda, they found that they often had to resort to images of white mill waifs to make audiences recognize that a public welfare problem existed. When Beldon met with Eufaula women to generate support for a local child welfare board, she found that they "could not even surmise for what purpose they were called together." But when she spoke in terms of the known symbol of children in need—the white mill child laborer—she secured her audience's interest. By transforming the anti–child labor campaign into a movement for state support for child welfare, with the mill child advertising its whiteness, reformers had remarkable success. "Sturdy future citizens who have been given their opportunity—saved from the grinding life of the child mill worker," declared the caption to a photograph of four robust white children in a CWD bulletin.[13]

Several additional factors, however, help to explain the legislature's near unanimous support for the creation of the CWD in 1919. Reformers' broader approach and the publication of *Child Welfare in Alabama* helped to expose poor children's enormous needs. This report dovetailed with a Russell Sage Foundation report on the state's penal system and social agencies commissioned by the previous governor, Charles Henderson, and delivered to Kilby at the beginning of his term. The study's author, Hastings Hart, condemned the conditions of Alabama's social agencies and deferred to the NCLC on evaluating child welfare conditions. He endorsed the committee's recommendation for the "establishment of a State department to take charge of the interest of this class of children, together with the enforcement of laws relating to child labor and school attendance." Growing support for public education in Alabama brought another group of reformers into the chorus clamoring for attention to child welfare needs, as the education movement provoked the formation of hundreds of school welfare organizations that worked with mothers' clubs for the betterment of the school and community.[14]

The Russell Sage report and the NCLC study landed on Kilby's desk shortly after his election. The new governor was personally responsive to reform and recognized that the time was right because of alarming social conditions that World War I had exposed. In his 1919 message to the legislature, Kilby noted that the "war changed attitudes away from accumulated wealth." "We came to the realization," he said, "of the fact that the Nation's chief asset was an upstanding, red-blooded, right-thinking, God-fearing, healthy young manhood." Alabama, he declared, was falling short, with 40 percent of its young men "unfit for military service." "In one school," he reported, "ninety percent of the children were found to have some physical defect—eighty percent of which were remedied."[15] Kilby publicized the public welfare problem and supported a state role in prevention and remediation.

Bush and Thomas M. Owen, head of the Alabama Department of Archives and History, designed the legislation for the new child labor bill and won the governor's approval. Although the original bill contained no provisions for creating a child welfare agency, Representative Alfred Moore Tunstall of Hale County offered an amendment to the bill that established the CWD and gave its officers inspection and enforcement powers. Kilby, who also increased spending for public education and public health to record levels for the state, became a strong supporter of the CWD, unsuccessfully advocating an appropriation increase from thirty thousand dollars to one hundred thousand dollars, the amount suggested by the NCLC and a second Russell Sage report.[16]

As constituted by the legislature, the CWD possessed the authority to "devise the plans and means for and have general oversight over the welfare work for minor children." It also had the power to advise judges in juvenile courts; to inspect various institutions caring for children; to oversee child-placement agencies; "to enforce all laws, regulating the employment of minor children, with full power of visitation and inspection of all factories, industries, and other establishments in which children may be employed." The legislature also charged the department with raising money in support of the development of child welfare work, with working with other departments and coordinating efforts relating to child welfare, and with establishing and maintaining homes for the care of dependent or neglected children. Governor Kilby thought so much of this department that he provided the department's full report in his 1923 message to the legislature, more space than he gave to any other issue.[17]

Victory by Forfeit

If the creation of the CWD and stronger child labor and compulsory education laws was the triumph of the child labor regulation campaign in the South, it was a victory by forfeit—manufacturers' opposition had declined in Alabama. The governor supported the child labor bill and linked it to the popular Prohibition issue, and public awareness on the subject was heightened. Kilby advocated the measure in part because it added a new educational requirement at a time when conscription for World War I had heightened public awareness of Alabama's high illiteracy rates. Alabama reformers also worked hard to avoid appearing antimanufacturing. As they broadened their campaign to oppose child labor everywhere but on farms and in domestic service, advocates of reform increasingly and publicly praised cotton manufacturers for complying with the law. The public could begin to believe in the enforcement of the law, with compulsory education increasing and steps under way for attendance officers and a child welfare department with enforcement powers.[18]

Mill men's declining opposition to anti–child labor legislation also reflected a sharp decline in the need for such workers. Between 1914 and 1919, the number of child laborers under the age of sixteen dropped from 16.7 percent of Alabama's total cotton manufacturing workforce to 1.8 percent. Changes in southern textile manufacturing such as an increased supply of adult workers, higher wages, and the maturity of the southern industry help explain the decline of manufacturers' need for young child labor. World War I had created a high demand for southern textile products, resulting in increased production and a larger pool of experienced operatives. With the war's end, such high production was no longer necessary, meaning that fewer jobs were available. At the same time, however, a new wave of labor organizing and protest in the Piedmont textile states erupted as workers sought to retain gains achieved during the war. High wartime wages consequently tended to persist, and manufacturers forced to pay higher wages preferred more experienced workers. Furthermore, higher wages enabled families to comply with child labor and compulsory education laws, since children's income was no longer necessary for family survival. Finally, the fact that northern companies owned many of Alabama's mills also contributed to the reduced commitment to child labor, as New England cotton industrialists came to advocate uniformity in child labor laws to eliminate the southern competitive advantage.[19]

By 1919, Alabama's child labor reform movement had much more political opportunity to develop into a broader Progressive child welfare initiative. Connections to leading national Progressive groups helped to give women reformers in particular credentials that were recognized even by manufacturers. Mill owners such as Donald Comer, the son of former governor Braxton Bragg Comer, recognized the importance of staying on good terms with the CWD. In 1922, Comer suggested a conference including CWD director Bush, cotton mill operators, manufacturers, and schoolteachers in mill localities, and he subsequently wrote to Governor Kilby, "Since I have become interested in manufacturing, I have felt that [child welfare] was a question that was of interest to the cotton manufacturers." Comer both acknowledged the potential power of the CWD and sought to maintain the power of the mill men when he told the governor, "If there is any change contemplated by Mrs. Bush's Department that will affect the cotton mill children of the State, we believe that a discussion with men like George Lanier of Lanette and Joe Bradley of Huntsville" should occur first.[20] Manufacturers moved into a more accommodating role because they believed both that they could afford to do so and that they could not afford to ignore this new government agency.

Under the CWD, three women trained as social workers began inspecting business establishments and enforcing the child labor law. The new department was very interested in developing the profession of social work among a native population familiar with Alabama conditions. "Many of our Alabama girls, going north to study, have remained to take positions there," an early report warned. The department felt that it was important to have "trained" inspectors with an "understanding of southern conditions."[21] While these new female child labor inspectors were militant about reporting any child under fourteen found working, the CWD's claims to have saved white cotton mill children exaggerated the agency's real impact since the industry's grip on young children had loosened, older children still worked, and mill families remained impoverished.

Ironically, the focus on certification and "eliminating from industry all children under fourteen" made it easy for cotton mills to be labeled good employers. The time and circumstances were right for mill men to mythologize themselves as saviors of the white working class. By 1921, southern reformers sometimes helped the manufacturers, eager to establish models of commercial enterprises accepting the laws. The CWD reported that the "attitude of manufacturers has been one of earnest cooperation." Furthermore, the CWD had begun to add the bureaucracy that made inspections more thorough, including requiring physicians to certify that children were old enough to work, and mills were more likely than smaller industries were to have a system for negotiating the increasingly complex process.[22]

Indeed, to the women of the CWD, who were eager to make sure all of the certification forms were filed correctly, the cotton mills began to look good in comparison to other employers oblivious to the law. The "law is grossly violated in Anniston," reported the CWD in 1920: "Aside from the cotton mills, little effort has been made to observe the law and little interest is manifested." The investigator, reflecting her lens of a larger Progressivism, was appalled at what the public ignored. "In Anniston this week,—a child of five years, a little girl, was made to dance and sing in a picture show—giving three performances in one day," she reported. Inspectors even worried that when the cotton mills refused to employ children, they found jobs that were not as easily regulated. For example, the inspector found "one boy who was unable to secure employment in a mill because he had not the schooling necessary for the issuance of an employment certificate." As a result, "he carried dinners all winter to the workers of a foundry."[23]

The CWD had strong roots in leading national Progressive groups and in Progressivism's support of new women. A cartoon from the *Montgomery Advertiser* illustrates the power of women in the CWD: an oversized, elegant, woman's hand supports a ladder, with bedraggled white children standing at its foot, looking expectantly upward. Governor Kilby appointed Bush as the CWD's first director, bypassing Lemuel Green, a man who lobbied for the job, and seven of Bush's eight staff members were female. ACLC members Murdoch, Elizabeth Fonde, and later Lura Harris Craighead served on the Alabama Child Welfare Commission, which oversaw the CWD. The CWD urged the hiring of young women social workers at the county level and continued to promote the child welfare work of women's clubs.[24]

To the National Conference of Social Workers, Bush proclaimed the creation of the CWD a watershed for Alabama, although she acknowledged that it "admittedly [remained] a backward state in social work." "Twenty years ago in Alabama," she said, "only a giant in soul and mind would have had the temerity to intimate that children had rights. . . . The field was inviting for corporations not averse to cheap labor—child labor. Children were exploited in Alabama—only God knows to what extent. And compulsory education! What an absurdity, what an interference with man's rights!" The establishment of the CWD, she argued, represented a departure from a state motto of "Here We Rest" to "Here We Work for the Birthright of Children."[25]

Bush and her cohorts believed that they were changing their state's destiny, setting its first modern welfare standards. The women's commitment can be explained by their interpretation of their work as a marked departure from the past and step toward the Progressive vision of a national right to childhood. Such female reformers described themselves as "builders of the New South." As one woman explained, women were the ones "carrying education into our benighted hill districts, the ones who have waged and won battles for industrial education, the ones who have won all that the South has of laws on the subject of child labor, . . . the ones who have done the thousand and one things for community betterment."[26]

The CWD's experimental, pioneering practices suggest that the feeling of membership in a larger reform culture sustained these women because local change was so slow. By 1924, only six counties maintained organized juvenile courts and thus had the welfare advisory boards that the CWD envisioned expanding the child welfare initiative in the state and providing the support to keep poor children in school. With so little funding and so few local child welfare boards, the CWD responded case by case to children brought to the agency's attention and relied heavily on clubwomen's isolated and limited child welfare work. Individual clubs reported holding "play days" in town parks, equipping a hospital with a baby bed, helping a destitute family find a home, installing a playground, and furnishing scholarships to a handful of children who would otherwise have had to leave school for work. The CWD nevertheless faithfully reported steps made and began to set modest goals for the entire state, even in the face of setbacks. By 1933, sixty-six of the state's sixty-seven counties, as shown on the CWD's map of county organizations, had "child welfare boards," but the CWD showed a map of twenty-five unorganized counties just the next year. The department attributed the decline to bureaucratic restructuring during the Great Depression as resources were shifted to the Alabama Relief Administration.[27]

The CWD's most significant goal was keeping children in school until they were literate rather than merely until they reached a certain age. Before the 1919 law's requirement that children complete the fourth grade went into effect, the CWD reported that in thirty-five counties,

30 percent of children who left school for work had never completed a grade and could not sign their names. Men served in Alabama's legislature with less formal education than required by the 1919 law. Self-educated Martin Luther Leith, lawyer, labor sympathizer, and representative from Jasper, for example, had attended school for only two months. The CWD utilized an elaborate certification process to enforce the grade requirement and within a few years reported that an increased number of children were completing the fourth grade before receiving work permits. In 1923, the department backed a new child labor measure that raised the education requirement to completion of sixth grade, effective in 1926. This represented the last significant change in Alabama's child labor laws until the New Deal.[28]

The CWD reflected Alabama's acceptance of a minimal but modern standard of child welfare, taking the state into previously unregulated areas. In addition to taking on the textile and other large industries, the CWD zealously tackled street trades and businesses with only a few child laborers. In one case, inspectors reprimanded two prominent judges who protested the removal of a thirteen-year-old boy whom the CWD had found working in a pool hall frequented by the judges.[29] The CWD prided itself on putting child welfare before business welfare.

The creation of the CWD reflected more than the growing activism of Alabama's clubwomen. Earlier clubwomen's actions, such as Lillian Orr's 1903 defense of child labor, had demonstrated that women from such organizations were not necessarily the most forward looking. Alabama women's leadership emerged through many intersections with male-led Progressive groups and leading women Progressives but was sustained by a transregional Progressive culture that relied on new women to institute many of its goals and standards.

The emergence of the CWD was the product of the growth of interregional reconciliation that took place during the Progressive Era and was facilitated by an insistence on the whiteness of child wage laborers. Edgar Gardner Murphy and his all-male ACLC helped forge this focus. Not all white child labor reformers saw the same thing when they spoke of whiteness, but they all understood that it was an important public stance for the movement. The whiteness of reform was critical in making child labor and child welfare work legitimate in Jim Crow Alabama.

Once legitimated, however, the Progressivism of the CWD focused less on whiteness and more on the intrinsic value of childhood. Progressivism's emphasis on the new woman meant an emphasis on her expertise —the child and the home. The CWD's description of Alabama's child labor law as "as deep, as wise, as kind as mother love itself" reflected the gendered nature of Progressivism's support for trained women's knowledge and authority. The department's literature focused on protecting the home and family and redefined the home's relationship to the community and the state. "If the home is the bulwark of the Christian nation, it must be rehabilitated when broken, rebuilt when weakened," contended one CWD report. The same report also redefined the home to justify the enforcement of the child labor law and the CWD's responsibility for it: "The home is not bound by four square walls. That is, its safety, its sanctity, and joyousness are dependent upon conditions that beat in from the outside: economic conditions, other homes, and influences of the entire community. And so the State, acting once more in her capacity as guardian to all the children, must provide a safeguard, a law which can assure the citizens of Alabama that no child will be prematurely exploited."[30]

The premium on honoring and protecting children and their childhood sometimes overcame the southern anti–child labor movement's ongoing emphasis on whiteness as uniquely worth saving. Greater acceptance of child welfare standards for white children diminished the need for the intense race-based rhetoric that reformers initially had used to draw attention to the "forgotten child of the people." Photographs in the CWD bulletins, however, quietly continued to keep child welfare a white issue by featuring only white children, and Bush accepted inferior standards for the welfare of black children. Yet transregional Progressivism also seemed to encourage a professionalism that looked beyond race, even as white reformers shared assumptions that a premium on whiteness facilitated reform progress. The CWD women, for example, had supported the NCLC's *Child Welfare in Alabama* report, which documented inferior standards for black children. Murdoch had worked with Beldon, who, despite warnings from Judge S. D. Murphy, had tried, albeit unsuccessfully, to make biracial advisory boards for juvenile courts. The CWD's first official bulletin lamented that "colored children are receiving no benefit from the law in the matter of certificating." This statement reflected the fact that the CWD had checked a thousand employment certificates that had been filed for fourteen-year-old white children, while a mere eight had been filed and checked for African American children the same age. African American children were overlooked not only because of racism but also because the exclusion of domestic service and agricultural work from the child labor laws meant that the majority of black children—and many white children—were not covered by the law. Efforts to enforce the law for African Americans generated protest, and reformers were pressured to avoid pushing racial boundaries. Murphy, for example, discouraged Beldon from inviting African Americans onto the boards by arguing that "unless the white people are made to realize their responsibility in the matter, nothing will be done for the white children, and certainly nothing for the colored."[31]

Nonetheless, as the CWD's mission expanded to include child labor in settings other than the cotton mill, its investigators became more likely to encounter African American child workers. Efforts to address black child labor provoked complaints, but Governor Kilby backed up the CWD. In 1920, Major W. F. Johnston of Anniston's Alabama Pipe and Foundry Company complained to the governor about the department's interest in black children. Johnston, who had been fined for employing Frank Smoot, an underaged African American child, protested, "I guess it is no use kicking, but this law, as enforced by these women, is most irksome. You doubtless realize that we cannot well keep up with these little negroes and their ages." Kilby responded, "I know that the Child Labor Law is many times irksome and perhaps, more or less, unjust to certain manufacturers. There are so many, however, who wink at the misrepresentations of the workers and their parents that it seems necessary to enforce rigid rules in the administration of the law." And despite the governor's support, in at least one instance the CWD was not willing to risk its status on advocacy on behalf of those who had violated racial etiquette: in 1922, the department refused to incur any expenses on behalf of a Red Cross volunteer who sought aid for a white girl who had given birth to a "negro child."[32]

Kilby clearly had great respect for Bush, who personally reported a number of the department's cases to the governor. At the end of his term, he wrote in his message to the legislature, "Perhaps no department of Government is doing more services for the State than this department under the able management of Mrs. L. B. Bush." He continued, "In Mrs. Bush, this State is fortunate in having one who has a vision and is developing rapidly this important work."[33]

The whiteness of child labor reform helped facilitate the emergence of a Progressivism devoted to child welfare in the South. The pressure for northern reformers to follow southern racial custom and accept white supremacy to make reform progress possible is perhaps most strongly seen in the actions of Jean Gordon, the NCL's secretary of southern states, who resigned her post in Louisiana over the appointment of two reformers associated with the Society for the Advancement of Colored People. One of them was Jeannette Rankin, whom Gordon complained had "carried her spirit of social equality to the point that she traveled to the Peace Conference at Geneva with a colored woman as her companion, even sharing the same bed-room." In a private resignation letter to Florence Kelley, Gordon wrote, "I am at a loss to understand if the appointment of these two parties is just from sheer lack of ability to understand the situation down here, or whether certain elements in the North are just going to defy the South on what they are pleased to call our prejudices and try in every way to force the negro upon us." In her official resignation letter, Gordon clearly stated her racial beliefs: "Being thoroughly convinced that race purity is the most important problem facing the American people to-day, I feel it imperative that I take my stand NOW, and refuse to work under any organization whose leaders believe in race amalgamation, and appoint as secretaries men and women who by their action or influence would remove those restrictions which we of the South have found to be absolutely necessary in order to preserve to future generations a white supremacy."[34]

On paper, the CWD professed to believe that "racial amity and civic integrity and community self-respect must be based upon strict and incorruptible justice." The CWD professed support for the concept of a color-blind law, as can be seen in its reported desire to see the "negro child . . . given the same measure of protection received by the white children in [juvenile] courts." "In fact, the heaviest financial burden assumed by any juvenile court was, as far as we know, incurred in the interest of five little negroes—and this in one of the Wiregrass counties of the state," Bush reported.[35] The CWD's public face, however, was that of sturdy white children. The reformers of the CWD believed that their progress was bound up in the perception of the progress of white people in the New South. The child laborers of the textile mills had been saved from being dismissed as little crackers, but African American children had no similar image resurrected to pronounce them as of value to the state of Alabama and the future of the nation. The CWD was the state's first public welfare agency, and its existence depended on the public perception that its work was for the welfare of white children.

White reformers invented the "forgotten child" as a white child laborer in a southern textile mill, the symbol of child welfare work in the New South. Ironically, after Edgar Gardner Murphy became ill and dropped out of the child labor reform movement, he lamented to Jane Addams about the indifference "that is slowly creeping over the North" regarding African Americans.[36] By putting whites first, Murphy had facilitated this decline. As Progressives sought national standards for child labor and child welfare, they had to honor and reinforce white supremacy in the South to win acceptance for reform and for the outsiders who helped the cause.

NOTES

Abbreviations

ADAH	Alabama Department of Archives and History, Montgomery
AFL Records	*American Federation of Labor Records: The Samuel Gompers Era.* Sanford, N.C.: Microfilming Corporation of America, 1979.
AJMP	Alexander J. McKelway Papers, Library of Congress
Annals	*Annals of the American Academy of Political and Social Science*
EGMP	Edgar Gardner Murphy Papers (microfilm), Southern Historical Collection, Wilson Library, University of North Carolina at Chapel Hill
NCL Records	National Consumers' League Records, Library of Congress
NCLC Papers	National Child Labor Committee Papers, Library of Congress

Introduction

1. Woodward, *Origins,* 369–95.

2. U.S. Bureau of Labor, *Woman and Child Wage-Earners,* 1:36.

3. Gompers's speech to the United Textile Workers of America, Washington, D.C., October 21, 1902, reel 110, *AFL Records.*

4. For considering the social construction of race or how race functions as ideology, I have found the following works helpful: Almaguer, *Racial Fault Lines;* Fields, "Ideology and Race"; Foley, *White Scourge;* Higginbotham, "African-American Women's History"; Omi and Winant, *Racial Formations;* Smedley, *Race.*

5. A. J. McKelway, "The Mill or the Farm," *Annals* 35 (January–June 1910): 52–57 (proceedings of the sixth annual meeting of the NCLC, supplement).

6. *Montgomery Advertiser,* January 20, 1903, 4; Foley, *White Scourge,* 6; Neal L. Anderson, NCLC minutes, February 15, 1905, minute book section 3, container 6, NCLC Papers; Watson, *Church and Cotton Mills,* 3; Van Vorst, *Cry,* 72, 99; Murphy, *Problems,* 46.

7. E. G. Murphy, *Basis,* 52. Almaguer, *Racial Fault Lines,* 7, examines historical contexts where race supersedes class as an "organizing principle."

8. E. G. Murphy, *Problems,* 156.

9. For more on the interests in disfranchising lower-class whites, see Kousser, *Shaping.*

10. E. G. Murphy, *Problems,* 94; clipping, "The Child Labor Bill Adversed by Committee," February 17, 1901, EGMP.

11. Chafe, *Paradox,* 16; Turner, *Women, Culture, and Community,* 187.

12. *Montgomery Advertiser,* February 11, 1903, 3.

13. "Roosevelt, Theodore—2 Addresses," Birmingham, 1911, and "Roosevelt Another Speech Birmingham 1911," container 1, folder Roosevelt addresses, NCLC Papers.

14. Sklar, "Two Political Cultures," 37, 51; Turner, *Women, Culture, and Community,* 188; *Proceedings of Annual Conventions of Alabama Equal Suffrage Association,* Huntsville, February 5, 1914, p. 32, box 3, Alabama Equal Suffrage Association Records, ADAH.

15. Gordon, "Putting Children First," 63–86.

Chapter One. Mill Men

1. For discussions of textile mill paternalism, see Carlton, "Paternalism," 17–26; Scranton, "Varieties."

2. Markham, Lindsay, and Creel, *Children in Bondage,* 48; Mitchell, *Rise,* 95; Freehling, *Prelude,* 323–29. Cash, *Mind,* remains the best source for a sense of the Old South of legend. Mitchell became a critic of child labor even before this book was published, however, and later wrote a "blistering attack" on mill owners' resistance to child labor reform (Carlton, introduction). The fact that he could initially assume that mill owners were philanthropists showed the strength of the idea that employment of families in a poor, rural region was a blessing despite the imperfection of child labor. See Hall, "Broadus Mitchell," for Mitchell's later denunciation of New South mill owners for their exploitation of child labor.

3. *Child Labor Bulletin* 2 (May 1913): 155; Dawley, *Child,* 461–62.

4. Dawley, *Child,* 464; *Child Labor Bulletin* 4 (May 1915): 42.

5. Perry, *Middle-Class Townsmen,* 156; Carlton, "Paternalism," 21; *Manufacturers' Record,* December 7, 1894, 1; U.S. Bureau of the Census, *Report of Manufacturing Industries,* 168.

6. Carlton, *Mill and Town,* 46, and chap. 2, "Mill Building as Town Building."

7. *Birmingham News,* January 16, 1895, 4; February 8, 1896, 4; Fuller, "Boom Towns," 40; Weil, "Developpement," 270–71 (article translated for the author by Suzanne Hurley). See Carlton, *Mill and Town,* chap. 2, for an in-depth study of how "town folk" got behind the promotion of mill building. By 1900, the commercial club had three hundred members (*Birmingham News,* April 23, 1900, 26). See also Hackney, *Populism,* 130. Braxton Bragg Comer and Rufus Rhodes of the *Birmingham News* were primary organizers of the club in 1893 (*Birmingham News,* May 26, 1902, special ed., 71).

8. Flynt, *Poor but Proud,* 93. Carlton, who studied the residences of mill directors in South Carolina mill corporations, found that the "overwhelming majority were South Carolinians" (*Mill and Town,* 43; see also 46–59). For more on mill development in Huntsville, see Perry, *Middle-Class Townsmen,* 110–14, 124.

9. Wright, *Old South, New South,* 135; Flynt, *Poor but Proud,* 93; U.S. Bureau of the

Census, *Census Reports,* vol. 8, *Manufactures,* pt. 2, *States and Territories,* 28; *Birmingham News,* March 12, 1895, 4; April 23, 1900, 23. See also Brennan, "Legislation," 96–99.

10. Scranton, "Varieties," 237.

11. Perry, *Middle-Class Townsmen,* 66; Weil, "Developpement," 566–74; *Birmingham Age-Herald,* January 13, 1895, 1.

12. A brief history of the Nichols family appears in the finding aid to the John Howard Nichols Collection, Baker Library, Harvard University.

13. Perry, *Middle-Class Townsmen,* 66; *In Memoriam,* 6, 29; McCluskey, "Howard Gardner Nichols," 28; Silber, *Romance,* 2. See also *Alabama,* 99, 151.

14. "Alabama City—Its Location and the Advantages It Offers the Workingmen, 1912," 4, "Gadsden—Industries—Textiles" vertical file, Gadsden Public Library; *Gadsden Times-News,* May 9, 1902, 1.

15. *In Memoriam,* 27, 30, 42; Flynt, *Poor but Proud,* 100. "Dwight Manufacturing Company, Alabama City, Alabama," recruitment pamphlet, 1903, "Gadsden—Industries—Textiles" vertical file, Gadsden Public Library; "Alabama City—Its Location and the Advantages It Offers the Workingmen, 1912," 4, "Gadsden—Industries—Textiles" vertical file, Gadsden Public Library; *Gadsden Times-News,* May 9, 1902, 1.

16. Howard Gardner Nichols to J. Howard Nichols, June 17, 1896, R. A. Mitchell to J. Howard Nichols, August 19, November 2, 1898, Dwight Manufacturing Company vertical file, Gadsden Public Library; Flynt, *Poor but Proud,* 98. All letters to J. Howard Nichols at Gadsden Public Library are copies of originals in the John Howard Nichols Collection, Baker Library, Harvard University. By 1901 the competition for labor had become such a problem that Alabama mill owners agreed not to provide workers with transportation to the mills (*Birmingham News,* June 26, 1902). Dwight faced particularly stiff competition for labor because its mills were in Etowah County, next door to Calhoun County, where Anniston already had a cotton mill and where three more were built by 1900 (*Birmingham News,* April 23, 1900, 39). One more county away, Huntsville's large Dallas and Merrimack Mills, also owned by Massachusetts companies, added to the competition for operatives.

17. "Alabama City—Its Location," 4; Charles Moody to J. Howard Nichols, July 11, 1896, O. B. Tilton to J. Howard Nichols, August 8, September 7, 1896, O. B. Tilton to C. F. Norris, October 17, 1896, Dwight Manufacturing Company vertical file, Gadsden Public Library.

18. Margaret E. Moody, typescript, March 1979, "Gadsden—Industries—Textiles" vertical file, Gadsden Public Library; O. B. Tilton to J. Howard Nichols, January 1, 1897, R. A. Mitchell to J. Howard Nichols, March 11, 1899, Dwight Manufacturing Company vertical file, Gadsden Public Library.

19. A. K. Walker, *Braxton Bragg Comer,* 78, 179, 180, 227; A. B. Moore, *History,* 915; Andrews, *Men and Mills,* 59. See also "Braxton Bragg Comer," in D. D. Moore, *Men,* 150–51.

20. *Manufacturers' Record,* April 2, 1897, 177; *Birmingham Age-Herald,* January 22, 1895; January 30, 1895, 4. For southern elites' efforts to claim credit for new enterprises, see Gaston, *New South Creed,* 98.

21. Andrews, *Men and Mills,* 59; Perry, *Middle-Class Townsmen,* 184; *Birmingham Age-*

Herald, January 22, 1895; Buechler, *Avondale Mills,* 16. For a list of mill directors, see *Manufacturers' Record,* April 2, 1897, 177; *Birmingham News,* March 25, 1897, 4.

22. A. K. Walker, *Braxton Bragg Comer,* 227; Buechler, *Avondale Mills,* 17; Andrews, *Men and Mills,* 59; Doster, "Alabama's Gubernatorial Election," 174; Kousser, *Shaping,* 230–31.

23. Flynt, *Poor but Proud,* 97; A. K. Walker, *Braxton Bragg Comer,* 16; *Birmingham News,* April 23, 1900, 39; Braxton Bragg Comer to J. McDonald Comer, March 11, 1908, Braxton Bragg Comer Papers, Southern Historical Collection, Wilson Library, University of North Carolina at Chapel Hill; Braxton Bragg Comer to J. Fletcher Comer, August 20, 1908, Comer Papers. For workers' testimony about improvements made by Donald Comer, see Flynt, *Poor but Proud,* 105. See also Breedlove, "Donald Comer"; *Alabama: The News Magazine of the Deep South,* October 2, 1942, in Avondale Mills clip file, Birmingham Public Library. For examples of Braxton Bragg Comer's continued micromanagement of the mill after becoming governor, see Braxton Bragg Comer to J. McDonald Comer, March 11, 24, 1908, Braxton Bragg Comer to J. Fletcher Comer, June 16, August 20, 1908, folder 168, vol. 1, oversized letterbook, Comer Papers.

24. J. McDonald Comer to Braxton Bragg Comer, April 3, 1907, folder RC2:G64, Governor Braxton Bragg Comer: Administrative Files, ADAH; Scarboro, interview; Webb, *Two-Party Politics,* 219.

25. McDonald, *Sweetwater,* 14, 15; *Birmingham News,* January 30, 1895, 4; Thorn, "Bell Factory," 28C. Woodward, *Origins,* 130–41, coined the phrase *new men* to refer to southern entrepreneurs who wanted to industrialize following a northern model.

26. *Florence Herald,* May 11, 1899, 1; "Florence as She Is," *Florence Times,* December 1903.

27. *Memorial Record of Alabama,* 357; *Florence Times,* December 1903, 34; *Florence Herald,* May 11, 1899, 1.

28. *Florence Herald,* "souvenir and industrial edition," December 21, 1900, 35; Bailey, interview. Bailey grew up in the mill village, and her grandmother and father worked in the Ashcraft Mill (later called the Florence Mill).

29. "Florence as She Is," *Florence Times,* December 1903; *Florence Herald,* "souvenir and industrial edition," December 21, 1900; *Birmingham News,* April 23, 1900, 39.

30. Carlton, *Mill and Town,* 61–66; *Manufacturers' Record,* January 25, 1895, 398. For an example of a harsh view of textile paternalism, see Scranton, "Culture, Politics, and Acquiescence"; see also Mitchell, interview. Mitchell admitted that *The Rise of Cotton Mills in the South* overemphasized mill men's philanthropic motivations, but his use of the term *old meanies* indicated his feeling that recent scholarship had overdrawn their ruthlessness.

31. *Birmingham News,* January 25, 1898, 5; Carlton, *Mill and Town,* 61.

32. *Gadsden Times-News,* September 16, 1898, 2; Miller, *Cotton Mill Movement,* 31; *Birmingham News,* January 30, 1895, 4; *Gadsden Tribune,* December 28, 1894, 4; *Gadsden Times-News,* June 3, 1979, "Gadsden—Industries—Textiles" vertical file, Gadsden Public Library; Carlton, *Mill and Town,* 67; *Anniston Hot Blast,* February 11, 1900, 4. Mitchell's *Rise of Cotton Mills* invited criticism by suggesting that mill men built mills out of a desire "to give" employment to "the necessitous masses of poor whites" (132). Antebellum mills were more

commonly seen as offering a means of sustenance for indigent women and children; Carlton, *Mill and Town*, 78, noted that pronouncements on the social benefits for indigents from economic development were not encountered often in literature on postbellum mills. See also Freeze, "Poor Girls."

33. Gaston, *New South Creed*, 7; Mitchell, *Rise*, 95.

Chapter Two. Factory Families

1. *Florence Herald,* July 5, 1900, 1; June 21, 1900, 1; July 19, 1900, 1.

2. Ibid., July 5, 1900, 1; December 28, 1899, 5.

3. U.S. Bureau of the Census, *Report of Manufacturing Industries,* 3; U.S. Bureau of the Census, *Census Reports,* vol. 8, *Manufactures,* pt. 2, *States and Territories,* 6, 1016, 4. This census shows that the average number of wage earners in Florence was 595.

4. U.S. census, 1910, Alabama, T624, reels 21, 13 (Lauderdale and Etowah Counties); U.S. census, 1900, Alabama, Etowah County, e.d. 165, sheets 1–27, pp. 273A–296B; U.S. Bureau of the Census, *Population,* 1901, 609. Newby, *Plain Folk,* 465, makes the distinction between what workers called "indoor work" and "outdoor work." Whites refused to do "indoor" work next to blacks. I located the Lauderdale and Etowah cotton mill populations using the soundex and the names of children who worked in the mill taken from Alabama Department for the Inspection of Mills, *Annual Report.* I thank Wallis Goodman and Christie Sample Wilson for their help with the work in the census data for Alabama City. Analysis of the Dwight Mill population is based on a table created of the entire population of Alabama City for 1900 with cotton mill households designated as any household that included a mill employee. Only eighteen men were identified as teamsters; they were hauling for the cotton mill company. Whether they had been hired by the cotton mill or by an independent company is debatable. After getting input from several labor historians, I decided to count these men as employed by the mills.

5. U.S. census, 1910, Alabama, T624, reel 21, e.d. 63, sheet 12A; e.d. 64, sheets 9A–B.

6. U.S. census, 1900, Alabama, Etowah County, e.d. 165, sheets 1–27, pp. 273A–296B; U.S. census, 1910, Alabama, T624, reel 13, e.d. 76, sheet 14A. U.S. Bureau of Labor, *Woman and Child Wage-Earners,* 1:524, gives the statistics of 7.1 as the size of the average southern family. On p. 466, this publication gives 5.1 as the average size for 252 southern textile families.

7. U.S. census, 1900, Alabama, Etowah County, e.d. 165, sheets 1–27, pp. 273A–296B.

8. U.S. Bureau of Labor, *Woman and Child Wage-Earners,* 1:29, 30, 36.

9. U.S. census, 1900, Alabama, Etowah County, e.d. 165, sheets 1–27, pp. 273A–296B; Alabama, *Report of the Department for the Inspection of Jails and Alms Houses and Cotton Mills,* 18; Hall et al., *Like a Family,* 61; U.S. Bureau of Labor, *Woman and Child Wage-Earners,* 1:35.

10. U.S. Bureau of Labor, *Woman and Child Wage-Earners,* 1:35–36, 239; U.S. census, 1900, Alabama, Etowah County, e.d. 165, sheets 1–27, pp. 273A–296B.

11. U.S. Bureau of Labor, *Woman and Child Wage-Earners,* 1:442; U.S. census, 1900, Ala-

bama, Etowah County, e.d. 165, sheets 1–27, pp. 273A–296B; U.S. census, 1910, Alabama, T624, reel 21, e.d. 63, sheet 7B.

12. U.S. Bureau of Labor, *Woman and Child Wage-Earners,* 1:123. For fuller pictures of mill village life, see Hall et al., *Like a Family;* Newby, *Plain Folk;* McLaurin, *Paternalism and Protest.* For more on the "tenancy ladder" and the status of landless farmers, see Kirby, *Rural Worlds Lost;* Daniel, *Breaking the Land.*

13. U.S. census, 1910, Alabama, T624, reel 21, e.d. 63, sheet 7B; R. A. Mitchell to J. Howard Nichols, November 2, 1898, Dwight Manufacturing Company vertical file, Gadsden Public Library; U.S. Bureau of Labor, *Woman and Child Wage-Earners,* 1:123. Newby, *Plain Folk,* 84, finds much interaction between farmers and mill workers. McHugh, *Mill Family,* uses census data from southern counties with cotton mills to show the interchange between farming and mill work.

14. *Florence Herald,* December 28, 1899, 5; March 8, 1900, 5; March 1, 1900, 5; March 10, 1904, 1.

15. Ibid., August 10, 1899, 1, 8; U.S. Bureau of Labor, *Woman and Child Wage-Earners,* 1:586. The *Florence Herald* dropped the "East Florence News" column by 1907.

16. Flynt, "Folks Like Us," 225.

17. Gates, *Model City,* 263.

18. *Birmingham Age-Herald,* January 13, 1895, 1; *Birmingham News,* February 8, 1895, 3.

19. Berney, *Hand-Book,* 482; *Birmingham Age-Herald,* February 10, 1895, 10; January 12, 1895, 4.

20. Lewis W. Parker, testimony, in U.S. House Committee, *Constitutional Amendment,* 9; *Birmingham News,* April 2, 1895, 2.

21. Newby, *Plain Folk,* 465l; Perry, *Middle-Class Townsmen,* 67. Carlton, *Mill and Town,* 244–45, found a flurry of interest in black operatives in South Carolina during the late 1890s. Frederickson, "Four Decades," argues that blacks had an expansive role as "mill laborers."

22. *Birmingham Age-Herald,* May 5, 1896, 1; Newby, *Plain Folk,* 469, 474. The *Birmingham News,* April 23, 1900, shows that the Speigner Convict Mills were developed.

23. Newby, *Plain Folk,* 481.

24. Ibid., 233. For the social bonds among mill workers, see Hall et al., *Like a Family.*

25. Newby, *Plain Folk,* 170.

26. *Anniston Hot Blast,* March 1, 1900, 1.

27. Newby, *Plain Folk,* 107, 506, 236–37. Prude, "Family," discusses how historians address the problem of evaluating the narrowing of the family's function in transition from "traditional" to "modern" society. He indicates that the nuclear family was more ubiquitous in past eras; thus, historians have made kin networks and family systems more central as they have related particular family systems to their historical settings. For more on contracts, see U.S. Bureau of Labor, *Woman and Child Wage-Earners,* 1:241–43.

28. Newby, *Plain Folk,* 89; Alabama Department for the Inspection of Mills, *Annual Report,* 16; Hall et al., *Like a Family,* 52.

29. U.S. Bureau of Labor, *Woman and Child Wage-Earners,* 7:46, 93. In the early twentieth century, more than 80 percent of Alabama factory families (including workers other than textile operatives) had insurance.

30. U.S. Bureau of Labor, *Woman and Child Wage-Earners;* Bailey, interview. For a description of an Alabama poor farm, see Tuten, "Regulating the Poor," 40–60.

31. See Newby, *Plain Folk,* 129–33, 118.

32. Ibid., 175; U.S. Bureau of Labor, *Woman and Child Wage-Earners,* 1:417. Although it is a community study of the Amoskeag Company in Manchester, New Hampshire, Hareven, *Family Time,* offers relevant observations on the interdependence that persisted between family members in rural and wage-employment settings. Southern textile families valued the arrangements that permitted movement between the mill and rural community origins to perpetuate kin networks. As long as paternalism harmonized with workers' familial orientation, allowing flexibility in the system for informal worker controls, workers showed little enthusiasm for unions.

33. U.S. Bureau of Labor, *Woman and Child Wage-Earners,* 1:122, 578, 7:106–7, 125.

34. Newby, *Plain Folk,* 505–6. For analysis of South Carolina textile workers' support of Blease in 1910–12, see Carlton, *Mill and Town,* 215–72. Blease was ambiguous about where he stood on child labor reform but opposed compulsory education and medical examinations of poor children. Blease played to mill workers' antagonism regarding the modern world's encroachment into their lives, drawing broad support among mill workers by developing campaign themes about how they could control their lives and those of their children.

35. R. A. Mitchell to J. Howard Nichols, November 18, 1898, Dwight Manufacturing Company vertical file, Gadsden Public Library.

36. R. A. Mitchell to J. Howard Nichols, n.d. [1897 or 1898], Dwight Manufacturing Company vertical file, Gadsden Public Library; U.S. census, 1900, Alabama, Etowah County, e.d. 165, sheets 1–27, pp. 273A–296B.

37. De Graffenried, "Georgia Cracker"; Whites, "De Graffenried Controversy," 451.

38. Whites, "De Graffenried Controversy," 470.

39. R. A. Mitchell to J. Howard Nichols, December 10, 26, 1898, February 24, 1899, Dwight Manufacturing Company vertical file, Gadsden Public Library. In 1897 the Mobile Society for the Propagation of Christian Knowledge had sponsored a handful of child labor bills, but these measures received little support or public notice (Davidson, *Child Labor Legislation,* 22–23).

40. *Florence Herald,* May 11, 1899, 4.

Chapter Three. Sentimentalism, Not Socialism

1. Davidson, *Child Labor Legislation,* 18–20, provides the history of the 1886–87 bill and its repeal.

2. *Birmingham Labor Advocate,* March 26, 1898, 4.

3. Ibid., June 26, 1897, 4; February 4, 1899, 4.

4. "The Textile Workers' Strike," *American Federationist* 4 (February 1898): 275.

5. *Birmingham Labor Advocate,* January 8, 1898, 1.

6. Gompers speech to the United Textile Workers of America Convention, Washington, D.C., October 21, 1902, reel 110, *AFL Records.*

7. Samuel Gompers, "The Crime of '94–95," *American Federationist* 4 (February 1898): 278.

8. Kessler-Harris, *Out to Work,* 203.

9. Bedford, *Socialism,* 79–81; "Textile Workers' Convention," *American Federationist* 4 (July 1897). For a fuller account of a merger between the southern controlled IUTW and northern craft unions that resulted in the United Textile Workers of America, see McLaurin, *Paternalism and Protest,* chap. 7. See also Prince Greene to Samuel Gompers, December 31, 1900, reel 143, *AFL Records.*

10. *Manufacturers' Record,* April 9, 1897, 183.

11. Edward Thimme, "Child Labor," *American Federationist* 1 (June 1894): 67–68; U.S. House Committee, *Uniform Hours,* 4, 5; R. Johnson and Brown, *Twentieth Century Biographical Dictionary.* For more on Lovering, see *Manufacturers' Record,* April 9, 1897, 187; Galambos, *Competition and Cooperation,* 26; U.S. Congress, *Memorial Addresses,* 33–34.

12. U.S. House Committee, *Uniform Hours,* 14, 19. For more on Orr, see Carlton, *Mill and Town,* 106, 138, 177, 182.

13. U.S. House Committee, *Uniform Hours,* 19, 28, 29.

14. Ibid., 52, 49, 53.

15. For how the AFL based its ideal of trade unionism on a male wage earner, see Milkman, "Organizing."

16. Laurie, *Artisans,* 192; Nardinelli, *Child Labor,* 136; Glickman, *Living Wage,* 47. For how Gompers and the AFL collaborated with Florence Kelley and Jane Addams to achieve the 1893 Factory Inspection Act, see Sklar, "Hull House." See also Brian Simon, *Education.* For Gompers's union strategies, see Laurie, *Artisans,* 177. Milkman, "Organizing," 123, suggests that bonds of skill had been the basis of unionism throughout the nineteenth century, thereby weakening the AFL's interest in organizing women in largely unskilled positions.

17. *American Federationist* 6 (May 1899): 57; "Textile Workers' Convention," *American Federationist* 4 (July 1897).

18. R. A. Mitchell to J. Howard Nichols, December 10, 1898, Dwight Manufacturing Company vertical file, Gadsden Public Library; Gompers to Alabama Union members, January 23, 1899, in Kaufman, *Samuel Gompers Papers,* 70; Ashby, *Child Labor,* 4.

19. McLaurin, *Paternalism and Protest,* chap. 7. See also Prince Greene to Samuel Gompers, December 31, 1900, reel 143, *AFL Records.*

20. Sam D. Nedrey to Gompers, June 11, 1901, reel 143, *AFL Records;* "Organizing the South," *American Federationist* 6 (June 1899): 77; Harry Walker to organized labor, April 2, 1900, and form letter from Greene, December 5, 1900, reel 143, *AFL Records; American*

Federationist 6 (September 1899): 126; *Birmingham Labor Advocate,* October 29, 1898, 4; "The Industrial Crime: Child Labor," *American Federationist* 10 (May 1903): 348.

21. *Birmingham Labor Advocate,* January 21, 1899, 4.

22. Ashby, *Child Labor,* 4; *Birmingham Labor Advocate,* November 24, 1900, 4; December 21, 1901, 4.

23. "Labor May Put Out an Independent Ticket in Jefferson County," *Birmingham News,* January 27, 1896, 5; Kelley, *Hammer and Hoe,* 1–10. For more on Birmingham and organized labor, see Ward and Rogers, *Labor Revolt.*

24. *Birmingham News,* November 23, 1895, 7; January 27, 1896, 5; *Birmingham Labor Advocate,* September 21, 1901, 1.

25. *Birmingham Labor Advocate,* November 19, 1898, 4; September 1, 1900, 4; November 26, 1898, 4; January 21, 1899, 4.

26. Ibid., January 13, 1900, 4; April 27, 1901, 1; July 19, 1902, 4. For more on the political work of trade unions, see Leidenberger, "Public," 189.

27. *Birmingham Labor Advocate,* April 27, 1901, 1; November 29, 1903, 4.

28. G. B. McCracken to Samuel Gompers, December 31, 1900, reel 143, *AFL Records;* R. A. Mitchell to J. Howard Nichols, Alabama City, December 10, 1898, Dwight Manufacturing Company vertical file, Gadsden Public Library; Davidson, *Child Labor Legislation,* 23.

29. Prince Greene to Samuel Gompers, December 31, September 6, 1900, reel 143, *AFL Records.* Mother Jones, a Socialist known for her efforts to abolish child labor, visited the Avondale Mills in 1908 and rebuked Gompers's conservatism by charging that he had failed the region's child workers and had acquiesced to the Democratic South. Instead, she claimed that she stood "for the overthrow of the entire system that murders childhood," advocating the "overthrow of a system that can give a $6,000 job to labor leaders who have betrayed these infants" (Mother Jones, "Governor Comer's Alabama Cotton Mills," in Steel, *Speeches and Writings,* 281; see also "Mother Jones, Labor's Joan of Arc," *Birmingham Labor Advocate,* June 16, 1900, 1).

30. Laurie, *Artisans,* 176–210, esp. 181, 189–90; Samuel Gompers, editorial, *American Federationist* 12 (1905): 74; McLaurin, *Paternalism and Protest,* chap. 7; Samuel Gompers, "An Address at the National Conference on the Foreign Policy of the United States," August 1898, in Kaufman, *Samuel Gompers Papers,* 6. At the 1894 AFL convention, a struggle broke out between socialist factions advocating a "political program," and Gompers's anti-Program Alliance. Socialists helped to prevent Gompers's reelection as AFL president, supporting John McBride, a miner. It was Gompers's only defeat in his thirty-eight years with the AFL (Laurie, *Artisans,* 190).

31. Prince Greene to Samuel Gompers, October 29, 1900, reel 143, *AFL Records.* The concept of an "industrial plantation," while invented for propaganda purposes, is misleading for a number of reasons but primarily because the workers were free. See Carlton, *Mill and Town,* 106; Carlton, "Paternalism," 17–26.

32. Ayers, *Promise,* 116–17; McLaurin, *Paternalism and Protest,* 177.

33. U.S. House Committee, *Uniform Hours,* 35.

34. Newby, *Plain Folk,* 522.

35. Milkman, "Organizing," 115–23; Glickman, *Living Wage,* 77, 65–66; McCurry, *Masters,* 72.

36. Gregory, *American Exodus,* 145–46. Although the subject of Gregory's work is the 1930s Okie subculture, some of his observations about what he calls "Plain-Folk Americanism" apply to the culture of white southern textile workers.

37. Davidson, *Child Labor Legislation,* 46; Alexander J. McKelway, "To the Board of Trustees," minute book section 3, container 6, March 23, 1905, NCLC Papers. Gompers promised to defer to Alexander J. McKelway, a southern member of the National Child Labor Committee, about when organized labor should advocate southern child labor legislation.

38. See Hall, *Revolt,* for a model examination of reform through co-opting prevailing middle-class norms.

39. Irene Ashby-Macfadyen to Nina Browne DeCottes, March 22, ca. December 1, 1902, William P. Browne Papers, ADAH; Samuel Gompers to Irene Ashby, January 3, 1901, in Kaufman, *Samuel Gompers Papers,* 315; Davidson, *Child Labor Legislation,* 25.

40. For an overview of Progressives' ideas, see Rodgers, "In Search of Progressivism."

41. *Birmingham News,* January 16, 1901, 3; July 8, 1896, 8 (for Commercial Club members); *Birmingham Labor Advocate,* December 1, 1900, 3. As discussed earlier, the Birmingham Commercial Club had promoted southern cotton mill development, including the repeal of the 1886 law limiting women and children's labor. The hard-core class issues raised by the issue of child labor would have to be restricted within the club's building.

42. Gompers, address to the United Textile Workers of America, October 21, 1902, reel 110, *AFL Records; Birmingham News,* January 18, 1901, 10.

43. *Birmingham Labor Advocate,* January 26, 1901, 4, 5.

44. Ibid.; *Birmingham News,* January 26, 1901, 2.

45. *Birmingham Labor Advocate,* February 7, 1901, 4; *Birmingham News,* January 16, 1901, 3; Davidson, *Child Labor Legislation,* 26–27.

46. Irene Ashby-Macfadyen to Nina Browne DeCottes, August 12, ca. December 1, 1902, Browne Papers; *Montgomery Advertiser,* May 19, 1901, 14.

47. Irene Ashby-Macfadyen to Nina Browne DeCottes, March 22, 1902, Browne Papers; *Montgomery Advertiser,* February 19, 1902, 2.

48. Kaufman, *Samuel Gompers Papers,* 5:349; Irene Ashby to Nina Browne DeCottes, August 21, 1901, Irene Ashby-Macfadyen to Nina Browne DeCottes, October 17, 1901, March 22, April 3, 10, 22, June 9, 1902, July 18, 1914, Browne Papers.

49. Irene Ashby-Macfadyen to Nina Browne DeCottes, April 22, ca. December 1, 1902, Browne Papers; Jane Addams to Anita McCormick Blaine, February 6, 1902, in Bryan, *Jane Addams Papers,* reel 4-266.

50. U.S. House Committee, *Constitutional Amendment,* 2.

51. Ibid., 29, 30.

52. Irene Ashby-Macfadyen to Nina Browne DeCottes, March 26, 1902, Browne Papers; U.S. House Committee, *Constitutional Amendment,* 47, 48, 49.

53. Ibid., 51, 52.

54. Ibid., 45, 46.

55. Irene Ashby to Nina Browne DeCottes, August 21, 1901, Browne Papers; U.S. House Committee, *Constitutional Amendment,* 47, 48, 49, 51, 52, 45, 46, 53, 59.

56. U.S. House Committee, *Constitutional Amendment,* 59.

57. Mathews, "Factoring," 601; Haltunen, *Confidence Men,* 189, 195.

58. M. K. Murphy, *Edgar Gardner Murphy,* 44; "Southern Prosperity Is Not Shackled to Children: An Interview, Edgar Gardner Murphy" (clipping), EGMP.

59. Craighead, *History,* 81, 87–88; *Birmingham News,* January 3, 1901, 20; Ashby, *Child Labor,* 8; *Montgomery Advertiser,* February 13, 1903, 5.

60. Baker, "Domestication"; Kerber, "Separate Spheres."

61. Thomas, *New Woman,* 101; Craighead, *History,* 106; *Birmingham News,* August 9, 1902, 13. Orr referred to the child labor bill as a "warm question" in the *Montgomery Advertiser,* February 11, 1903, 3.

62. *Birmingham News,* May 15, 1903, 31; May 26, 1902 (industrial arts edition), 73; August 9, 1902, 13; *Florence Herald,* January 30, 1903, 1; Hackney, *Populism,* 130; *Montgomery Advertiser,* February 12, 1903, 8. For a history of the industrial school, see "Making Good Men Out of Bad Boys," *Birmingham News,* industrial arts edition, May 26, 1902, 73.

63. *Birmingham News,* August 16, 1903, 12; July 5, 1902, 13; *Montgomery Advertiser,* February 28, 1902, 2. On Albert Goodwyn's controversial gubernatorial candidacy, see *Birmingham Age-Herald,* May 9, 1896, 4; May 22, 1896, 4; *Montgomery Advertiser,* February 11, 1903, 9; February 13, 1903, 5.

64. *Montgomery Advertiser,* February 11, 1903, 3. For debate on the relationship between women's culture and feminism and politics, see DuBois et al., "Politics and Culture." Frankel and Dye, *Gender,* includes essays that illuminate the diversity of women's reform with special attention to region, race, and class and thus are part of the challenge to the trajectory of women's reform emerging from "women's sphere." Muncy, *Creating a Female Dominion,* shows the importance of institutions such as Hull House for the emergence of female reform initiative.

65. Irene Ashby-Macfadyen to Nina Browne DeCottes, ca. December 1, 1902, Browne Papers; E. G. Murphy, *Problems,* 135. Murphy discussed this problem with NCLC reformer Alexander J. McKelway (Murphy to McKelway, January 23, 1905, EGMP).

Chapter Four. Inventing the "Forgotten Child"

1. For an excellent case study of how southern women's reform efforts evolved in relation to emerging national groups such as the Women's Christian Temperance Union and the General Federation of Women's Clubs, see McArthur, *Creating the New Woman,* 7–30. See also Thomas, *New Woman,* 13.

2. Child labor reform follows a slightly different trajectory than is typical for southern women's increasing politicization. McArthur, *Creating the New Woman,* exemplifies the historiography that stresses traditions of women's voluntarism, the construction of increasingly elaborate female networks, and the unique public opportunities available to southern women because of weak southern governments. Child labor reform in Alabama eventually conforms to this pattern for the emergence of the new southern woman, but on this issue, intersections with male reform groups and national attention to the problem also played an important role in politicizing southern women's child welfare work.

3. Edgar Gardner Murphy to Jane Addams, November 7, 1909, in Bryan, *Jane Addams Papers,* reel 5-916.

4. E. G. Murphy, *Child Labor and Business,* 4; "The Ministers' Union Takes Action in Reference to Street Fair" (clipping), February 4, 1901, EGMP. Murphy's church helped establish a library for mill children (unidentified clipping, December 1, 1900, and "Notes from St. John's," February 1, 1901, EGMP). Another church started a night school and Sunday School for workers in the factory district of west Montgomery (Ashcroft, Anderson, and Knox, *In Remembrance,* 14). See also Murphy, *South and Her Children,* 10.

5. E. G. Murphy, *Child Labor and Business,* 4. Hubbard, "Eye-Witness," 6, suggests that manufacturers opposed to reform continued to use the term *sentimentalist* to denounce child labor reformers. Murphy's letters to his son illuminate the playful, sentimental, rhetoric of the middle-class private sphere. "This is just a Christmas page of kisses and hugs, my dearest eleven year old, my precious, my joy!" he wrote in 1906 (Edgar Gardner Murphy to Gardner Murphy, December 22, 1906, EGMP). Five years later, the rubric of contemporary middle-class familial affection continued: "O! how glad we shall be to see thee—hug thee—kiss thee—scold thee . . . greet thee . . . love thee—have thee *again!!!*" (Edgar Gardner Murphy to Gardner Murphy, March 19, 1911, EGMP).

6. "Southern Prosperity Is Not Shackled to Children: An Interview, Edgar Gardner Murphy" (clipping), EGMP; Foucault, *History,* 82, 89. Sawicki, *Disciplining Foucault,* 99, emphasizes the transformative potential of Foucault's understanding of power exercised through discourse. ACLC member and former Alabama Governor Thomas G. Jones was an exception, wielding both political and cultural power.

7. Craighead, *History,* 47, 53, 95.

8. Edgar Gardner Murphy to Major Barron, June 11, 1907, in response to Barron's misinterpretation of the term *success* in Murphy's editorial "Education for the Unsuccessful" (*Montgomery Advertiser,* June 11, 1907), EGMP; Bailey, *Edgar Gardner Murphy,* 2; M. K. Murphy, *Edgar Gardner Murphy,* 6.

9. Edgar Gardner Murphy to Gardner Murphy, June 15, 1911, EGMP.

10. Bailey, *Edgar Gardner Murphy,* 13; M. K. Murphy, *Edgar Gardner Murphy,* 12; Levine, "Edgar Gardner Murphy," 101.

11. Bailey, *Edgar Gardner Murphy,* 19.

12. For accounts of Smith's lynching, see Williamson, *Rage.* For contemporary accounts, see Royster, *Southern Horrors.* Bailey, *Edgar Gardner Murphy,* 9, and Williamson, *Rage,*

209, discuss Murphy's resolution against lynching. See also "Resolutions on 'Paris Lynching,'" 1893, EGMP.

13. E. G. Murphy, *Problems,* 12, 49; *Montgomery Advertiser* clipping, November 28, 1901, EGMP.

14. "Backward or Forward?" *South Atlantic Quarterly* 8 (January 1909): 19, copy in EGMP; E. G. Murphy, *Problems,* 156. For an overview of various interpretations of the causes of racial violence, see Tolnay and Beck, *Festival,* esp. chap. 4, "Social Threat, Competition, and Mob Violence," 55–85.

15. E. G. Murphy, *Problems,* 10.

16. Bederman, *Manliness and Civilization,* 10–15, 18, 27.

17. Ibid., 29, 28. See also Omi and Winant, *Racial Formations,* 59.

18. Bederman, *Manliness and Civilization,* 28–29; E. G. Murphy, *Problems,* 3.

19. Hoffschwelle, *Rebuilding,* 16; Bailey, *Edgar Gardner Murphy,* 30. For lists of members of the ACLC, see Ashby, *Child Labor,* 3; Eva McDonald Valesh, "Three Notable Lines of Labor Work," *American Federationist* 8 (November 1901): 459; E. G. Murphy, Nichols, and Sears, *Child Labor,* 24. For a list of Southern Society members, see "The Montgomery Conference: Under the Auspices of the Southern Society for the Promotion of the Study of Race Conditions and Problems in the South" (program), May 8–10, 1900, EGMP. These lists of ACLC members are not identical, and the number sixteen includes all names that appear in any of the sources.

20. Ashcroft et al., *In Remembrance,* 9; T. A. Owen, *History,* 1276; Ashby, *Child Labor,* 3; E. G. Murphy, Nichols, and Sears, *Child Labor,* 3. The South Alabama Presbytery assigned Anderson as the minister of Montgomery's First Presbyterian Church in late 1891 (H. R. McDonald to Alexander McIver, March 3, 1900, Alexander McIver Papers, Southern Historical Collection, Wilson Library, University of North Carolina at Chapel Hill).

21. "The Montgomery Conference: Under the Auspices of the Southern Society for the Promotion of the Study of Race Conditions and Problems in the South" (program), May 8–10, 1900, EGMP. See also "The Southern Society" (clipping), February 3, 1900, EGMP. On Baldwin's commitment to public education, see Edgar Gardner Murphy to George Foster Peabody, March 14, 1903, Southern Education Board Papers, Southern Historical Collection, Wilson Library, University of North Carolina at Chapel Hill. Jones, a member of Murphy's congregation, had been elected governor in 1892 and 1894. For Washington's philosophy, see Woodward, *Origins,* 357–60. On the Southern Society, see "The Race Problem" (clipping), January 17, 1900, "A Notable Conference," and "A Southern Conference: Official Statement," EGMP. Many members of the Southern Society, including Murphy, knew Washington.

22. Clipping from the *Montgomery Advertiser,* November 28, 1901, EGMP; Edgar Gardner Murphy, "An Interview: A Talk about the Work of the Southern Education Board" (clipping), *Montgomery Advertiser,* 1901, EGMP; "The Montgomery Conference: Under the Auspices of the Southern Society for the Promotion of the Study of Race Conditions and Problems in the South" (program), May 8–10, 1900, EGMP. Murphy served as the SEB's

executive secretary until 1908 although he was at times incapacitated by ill health (Claxton, *Work,* 1). For a full list of SEB members, see Harlan, "Southern Education Board," 190. Other notable SEB members included Walter Hines Page, J. L. M. Curry, Charles W. Dabney, Charles D. McIver, Wallace Buttrick, and Hollis B. Frissell. The SEB had eleven northern and fifteen southern members in its thirteen-year history. Robert C. Ogden, William H. Baldwin Jr., and George Foster Peabody had the most long-standing connection to Negro industrial schools and raised a modest budget for the board from Andrew Carnegie and the General Education Board, a group initially funded by a donation from the Rockefellers that between 1903 and 1965 supported education efforts for both blacks and whites, primarily in rural areas.

23. E. G. Murphy, *Problems,* 6; Harlan, "Southern Education Board," 191, 201.

24. Kate Gordon to members of the Official Board of the National Women's Suffrage Association, June 23, 1915, copy from the Library of Congress in folder 94.1.1, Pattie Ruffner Jacobs Papers, Birmingham Public Library; "The Child Labor Bill Adversed by Committee" (clipping), February 17, 1901, EGMP.

25. "The Child Labor Bill Adversed by Committee" (clipping) February 17, 1901, EGMP.

26. Edgar Gardner Murphy, "The Schools of the People," address delivered to the General Session of the National Educational Association, Boston, July 10, 1903, reprinted in E. G. Murphy, *Problems,* 43; E. G. Murphy, *Problems,* 47; Edgar Gardner Murphy, "The Industrial Revival and Child Labor," in *Problems,* 123; E. G. Murphy, *Pictures,* 12.

27. *Florence Herald,* March 22, 1907, 1; *Birmingham News,* April 28, 1902, 8.

28. E. G. Murphy, *Child Labor and the Public;* U.S. Bureau of Education, *Report, 1904–5,* 1:70, table 8; *Gadsden Times-News,* February 6, 1903, 2 (reprinted from the *Anniston Hot Blast*); *Florence Herald,* November 27, 1903, 2. According to the U.S. Bureau of Education report, the average number of days the schools were open in Alabama was 73.5 in 1900, 96 in 1901–2, and 103 in 1903–4. But the average number days of attendance was much lower. The average number of days of school for every child between ages five and eighteen in 1903–4 was only 38 because so many children did not enroll at all. The average number of days attended by each *enrolled* pupil for that year was 67, still far below the 103 days that school was open.

29. *Florence Herald,* January 30, 1903, 1; October 9, 1903, 4; July 3, 1903, 1; Bailey, interview; *Birmingham News,* April 4, 1903, 11 (a reprint of Lindsay's Florence report). Birmingham mill operator Braxton Bragg Comer also sponsored a free kindergarten (*Birmingham News,* October 10, 1903, 28).

30. *Florence Herald,* January 16, 1903, 2.

31. *Manufacturers' Record,* November 5, 1903, 301; July 4, 1901, 443; Patton, "Southern Reaction," 72; see also various issues of the *Manufacturers' Record,* 1903. Murphy and the SEB tried hard to disassociate themselves from proposals for national aid. See "A Significant Confession," container 3, folder 26, AJMP.

32. E. G. Murphy, *Problems,* 135; Edgar Gardner Murphy, address to the National Con-

ference of Charities and Correction, Atlanta, May 9, 1903, reprinted in E. G. Murphy, *Problems,* 135.

33. E. G. Murphy, *Pictures;* E. G. Murphy, *Problems,* 115.

34. E. G. Murphy, *Problems,* 137, 115–16.

35. E. G. Murphy, *Pictures;* E. G. Murphy, *Problems,* 109; *Florence Herald,* November 16, 1894, 2; *Montgomery Advertiser,* January 7, 1902, 2. Given her alliance with Irene M. Ashby-Macfadyen, DeCottes may have been unusually likely to report mill accidents in a way that focused responsibility on the mill. It is hard to gauge the accuracy of Murphy and the ACLC's estimates of the number of very young children working in mills because census reports did not distinguish between employed children under twelve and those under sixteen. Census takers did not collect occupation data on children under ten, and families were always likely to underreport the work of young children.

36. Ashby, *Child Labor,* 10; E. G. Murphy, Nichols, and Sears, *Child Labor,* 15.

37. E. G. Murphy, *Pictures;* E. G. Murphy, *Problems,* 107–8.

38. E. G. Murphy, *Pictures.*

39. E. G. Murphy, *South and Her Children,* 6, 17; E. G. Murphy, Nichols, and Sears, *Child Labor,* 3, 10.

40. E. G. Murphy, Nichols, and Sears, *Child Labor,* 17, 19; Davis, "Reflections," 803.

41. Davidson, *Child Labor Legislation,* 49–50.

42. Ibid.; *Montgomery Advertiser,* February 11, 1903, 3; Craighead, *History,* 107; Thomas, *New Woman,* 100.

43. *Montgomery Advertiser,* February 13, 1903, 9; *Gadsden Times-News,* January 30, 1903.

44. E. G. Murphy, *Problems,* 94, 281.

Chapter Five. Whiteness of Reform

1. Neal L. Anderson, speech, February 15, 1905, 18, minute book section 3, container 6, NCLC Papers.

2. *Montgomery Advertiser,* April 20, 1901, 4. The same quotation appears in E. G. Murphy, *Open Letter,* 9.

3. Neal L. Anderson, speech, February 15, 1905, 18, minute book section 3, container 6, NCLC Papers; E. G. Murphy, *Problems,* 156.

4. Omi and Winant, *Racial Formations,* 64, 69.

5. Bederman, *Manliness and Civilization,* 29. Bederman provides evidence of twentieth-century sensibilities of race and civilization and their relationship to Darwinism and Lamarckian biological theories about human heredity.

6. Almaguer, *Racial Fault Lines,* 13; Foley, *White Scourge,* 6; Hale, *Making Whiteness,* 3–11; *Manufacturers' Record,* July 4, 1901, 443. Almaguer provides a detailed discussion of the historical underpinnings of the association of nonwhite groups with degrading labor conditions and second-class citizenship. See Roediger, *Wages,* on the growing emphasis in labor

history on how workers recognized that claiming whiteness could be a basis for rights and privileges.

7. Two works that have dealt with the public preoccupation of the whiteness of rural southerners are Whisnant, *All That Is Native and Fine,* and Silber, *Romance,* 143–46. Both Whisnant and Silber show how the mountain white was romanticized as a figure with untarnished traits of Anglo-Saxonism.

8. Almaguer, *Racial Fault Lines,* 7, examines historical contexts where race supersedes class as an "organizing principle." Smedley, *Race,* 21, is also helpful for understanding how race can be a way of dividing humanity.

9. E. G. Murphy, *Basis,* 52.

10. Ibid., 52–53.

11. Ibid., 56; Bederman, *Manliness and Civilization,* 28–29; E. G. Murphy, *Problems,* 19–21. Pascoe, "Miscegenation Law," evaluates the emergence of modernist racial ideology during the 1920s, in the process identifying the turn-of-the-century biologically grounded racialism that culturalists challenged. This racialism shaped Murphy's fear of miscegenation. In *The Black Image in the White Mind,* Fredrickson applied the term *Herrenvolk* democracy to the U.S. South to describe political democracy for the master race. Murphy also held a concept of democracy as the privilege of the master race from which irresponsible whites could be excluded and in which responsible African Americans might eventually be included. Williamson, *Rage,* 212, discusses how Murphy argued that "segregation was not degradation."

12. E. G. Murphy, *Basis,* 23.

13. E. G. Murphy, "Child Labor as a National Problem," *Charities,* May 16, 1903, 491; NCLC minute book, April 1904–April 1906, pp. 1–3, container 6, NCLC Papers. For a history of the NCLC, see Trattner, *Crusade.* Alexander J. McKelway, eulogy for Edgar Gardner Murphy, container 4, folder 102, AJMP, indicates Murphy's influence on McKelway. For more on McKelway, see Doherty, "Alexander J. McKelway."

14. *Birmingham News,* August 9, 1902, 13; *Manufacturers' Record,* July 4, 1901, 443; W. H. Swift, "Why Is It Hard to Get Good Child Labor Laws in the South?" *Child Labor Bulletin* 3 (May 1914): 73.

15. Edmonds, *Cotton Mill Labor Conditions,* 3–4; *Annals* 20 (July–December 1902): 186.

16. Alexander J. McKelway, "The Menace of Race-Degeneracy in America" (speech), container 4, folder 64, AJMP; Hubbard, "Eye-Witness," 3; Mrs. A. O. Granger, "The Effect of Club Work in the South," *Annals* 28 (July–December 1906): 253.

17. Rafter, *White Trash,* 5; Oscar C. McCulloch, "The Tribe of Ishmael: A Study in Social Degradation" in Rafter, *White Trash,* 50–51, 54. Rafter has collected some of these eugenics studies in *White Trash.* These studies did not exclusively examine southerners.

18. Elizabeth S. Kite, "Two Brothers," in Rafter, *White Trash,* 80. Rafter, *White Trash,* discusses eugenicists who coined the term *cacogenic* to describe families with bad genes. Larson, *Sex, Race, and Science,* argues that during the second decade of the twentieth century, women's clubs, birth control advocates, and mental health reformers sought to "purify

the race" by advocating stricter marriage laws, institutionalization of those deemed degenerate, and involuntary sterilization.

19. McCulloch, "Tribe," 54.

20. Hugh G. Fox, "Child Labor in the South," *Charities,* June 6, 1903, 553. Pascoe, "Miscegenation Law," argues that eugenicists were prominent participants in the debate on the meaning of biology in a context where culturalists challenged physical characteristics as indicators of race. Eugenicists argued that certain traits were inherited and therefore were obsessed with the problems that mixed-race individuals allegedly would pose.

21. Alexander J. McKelway, "The Menace of Race-Degeneracy in America" (speech), 3, container 4, folder 64, AJMP.

22. Untitled list of answers to objections to child labor laws, pp. 9, 10, container 3, folder 42, AJMP; Alexander J. McKelway, "Child Labor in the South," n.d. [probably 1907], 8, 9, container 4, folder 72, AJMP.

23. *Montgomery Advertiser,* January 20, 1903, 4; Watson, *Church and Cotton Mills,* 14.

24. Alexander J. McKelway, "Child Labor," paper presented to the Presbyterian Ministers' Association, Atlanta, Georgia, June 26, 1905, container 3, folder 42, AJMP; *Birmingham News,* May 30, 1901, 4.

25. *Birmingham News,* August 9, 1902, 13; see Neal L. Anderson, speech, February 15, 1905, 18, minute book section 3, container 6, NCLC Papers; Watson, *Church and Cotton Mills,* 3; E. G. Murphy, *Problems,* 46, 91, 123, 169; Van Vorst, *Cry,* 72, 99.

26. E. G. Murphy, "'The Grandfather Clause': Do Our People Want It?" (clipping), June 26, 1901, EGMP.

27. E. G. Murphy, *Problems,* 17. A number of clippings of book reviews are in the EGMP.

28. E. G. Murphy, *Open Letter,* 10. A sermon that Murphy gave at the climax of the Populist challenge suggests his association of political insurgency in the South with corruption at the polls and social disorder. See "Preached Sunday before Election" (clipping), November 1896, EGMP. For an example of a struggle of small white farmers and landless farmers to gain control of the Democratic Party, see Kirwan, *Revolt.* Murphy discusses the need for a "particular form of public order" before democratizing in *Problems,* 190. On Alabama politics and incidents of ballot fraud and intimidation of black and illiterate white voters, see Hackney, *Populism,* 63.

29. E. G. Murphy, *White Man,* 24–25; E. G. Murphy, "'The Grandfather Clause': Do Our People Want It?" (clipping), June 26, 1901, EGMP.

30. E. G. Murphy, *Open Letter,* 11; E. G. Murphy, *Problems,* 3.

31. *Montgomery Advertiser,* July 11, 1901, 4; *Birmingham News,* July 15, 1901, 4; N. R. Baker, "Investigation as to Causes of Non Enrollment and Irregular Attendance in Talladega County, Alabama," n.d. [ca. 1908–10], Southern Education Board Papers.

32. J. T. Hefflin quoted by Bond, *Negro Education,* 190. The full quotation appears in Alabama Constitutional Convention, *Official Report,* day 72. Gilmore, *Gender and Jim Crow,* 21, shows the array of African American resistance to Jim Crow segregation and oppression and illuminates how the competition between whites and blacks that may have worried the

white middle classes the most was not between the poor of each race but between professionals.

33. *Alabama Baptist,* February 13, 1907, 7; Neal L. Anderson, speech, February 15, 1905, 18, minute book section 3, container 6, NCLC Papers.

34. Untitled list of answers to objections to child labor laws, p. 12, container 3, folder 42, AJMP; Page, *Rebuilding,* 22, 4, 26. Leloudis, "School Reform," 897. Page edited the *Raleigh State Chronicle* in the 1880s before leaving the region and working for the *Forum* (New York) and *Atlantic Monthly* (Boston), and starting his own magazine, *World's Work* (New York) in 1900. An ally of the southern public education movement and a correspondent of various reformers, including Murphy, Page encapsulated in his phrase regional reformers' hopes that the South would fulfill its traditions of democracy and free institutions that made it more akin than unrelated to the North. For more on Page's relationship with leading education reformers and the impact of his speech, see Hendrick, *Life and Letters,* 64–101. For the full text of the speech, see Page, *Rebuilding,* 2–35.

35. E. G. Murphy, *Problems,* 94; Page, *Rebuilding,* 34.

36. A. J. McKelway, "Child Labor and Citizenship" (speech), n.d., container 3, AJMP.

37. E. G. Murphy, *Problems,* 106; Hayes Robbins, "The Necessity for Factory Legislation in the South," *Annals* 20 (July–December 1902): 186; Prunella Guilgord, "The Price of a Garden," *Stories about the Other Child,* supplement to the *Child Labor Bulletin* 2 (December 1913): 37.

38. U.S. Bureau of Labor, *Woman and Child Wage-Earners,* 1:29; W. H. Hand, "Need of Compulsory Education in the South," *Child Labor Bulletin* 1 (June 1912): 78. Kelley, *Race Rebels,* is a model work for its sensitivity to the ways in which gender could be manipulated to reinforce or resist racial stereotyping.

39. Bond, *Negro Education,* 192.

40. E. G. Murphy, *Problems,* 193; Alabama Constitutional Convention, *Official Report,* Article 8, Suffrage, day 82.

41. E. G. Murphy, *Alabama's First Question,* 2, 6; J. H. Phillips, "Local Taxation for Schools," in Murphy, *Alabama's First Question,* 10. The constitution provided for a state school fund with revenues raised from any property sold by the state, all poll taxes, a special annual tax of thirty cents on each one hundred dollars of taxable property, and the ability of counties to levy a tax not exceeding ten cents on each one hundred dollars of taxable property after approval of three-fifths of county electors (Alabama Constitutional Convention, *Official Report,* Article 14, day 82). For more on reformers' concerns about the inadequacies of education revenues, see Phillips, "Local Taxation," 8. Phillips based his illiteracy statistics on the 1900 U.S. census. The accuracy of Murphy's "five cents a day" statistic is questionable—other sources suggest that if anything, it was a bit high. "School per Capita Is Decreased," *Birmingham News,* October 9, 1903, reported that $1.38 per year was spent on each school-age child in Alabama. The U.S. Bureau of Education, *Report of the Commissioner of Education, 1900–1901,* vol. 1, table 16, reported that four dollars was the average yearly expenditure per Alabama pupil.

42. Bond, *Negro Education*, 192; E. G. Murphy, "Alabama's First Question," 5. The eight counties mentioned were St. Clair, Winston, Franklin, Chilton, Cherokee, and Cleburne in the northern half of the state and Coffee and Covington in the south. That Black Belt counties gave the majority of their school funds to their minority population is demonstrated by the shift in funding for teachers' salaries after 1891. Expenditures for white teacher salaries in Wilcox County, for example, rose from $4,397 in 1890–91 to $28,108 in 1907–08, while funds for black teachers fell from $6,545 to $3,940 (Bond, *Negro Education*, table 6, "Expenditures and School Population in the Black Belt County of Wilcox, by Race, 1876–1930").

43. *Birmingham News,* June 14, 1902, 13; Movements, *Save the Little Americans,* 5. Ogden was a sponsor of the Southern Education Board and hosted train trips to the South on which he invited northern and later southern male and female philanthropists and educators, courting support for efforts to improve education (see, for example, container 6, folder February 1904, Robert C. Ogden Papers, Library of Congress). A letter from J. E. Chamberlain to Ogden, May 2, 1904, container 7, May 1904 folder, Ogden Papers, shows that Ogden was under pressure to show that he sought to help both races, not just blacks.

44. Braeman, *Albert J. Beveridge,* 117; Albert Shaw to Albert J. Beveridge, January 26, 1907, container 282, folder 1906–7, Beveridge Papers; Albert J. Beveridge to Jane Addams, December 13, 1906, in Bryan, *Jane Addams Papers,* reel 4-1525. For Beveridge's speech, see *Congressional Record—Senate,* January 23, 1907, 1552–57; January 28, 1907, 1794–97; January 29, 1907, 1866–82.

45. *Congressional Record—Senate,* January 28, 1907, 1795; Beveridge, *Meaning,* 331, 341. Bremner, *Discovery,* 224, credits Beveridge with adding to the child labor debate the warning that white superiority was at stake; however, the child labor movement's race-based rhetoric had much earlier roots.

46. Braeman, *Albert J. Beveridge,* 118; Beveridge, *Meaning,* 324.

47. E. G. Murphy, *Federal Regulation;* Florence Kelley to son, November 10, 1907, reel 4, Florence Kelley Papers, microfilm, New York Public Library. For Murphy's resignation from the NCLC, see E. G. Murphy to Felix Adler, December 18, 1906 (handwritten letter inserted into minute book), minute book 1906–8, container 6, NCLC Papers. For the committee's acceptance of Murphy's letter of resignation, see minute book section 13, Board of Trustees meeting, January 29, 1907, NCLC Papers. For the NCLC's withdrawal of its support for the Beveridge bill, see Robert W. de Forest to Mr. Warburg, December 6, 1906, minute book section 19, container 6, NCLC Papers. De Forest argued that the NCLC should not endorse the bill because it would alienate the South, where he thought the committee should focus. After having dinner with Beveridge, the NCLC Board of Trustees debated the issue and voted not to endorse the bill (Board of Trustees minutes, December 6, 1906, minute book section 19, container 6, NCLC Papers). Kelley warned Beveridge that the NCLC would "reverse its position" on his bill (Florence Kelley to Albert J. Beveridge, October 31, 1907, container 156, Beveridge Papers).

48. E. G. Murphy, *Federal Regulation,* 7, 20.

49. Florence Kelley to son, March 17, 1907, reel 4, Kelley Papers; Samuel McCune Lindsay to Albert J. Beveridge, November 8, 1907, in container 156, Beveridge Papers.

50. Van Vorst, *Cry,* 26, 34; Van Vorst and Van Vorst, *Woman.* The earlier piece lacks this racial language.

51. Rafter, *White Trash,* 26–27; Van Vorst, *Cry,* 30, 61.

52. Whites, "De Graffenried Controversy," 451; Van Vorst, *Cry,* 99; Van Vorst and Van Vorst, *Woman,* 300.

Chapter Six. Transregional Progressivism

1. Van Vorst, "Cry," 2; Van Vorst, *Cry,* 20.

2. Scott, *Southern Lady;* Berkeley, "First Southern Conference," 900.

3. McArthur, *Creating the New Woman,* 143; Turner, *Women, Culture, and Community,* 191; Sims, "Feminism and Femininity," 159.

4. *Child Labor Bulletin* 5 (August 1916): 87.

5. Muncy, *Creating a Female Dominion,* 108, shows the emergence of women's influence on state child welfare policy through such groups as the U.S. Children's Bureau.

6. *Birmingham News,* November 22, 1905, 9.

7. Craighead, *History,* 218; Alabama Child Labor Law, no. 776, August 9, 1907, box SP165, Child Welfare Department Records, ADAH.

8. *Birmingham News,* August 18, 1906, 5; Hackney, *Populism,* 306.

9. Craighead, *History,* 217; Braxton Bragg Comer, "Movements for Education from the Log School to the University—Money Spent to Give the Boys and Girls a Chance" (speech), June 1, 1910, series 1, folder 3, Comer Papers; U.S. Bureau of Labor, *Woman and Child Wage-Earners,* 1:570; Shirley Bragg to Braxton Bragg Comer, May 31, 1907, May 1908, folder "Prisons, Almshouses, Cotton Mills Inspection Reports," RC2: G70, Comer Administrative Files.

10. Alabama Inspector of Jails and Alms Houses, *Annual Report,* 12; "Instructions to Superintendents, Principals and Other School Authorities," 3, box SP165, Child Welfare Department Records.

11. Alabama Department for the Inspection of Mills, *Annual Report,* 138; Carlton, *Mill and Town,* 202.

12. Carlton, *Mill and Town,* 203; Bailey, interview. According to Flynt, *Poor but Proud,* "In 1924, Alabama's cotton textile workers earned about half of what Massachusetts operatives made" (102).

13. Alabama Inspector of Jails and Alms Houses, *Annual Report,* 9; Alabama Child Labor Law, no. 776, August 9, 1907, box SP165, Child Welfare Department Records. The inspector and his clerk were overburdened with the responsibility of conducting four inspections for all seventy-one manufacturing establishments, along with the sixty-nine jails and fifty-five almshouses that were the original charge of the prison inspector's office.

14. Alabama Inspector of Jails and Alms Houses, *Annual Report*, 10; Alabama Department for the Inspection of Mills, *Annual Report*, 8.

15. Alabama Department for the Inspection of Mills, *Annual Report*, 44, 82. For the best evidence of mill families' eagerness for education when it was offered on terms that did not interfere with their livelihoods, see Alabama Department of Education, *First Report*, 38.

16. U.S. Bureau of Labor, *Woman and Child Wage-Earners*, 1:537–39, 246, 488; Markham, Lindsay, and Creel, *Children in Bondage*, 212; Lindenmeyer, *"Right,"* 113.

17. U.S. Bureau of Labor, *Woman and Child Wage-Earners*, 1:336; Markham, Lindsay, and Creel, *Children in Bondage*, 42.

18. Markham, Lindsay, and Creel, *Children in Bondage*, 42, 41; Florence Kelley to Albert J. Beveridge, August 5, 1907, container 156, Beveridge Papers. See also Conant, "Eight-Hour Day," 3.

19. *Child Labor Bulletin* 3 (May 1914): 17.

20. Fenollosa, *Red Horse Hill*, 50, 64.

21. Clippings scrapbook for the seventh and eighth conferences, container 49, NCLC Papers; Theodore Roosevelt, first address, 1911, and Theodore Roosevelt, "Roosevelt Another Speech Birmingham 1911," both in container 1, folder "Roosevelt, Theodore—2 Addresses," NCLC Papers.

22. "Attendance Large at Formal Opening of National Child Labor Conference," *Birmingham News*, March 9, 1911, and *Birmingham News*, March 9, 10, 1911, all in clippings scrapbook for the seventh and eighth conferences, container 49, NCLC Papers; *Birmingham News*, March 4, 1911, 12.

23. "Something about 'Personnel' of the Child Labor Conference," *Birmingham Age-Herald*, March 9, 1911, clippings scrapbook for the seventh and eighth conferences, container 49, NCLC Papers.

24. Ibid.

25. "McKelway Flays Mill Interests," *Boston Transcript*, March 10, 1911, and "Child Labor Conference and Its Results," *Birmingham Ledger*, March 9, 1911, both in clippings scrapbook for the seventh and eighth conferences, container 49, NCLC Papers; Alexander McKelway, "The Herod among Industries" (speech), March 9, 1911, container 3, AJMP.

26. "Reception for Miss Jane Addams at Country Club," *Birmingham Age-Herald*, March 5, 1911, and "Something about 'Personnel' of the Child Labor Conference," *Birmingham Age-Herald*, March 9, 1911, both in clippings scrapbook for the seventh and eighth conferences, container 49, NCLC Papers.

27. "As a Woman Sees It," *Birmingham News*, March 7, 1911, 10; Nellie Kimball Murdoch to Florence Kelley, June 30, 1931, and Florence Kelley to Nellie Kimball Murdoch, July 11, 1931, reel 4, Kelley Papers; Nellie Kimball Murdoch to Dr. John Howland Lathrop, February 15, 1943, reel 29, NCL Records.

28. Thomas, *New Woman*, 106; *Birmingham City Directory*, 1914; Bordin, "'Baptism'"; *Birmingham Labor Advocate*, October 15, 1898, 4. Both *Murdock* and *Murdoch* appear in various records for Nellie Kimball, but the city directory identifies the couple as *Murdoch*. W. L.

Murdoch does not appear in any standard biographical sources or in the surname clippings file at the ADAH. Although Bordin's work is on an earlier period, she evaluates the temperance crusade as women's first experience with public power. See also Baker, "Domestication," for the WCTU as a descendant of the temperance movement but also flexible enough to accommodate a broad array of women's local concerns for the public good. On the Alabama WCTU, see Thomas, *New Woman*, 10–40.

29. Thomas, *New Woman*, 27–28; LaMonte, *Politics and Welfare*, 46, 50; Alabama Department of Education, *First Report*, 117. LaMonte identifies the women of the Boys' Club as initiators of the Children's Aid Society. Alabama Child Welfare Department reports identify the Children's Aid Society as the private organization that was the precursor to this first public welfare department.

30. Thomas, *New Woman*, 135–37; Nellie Kimball Murdoch to Elizabeth S. McGee, 1949, July 4, 1943, reel 29, NCL Records. Murdoch held study groups in her home after the 1911 NCLC conference. During these meetings, the BESA was created, and Murdoch served as its third vice president. She became the corresponding secretary for the AESA when it formed a year later. The Selma association was created in 1910 after the constitutional amendment for Prohibition failed. The AESA was affiliated with the National American Woman Suffrage Association. The NCL helped the U.S. Bureau of Labor gather information for the *Woman and Child Wage-Earners* report. See Josephine Goldmark, "Report of the Committee on Legislation and the Legal Defense of Labor Laws," *National Consumers' League Thirteenth Report,* January 19, 1912, p. 4, reel 4, NCL Records. Gordon's title became secretary for the southern states, reflecting how her involvement signaled a new regional focus within the NCL.

31. *Child Labor Bulletin* 2 (May 1913): 160; Sklar, "Two Political Cultures," 45. Gender politics refers to the way that women exploited contemporary assumptions about men and women's innate qualities to argue for greater authority for women on public issues that related to traditional womanly concerns about children and family. Women made a politics out of claiming that their gender difference gave them the authority to argue for the protection of children and the home from the relentless needs of industrial capitalism (Sklar, "Two Political Cultures," 36–62).

32. Sklar, "Two Political Cultures," 48, 49.

33. *Proceedings of Annual Conventions of Alabama Equal Suffrage Association,* Huntsville, February 5, 1914, p. 32, box 3, Alabama Equal Suffrage Association Records.

34. Davidson, *Child Labor Legislation,* 229. Murdoch wrote to Davidson in 1931 and explained that some club leaders connected to prominent manufacturers continued to resent criticism of the cotton manufacturers.

35. Thomas, *New Woman,* 137; *Child Labor Bulletin* 3 (May 1914): 192. Worthington served as secretary of the ACLC until the NCLC's agent, Herschel Jones, took over the position.

36. Thomas, *New Woman,* 141–42. Phillips reinstated Worthington to the course after the AESA came to her defense.

37. *Congressional Record,* February 15, 1909, as quoted by Lindenmeyer, *"Right,"* 23; *Child Labor Bulletin* 2 (May 1913): 171; Nellie Kimball Murdoch to Julia Lathrop, October 11, 1914, folder 94.1.3, Jacobs Papers. Lindenmeyer, *"Right,"* 11, says that historians attribute the bureau's origins to Kelley and to Lillian D. Wald. Lindenmeyer, *"Right,"* 41, reports that when the U.S. Children's Bureau was transferred into the newly created Department of Labor in 1913, the bureau was actively gathering and coordinating information on child labor. While Lathrop and many of the reformers who worked for the bureau supported a federal child labor law, President Woodrow Wilson pressured the bureau to avoid seeming to advocate federal regulation of child labor. Wilson subsequently changed his mind and supported a federal child labor law in 1916 after the Republican Party platform adopted passage of the Keating-Owen bill, giving Congress the power to regulate child labor by prohibiting the interstate sale of products made by children under fourteen and in some cases children under sixteen (Lindenmeyer, *"Right,"* 118). Southern opposition to Keating-Owen focused primarily on the bill's eight-hour-day requirement. See testimony by David Clark of Charlotte, North Carolina, editor of the *Southern Textile Bulletin,* in U.S. Congress, *Hearings,* 7–12. The U.S. Congress passed the measure in 1916, but the U.S. Supreme Court ruled the law unconstitutional two years later.

38. *Child Labor Bulletin* 2 (May 1913): 99.

39. Alabama Department for the Inspection of Mills, *Annual Report,* 8, 9; *Child Labor Bulletin* 2 (May 1913): 155, 156, 164, 157, 124. See also Oates's article in the *Child Labor Bulletin* 2 (May 1913): 117–20.

40. Alabama Department for the Inspection of Mills, *Annual Report,* 8; Lewis Hine, "General Statement, Investigation of Merrimack," November–December 1913, container 3, folder "Alabama Mills," NCLC Papers; Davidson, *Child Labor Legislation,* 230. Hine's report includes his observations on several Alabama mills, with a special comparison of the Merrimack Mills in Huntsville to the company's mills in Lowell, Massachusetts.

41. Jones, *Child Labor,* 5, 6.

42. Craighead, *History,* 370; Davidson, *Child Labor Legislation,* 231, 232, 234; *Montgomery Advertiser,* January 28, 1915, 1; January 29, 1915, 3; January 18, 1915, 2. John B. Weakly of Jefferson County introduced the bill in the Alabama House, and H. T. Hartwell of Mobile introduced the same measure in the Senate. Testifying in 1916 before a congressional hearing on the proposed federal child labor bill, Alabama manufacturer Joseph J. Bradley from Huntsville's Merrimack Mills admitted that manufacturers no longer cared about the minimum age. But they opposed limits on the hours of the fourteen- to sixteen-year-old girls who were a significant proportion of the spinning labor force and who worked more continuously than boy doffers. Bradley argued that the mill would have to buy more efficient machinery to make up for the lost labor of girl spinners (U.S. House, *Hearings,* 54–55).

43. *Montgomery Advertiser,* January 29, 1915, 3; January 17, 1915, 20; January 20, 1915, 7.

44. Ibid., January 17, 1915, 20.

45. Davidson, *Child Labor Legislation,* 232, remarks that the argument that child labor

regulation would offer an opening for organized labor was entirely absent from the 1915 debates.

46. LaMonte, *Politics and Welfare*, 60; *Child Labor Bulletin* 4 (May 1915): 14.

47. Florence I. Taylor, "Child Labor Law Administration," in Clopper, *Child Welfare*, 132, 137, 136.

48. Ibid., 134; Alabama Department for the Inspection of Mills, *Annual Report*, 8. Even Birmingham did not hire an attendance officer (Clopper, *Child Welfare*, 84, 131).

Chapter Seven. New Women and Child Welfare

1. Case no. 464, March 1932, Katherine Du Pre Lumpkin Papers, Southern Historical Collection, Wilson Library, University of North Carolina at Chapel Hill.

2. M. B. Owen, *Story*, 20; Webb and Armbrewster, *Alabama Governors*, 166; Thomas E. Kilby to Owen R. Lovejoy, June 9, 1922, folder 3, Governor Thomas E. Kilby: Administrative Files, ADAH.

3. Alabama Legislature, *General Laws 1915*, 587–88, 577; Murdoch, "Juvenile Courts and Probation," in Clopper, *Child Welfare*, 150; Evelina Beldon, "Alabama Juvenile Courts," folder 94.1.6, Jacobs Papers. Green, *Before the New Deal*, 92, shows southern reformers in New Orleans going through a similar process of shifting toward a more ambitious agenda of social reform.

4. Evelina Beldon, "Alabama Juvenile Courts," folder 94.1.6, Jacobs Papers.

5. Samuel D. Murphy to Evelina Beldon, April 21, 1916, Evelina Beldon to Julia Lathrop, April 6, 1916, and Nellie Kimball Murdoch to Julia Lathrop, December 27, 1915, all in folders 94.1.7 and 94.1.5, Jacobs Papers.

6. Bush, "How Alabama Organized," 130; typed history, folder "Short History of the CWD," [1919?], box SP166, Child Welfare Department Records; Clopper, *Child Welfare*, 7; *Alabama Childhood: The Official Bulletin of the State Child Welfare Department of Alabama* 1, no. 1 (April–May–June 1921): 39. NCLC members wrote five of the articles in *Child Welfare in Alabama*, and Murdoch authored the remaining one.

7. Owen R. Lovejoy to Thomas E. Kilby, November 20, 1919, box SG22121, folder 1, Kilby Administrative Files; Clopper, *Child Welfare*, 145, 6.

8. Owen R. Lovejoy to Thomas E. Kilby, November 20, 1919, box SG22121, folder 1, Kilby Administrative Files; M. B. Owen, *Story*, 20; typed history, folder "Short History of the CWD," [1919?], box SP166, Child Welfare Department Records; Clopper, *Child Welfare*, 202. See also Loraine Bedsole Bush to Thomas E. Kilby, November 23, 1919, SG22121, folder 1, Kilby Administrative Files; Davidson, *Child Labor Legislation*, 235. Clopper, *Child Welfare*, 201, says the Children's Aid Society started in 1917. In 1922, the Children's Aid Society was incorporated into the Child Welfare Department as the Children's Aid Division, headquartered in Montgomery (Alabama Child Welfare Department, *Child Welfare Department*, 14).

9. Loraine Bedsole Bush to Owen R. Lovejoy, n.d., and Loraine Bedsole Bush to

Thomas E. Kilby, November 23, 1919, box SG22121, folder 1, Kilby Administrative Files; Bush, "How Alabama Organized," 131.

10. M. B. Owen, *Story,* 20; Mollie Dowd to Florence Kelley, December 27, 1920, reel 4, Kelley Papers.

11. For the education, child welfare, and child labor laws, see Alabama Legislature, *General Laws 1919,* 616, 694, 868, 871, 615.

12. *Alabama Childhood: The Official Bulletin of the State Child Welfare Department of Alabama* 1, no. 1 (April–May–June 1921): 52; Davidson, *Child Labor Legislation,* 229; "Governor's Message," in Alabama Legislature, *General Laws 1923,* xcvi.

13. Nellie Kimball Murdoch to Miss Flemming, August 3, 1920, and Evelina Beldon to Nellie Kimball Murdoch, April 3, 1916, folders 94.1.9 and 94.1.7, Jacobs Papers; *Alabama Childhood: The Official Bulletin of the State Child Welfare Department of Alabama* 1, no. 1 (June 1921 supplement): 51.

14. Alabama Legislature, House of Representatives, *Journal,* 2524; Hart, *Social Progress,* 5; Alabama Legislature, *General Laws 1923,* xviii. The House approved a version of Senate bill 247 establishing the CWD with an amendment to give the new department inspection power by a vote of sixty-three to two. The Russell Sage Foundation, started in 1907 with a sixty-five-million-dollar gift from Margaret Olivia Sage, was the "nation's pioneer independent institute for social research" (Hammack and Wheeler, *Social Science,* 35).

15. Alabama Legislature, House of Representatives, *Journal,* 35–36.

16. Davidson, *Child Labor Legislation,* 235; Alabama Legislature, House of Representatives, *Journal,* 2524; Alabama Legislature, *General Laws 1923,* lxxxv. Tunstall's amendment shifted responsibility for ensuring compliance from the state prison inspector to the new department. Bush married Tunstall in 1924. Although there is no evidence that the two had a relationship as early as 1919, her work on the bill suggests that she would have been looking for a receptive representative to strengthen the department's powers. The new law did not apply to children employed in farming or domestic service, and Murdoch was aware that agricultural work remained the biggest barrier to Alabama children attending school. She understood, however, that support for child welfare had to be secured before reformers could contemplate expanding their goals. "It is going to take a vigorous campaign of education for the farmer, himself, to change this situation," she had told reformers at the 1913 NCLC annual meeting (*Child Labor Bulletin* 2 [May 1913]: 125). In 1919, the NCLC was only beginning to branch out to address agricultural labor, and Murdoch followed plans to reach the most easily identified groups of working children in cities and mill villages.

17. Alabama Legislature, *General Laws 1919,* 694–95; Alabama Legislature, *General Laws 1923,* lxxxv–xcviii.

18. Alabama Legislature, *General Laws 1919,* 871. Both houses of the Alabama legislature unanimously approved an amendment that kept children under twenty-one out of places where "intoxicating liquors" were manufactured or sold (Alabama Legislature, House of Representatives, *Journal,* 2117, 2670). The actions of Alabama's politicians re-

flected the decline in opposition to child labor regulation among the state's mill men. It was the only southern state to pass legislation that instituted the eight-hour workday for children, and whereas all twelve North Carolina representatives and senators and all nine South Carolina congressmen opposed the federal Keating-Owen Act, five Alabama congressmen supported it and only three opposed it.

19. U.S. Bureau of the Census, *Census Reports,* vol. 10, *Manufactures,* pt. 4, *Special Reports on Selected Industries,* 161; Hall et al., *Like a Family,* 60, 183–98; Lea, "Cotton Textiles," 486. The use of child labor declined across the southern Piedmont but was sharpest in Alabama. The author would like to thank David Carlton for his help in understanding the decline in child labor.

20. Donald Comer to Thomas Kilby, June 12, May 19, 1922, and Thomas Kilby to Donald Comer, June 9, 1922, all in box SG22121, folder 3, Kilby Administrative Files.

21. Alabama Child Welfare Department, *Report.*

22. *Alabama Childhood: The Official Bulletin of the State Child Welfare Department of Alabama* 1, no. 1 (April–May–June 1921): 8, 13; Alabama Child Welfare Department, *Instructions.* During the first year of its existence, the CWD inspected 197 cotton mills, 16 bakeries, 15 bottling plants, 16 candy factories, 17 foundries, 20 mines, 18 railroad shops, 38 sawmills, and 14 overall factories, for a total of 351 establishments.

23. "Child Welfare, Calhoun County, Tentative Report—Investigation Not Complete," 1920, pp. 9–10, box SG22121, folder 1, Kilby Administrative Files.

24. Alabama Child Welfare Department, *Report,* drawing on cover by Frank Spangler of the *Montgomery Advertiser,* 10; Lemuel B. Green to Thomas E. Kilby, September 27, 1919, and William H. Thomas to Thomas E. Kilby, October 17, 1919, box SG22121, folder 1, Kilby Administrative Files; *Alabama Childhood: The Official Bulletin of the State Child Welfare Department of Alabama* 1, no. 1 (April–May–June 1921): 1; Alabama Child Welfare Department, *Children's Aid Division,* cover; Alabama Child Welfare Department, *Report,* 66. Green, one of two inspectors of institutions, was the sole male employee. The commission also included such important state figures as the governor; the superintendent of education, Dr. John W. Abercrombie; the state health officer, Dr. S. W. Welch; and three judges, Lawrence H. Lee, W. T. Murphree, and T. J. Bedsole.

25. Bush, "How Alabama Organized," 129, 133.

26. *Birmingham News,* April 7, 1911, 10.

27. Alabama Child Welfare Department, *Report,* 19, 61; Mrs. Joseph Brevard Jones, "The Alabama Federation and the Child Welfare Work," *Alabama Childhood: The Official Bulletin of the State Child Welfare Department of Alabama* 1, no. 1 (April–May–June 1921): 36–37; Alabama Child Welfare Department, *Annual Report,* 28–29.

28. Alabama Child Welfare Department, *Annual Report,* 8–9; Alabama Child Welfare Department, *Report,* 59; "Child Labor Law," from the Code of Alabama, 1923, p. 4, box SP165, Child Welfare Department Records; D. D. Moore, *Men,* 93.

29. *Alabama Childhood: The Official Bulletin of the State Child Welfare Department of Alabama* 1, no. 1 (April–May–June 1921): 14.

30. Alabama Child Welfare Department, *Child Welfare Department,* 51; Alabama Child Welfare Department, *Report,* 12, 51.

31. E. G. Murphy, *Problems,* 94; Loraine Bedsole Bush to Thomas E. Kilby, March 5, 1921, box SG22121, folder 2, Kilby Administrative Files; Evelina Beldon to Julia Lathrop, March 31, 1916, and Samuel D. Murphy to Evelina Beldon, April 10, 1916, folders 94.1.6 and 94.1.7, Jacobs Papers; *Alabama Childhood: The Official Bulletin of the State Child Welfare Department of Alabama* 1, no. 1 (April–May–June 1921): 7–8.

32. W. F. Johnston to Thomas E. Kilby, November 18, 1920, Thomas E. Kilby to W. F. Johnston, November 22, 1920, and Mary Andrew to Thomas E. Kilby, November 23, 1922, all in box SG22121, folders 2, 3, Kilby Administrative Files.

33. "Governor's Message," in Alabama Legislature, *General Laws 1923,* cxxxviii.

34. Jean Gordon to the president and board of the New Orleans Branch of the National Consumers' League, January 8, 1921, and Jean Gordon to Florence Kelley, January 11, 1921, both in reel 4, Kelley Papers.

35. *Alabama Childhood: The Official Bulletin of the State Child Welfare Department of* Alabama 1, no. 2 (July–August–September 1921): 19.

36. Edgar Gardner Murphy to Jane Addams, November 7, 1909, in Bryan, *Jane Addams Papers,* reel 5-916.

BIBLIOGRAPHY

Manuscript Collections

Alabama Department of Archives and History, Montgomery. Alabama Education Association Records. Alabama Equal Suffrage Association Records. Alabama Federation of Women's Clubs Association Records. William P. Browne Papers. Child Welfare Department Records. Governor Braxton Bragg Comer: Administrative Files. Illiteracy Commission: State Records. Governor Thomas E. Kilby: Administrative Files.

Baker Library, Harvard University, Cambridge, Massachusetts. John Howard Nichols Collection.

Birmingham Public Library, Birmingham, Alabama. Avondale Mills clip file. Pattie Ruffner Jacobs Papers.

Gadsden Public Library, Gadsden, Alabama. Dwight Manufacturing Company Vertical File. Gadsden—Industries—Textiles Vertical File.

Library of Congress, Washington, D.C. Albert J. Beveridge Papers. Alexander J. McKelway Papers. National Child Labor Committee Papers. National Consumers' League Records, microfilm. Robert C. Ogden Papers. Theodore Roosevelt Papers, Library of Congress, microfilm edition, 1964.

New York Public Library, New York. Florence Kelley Papers, microfilm.

Southern Historical Collection, Wilson Library, University of North Carolina at Chapel Hill. Braxton Bragg Comer Papers. Charles W. Dabney Papers. Katherine Du Pre Lumpkin Papers. Alexander McIver Papers. Edgar Gardner Murphy Papers (microfilm). Southern Education Board Papers.

Periodicals

Alabama Baptist, 1903–7

American Federationist, 1894–1907

Annals of the American Academy of Political and Social Science, 1901–12

Anniston (Alabama) Hot Blast, 1900

Baltimore Manufacturers' Record, 1894–1907

Birmingham (Alabama) Age-Herald, 1895–96, 1900–1901

Birmingham (Alabama) Labor Advocate, 1895–1909

Bibliography

Birmingham (Alabama) News, 1895–1911, 1915
Charities, 1903–5
Child Labor Bulletin, 1910–19
Florence (Alabama) Herald, 1899–1907
Florence (Alabama) Times, 1903
Gadsden (Alabama) Times-News, 1894–1909
Montgomery (Alabama) Advertiser, 1901–3, 1906–7, 1911, 1915

Interviews

Bailey, Patricia. Interview with author. Florence, Alabama, July 1996.
Mitchell, Broadus. Interview with D. Singal, November 11, 1971 (B-023), and M. Frederickson, August 14, 1977 (B-024). Southern Oral History Program Collection #4007, Southern Historical Collection, Wilson Library, University of North Carolina at Chapel Hill.
Scarboro, Robert. Telephone interview with author, 9 April 1997.

Other Works

Agee, James, and Walker Evans. *Let Us Now Praise Famous Men*. 1939; reprint, Boston: Houghton Mifflin, 1988.
Alabama: A Drama in Four Acts. Chicago: Dramatic Publishing, 1901.
Alabama Child Welfare Department. *Alabama Childhood: Report of the Work of the Child Welfare Department from October 1, 1920, to July 31, 1921*. Montgomery: Brown Printing, 1921.
———. *Annual Report of State Child Welfare Department*. Montgomery: Wetumpka Printing, 1934.
———. *Children's Aid Division, State Child Welfare Department of the State of Alabama*. Montgomery: n.p., 1923.
———. *The Child Welfare Department of the State of Alabama*. Montgomery: Brown Printing, 1923.
———. *Instructions to Superintendents, Principals, and Other School Authorities for the Issuance of Employment Certificates and Newsboys' Badges as Is Required by the Alabama Child Labor Law*. Montgomery: Alabama Child Welfare Department, 1921.
———. *Report of Child Welfare Department, 1923–1927*. Birmingham: Brown Printing, 1927.
Alabama Constitutional Convention. *Official Report of the Proceedings of the Constitutional Convention of the State of Alabama*. Montgomery: Birmingham Printing, 1901.
Alabama Department for the Inspection of Mills, Factories, and Manufacturing Establishments. *Annual Report of the Factory Inspector of the State of Alabama for the Year Ending December 31, 1912*. Montgomery: Brown Printing, 1913.
Alabama Department of Education. *First Report of the Alabama Illiteracy Commission*. Montgomery: Brown Printing, 1916.

Bibliography

Alabama Inspector of Jails and Alms Houses. *Report of the Department for Inspection of Jails and Alms Houses and Cotton Mills, Factories, Etc.* Montgomery: Brown Printing, 1910.

Alabama Legislature. *General Laws of the Legislature of Alabama Passed at the Session of 1915.* Montgomery: Brown Printing, 1915.

———. *General Laws of the Legislature of Alabama Passed at the Session of 1919.* Montgomery: Brown Printing, 1919.

———. *General Laws of the Legislature of Alabama Passed at the Session of 1923.* Montgomery: Brown Printing, 1923.

Alabama Legislature. House of Representatives. *Journal, Session of 1919.* Montgomery: Brown Printing, 1920.

Almaguer, Tomas. *Racial Fault Lines: The Historical Origins of White Supremacy in California.* Berkeley: University of California Press, 1994.

American Federation of Labor Records: The Samuel Gompers Era. Sanford, N.C.: Microfilming Corporation of America, 1979.

Andrews, Mildred Gwin. *The Men and the Mills: A History of the Southern Textile Industry.* Macon, Ga.: Mercer University Press, 1987.

Ashby, Irene M. *Child Labor in Alabama: Report to the Executive Committee of the State, on the History of Child Labor Legislation in Alabama.* Montgomery: n.p., 1901.

Ashcroft, Bruce, Mark Anderson, and Mrs. Allen L. Knox. *In Remembrance: The Centennial History of Trinity Presbyterian Church.* Montgomery, Ala.: Trinity Presbyterian, 1989.

Ayers, Edward L. *The Promise of the New South: Life after Reconstruction.* New York: Oxford University Press, 1992.

Bailey, Hugh C. *Edgar Gardner Murphy: Gentle Progressive.* Coral Gables, Fla.: University of Miami Press, 1968.

Baker, Paula. "The Domestication of Politics: Women and American Political Society, 1780–1920." *American Historical Review* 89 (June 1984): 620–47.

Bederman, Gail. *Manliness and Civilization.* Chicago: University of Chicago Press, 1995.

Bedford, Henry F. *Socialism and the Workers in Massachusetts, 1886–1912.* Amherst: University of Massachusetts Press, 1966.

Bender, Thomas. "Wholes and Parts: The Need for Synthesis in American History." *Journal of American History* 73 (June 1986): 120–36.

Berkeley, Kathleen C. "The First Southern Conference on Women's History." *Signs* 14 (summer 1989): 900–901.

Berney, Saffold. *Hand-Book of Alabama.* Birmingham, Ala.: Roberts and Son, 1892.

Beveridge, Albert J. *The Meaning of the Times and Other Speeches* Indianapolis: Bobbs-Merrill, 1908.

Billings, Dwight B., Jr. *Planters and the Making of a "New South": Class Politics and Development in North Carolina, 1865–1900.* Chapel Hill: University of North Carolina Press, 1978.

Bond, Horace Mann. *Negro Education in Alabama: A Study in Cotton and Steel.* Washington, D.C.: Associated Publishers, 1939.

185

Bordin, Ruth. "'A Baptism of Power and Liberty': The Women's Crusade of 1873–1874." *Ohio History* 87 (autumn 1978): 393–404.

Bowman, Shearer Davis. *Masters and Lords: Mid-Nineteenth-Century U.S. Planters and Prussian Junkers.* New York: Oxford University Press, 1993.

Braeman, John. *Albert J. Beveridge: American Nationalist.* Chicago: University of Chicago Press, 1971.

Breedlove, Michael. "Donald Comer: New Southerner, New Dealer." Ph.D. diss., American University, 1990.

Bremner, Robert H. *The Discovery of Poverty in the United States.* New Brunswick, N.J.: Transaction Publishers, 1992.

Brennan, James A. "Legislation for the Working Children of Alabama: Growth and Reform of the Cotton Textile Mills to 1903." Master's thesis, Samford University, 1970.

Brinkley, Alan. "In Retrospect: Richard Hofstadter's *The Age of Reform:* A Reconsideration." *Reviews in American History* 13 (September 1985): 462–80.

Bryan, Mary Lynn McCree, ed. *The Jane Addams Papers, 1860–1960.* Ann Arbor, Mich.: University Microfilms International.

Buechler, Joseph P. *Avondale Mills: The First Fifty Years.* Honors thesis, Auburn University, 1985.

Bush, Loraine B. "How Alabama Organized Her Work for Children." In *Proceedings of the National Conference of Social Work.* Chicago: University of Chicago Press, 1920.

Byerly, Victoria. *Hard Times Cotton Mill Girls: Personal Histories of Womanhood and Poverty in the South.* Ithaca, N.Y.: ILR Press, 1986.

Carlton, David L. Introduction to *The Rise of Cotton Mills in the South,* by Broadus Mitchell. 1921; Columbia: University of South Carolina Press, 2001.

———. *Mill and Town in South Carolina, 1880–1920.* Baton Rouge: Louisiana State University Press, 1982.

———. "Paternalism and Southern Textile Labor: A Historical Review." In *Race, Class, and Community in Southern Labor History,* edited by Gary M. Fink and Merl E. Reed. Tuscaloosa: University of Alabama Press, 1994.

Cash, W. J. *The Mind of the South.* New York: Random House, 1941.

Chafe, William. *The Paradox of Change: American Women in the Twentieth Century.* New York: Oxford University Press, 1991.

Claxton, P. P. *The Work of the Conference for Education in the South: A Record of Progress for Sixteen Years.* Washington, D.C.: Executive Board of the Southern Conference for Education, 1914.

Clopper, Edward N. *Child Welfare in Alabama.* New York: National Child Labor Committee, 1918.

Comer, Donald. *Braxton Bragg Comer: An Alabamian Whose Avondale Mills Opened New Paths for Southern Progress.* New York: Newcomen Society of England, American Branch, 1947.

Cooper, John Milton, Jr. *Walter Hines Page: The Southerner as American, 1855–1918*. Chapel Hill: University of North Carolina Press, 1977.

Cott, Nancy. *The Grounding of Modern Feminism*. New Haven: Yale University Press, 1987.

Craighead, Lura Harris. *History of the Alabama Federation of Women's Clubs*. Vol. 1, 1895–1918. Montgomery, Ala.: Paragon, 1936.

Crofts, Daniel. "The Black Response to the Blair Education Bill." *Journal of Southern History* 37 (February 1971): 41–65.

Cruikshank, George M. *A History of Birmingham and Its Environs*. Chicago: Lewis Publishing, 1920.

Crunden, Robert M. *Ministers of Reform: The Progressives' Achievement in American Civilization, 1889–1920*. New York: Basic Books, 1982.

Daniel, Pete. *Breaking the Land: The Transformation of Cotton, Tobacco, and Rice Cultures since 1880*. Urbana: University of Illinois Press, 1985.

Davidson, Elizabeth. *Child Labor Legislation in the Southern Textile States*. Chapel Hill: University of North Carolina Press, 1939.

Davis, David Brion. "Reflections on Abolitionism and Ideological Hegemony." *American Historical Review* 92 (October 1987): 797–812.

Dawley, Thomas Robinson, Jr. *The Child That Toileth Not: The Story of a Government Investigation*. New York: Gracia Publishing, 1912.

De Graffenried, Clare. "The Georgia Cracker in the Cotton Mills." *Century Magazine* 41 (February 1891): 483–98.

Doane, David. "Regional Cost Differences and Textile Location." *Explorations in Economic History* 9 (fall 1971): 3–34.

Doherty, Herbert. "Alexander J. McKelway: Preacher to Progressive." *Journal of Southern History* 25 (May 1958): 177–90.

Doster, James F. "Alabama's Gubernatorial Election of 1906." *Alabama Review* 7 (July 1995): 165–78.

DuBois, Ellen, Mari Jo Buhle, Temma Kaplan, Gerda Lerner, and Carroll Smith-Rosenberg. "Politics and Culture in Women's History: A Symposium." *Feminist Studies* 6 (spring 1980): 26–64.

Edmonds, Richard Woods. *Cotton Mill Labor Conditions in the South and New England*. Baltimore: Manufacturers' Record Publishing, 1925.

Fenollosa, Mary [Sidney McCall, pseud.]. *Red Horse Hill*. Boston: Little, Brown, 1909.

Few, William P. "The Constructive Philanthropy of a Southern Cotton Mill." *South Atlantic Quarterly* 8 (January 1909): 82–90.

Fields, Barbara J. "Ideology and Race in American History." In *Region, Race, and Reconstruction: Essays in Honor of C. Vann Woodward*, edited by J. Morgan Kousser and James M. McPherson. New York: Oxford University Press, 1982.

Fink, Gary M., and Merl E. Reed. *Race, Class, and Community in Southern Labor History*. Tuscaloosa: University of Alabama Press, 1994.

Flamming, Douglas. *Creating the Modern South: Millhands and Managers in Dalton, Georgia, 1884–1984.* Chapel Hill: University of North Carolina Press, 1992.

Flynt, J. Wayne. "Alabama White Protestantism and Labor, 1900–1914." *Alabama Review* 25 (July 1972): 192–217.

———. "Dissent in Zion: Alabama Baptists and Social Issues, 1900–1914." *Journal of Southern History* 35 (November 1969): 523–42.

———. "Folks Like Us: The Southern Poor White Family, 1865–1935." In *The Web of Southern Social Relations,* edited by Walter L. Fraser Jr., R. Frank Saunders, and Jon L. Wakelyn. Athens: University of Georgia Press, 1985.

———. *Poor but Proud: Alabama's Poor Whites.* Tuscaloosa: University of Alabama Press, 1989.

———. "Spindle, Mine, and Mule: The Poor White Experience in Post–Civil War Alabama." *Alabama Review* 34 (October 1981); 243–86.

Foley, Neil. *The White Scourge: Mexicans, Blacks, and Poor Whites in Texas Cotton Culture.* Berkeley: University of California Press, 1997.

Foucault, Michel. *The History of Sexuality.* Vol. 1, *An Introduction.* New York: Random House, 1980.

Frankel, Noralee, and Nancy S. Dye, eds. *Gender, Class, Race, and Reform in the Progressive Era.* Lexington: University of Kentucky Press, 1991.

Frederickson, Mary. "Four Decades of Change: Black Workers in Southern Textiles, 1941–1981." *Radical America* 16 (November–December 1982): 27–44.

Fredrickson, George. *The Black Image in the White Mind: The Debate on Afro-American Character and Destiny, 1817–1914.* New York: Harper Torchbooks, 1972.

Freehling, William. W. *Prelude to Civil War: The Nullification Controversy in South Carolina, 1816–1836.* New York: Harper and Row, 1966.

Freeze, Gary. "Poor Girls Who Might Otherwise Be Wretched: The Origins of Paternalism in North Carolina's Mills, 1836–1880." In *Hanging by a Thread: Social Change in Southern Textiles,* edited by Jeffrey Leiter, Michael D. Schulman, and Rhonda Zingraff. Ithaca: ILR Press, 1991.

Fuller, Justin. "Boom Towns and Blast Furnaces: Town Promotion in Alabama, 1885–1893." *Alabama Review* 29 (January 1976): 37–47.

Galambos, Louis. *Competition and Cooperation: The Emergence of a National Trade Association.* Baltimore: Johns Hopkins Press, 1966.

Gaston, Paul M. *The New South Creed: A Study in Southern Mythmaking.* New York: Knopf, 1970.

Gates, Grace Hooten. *The Model City of the New South: Anniston, Alabama, 1872–1900.* Tuscaloosa: University of Alabama Press, 1996.

Gilmore, Glenda Elizabeth. *Gender and Jim Crow: Women and the Politics of White Supremacy in North Carolina, 1896–1920.* Chapel Hill: University of North Carolina Press, 1996.

Glickman, Lawrence B. *A Living Wage: American Workers and the Making of Consumer Society.* Ithaca: Cornell University Press, 1997.

Gordon, Linda. "Putting Children First: Women, Maternalism, and Welfare in the Early

Twentieth Century." In *U.S. History as Women's History: New Feminist Essays,* edited by Linda Kerber. Chapel Hill: University of North Carolina Press, 1995.

Grantham, Dewey. *The South in Modern America: A Region at Odds.* New York: HarperCollins, 1995.

Green, Elna C., ed. *Before the New Deal: Social Welfare in the South, 1830–1930.* Athens: University of Georgia Press, 1999.

Gregory, James N. *American Exodus: The Dust Bowl Migration and Okie Culture in California.* New York: Oxford University Press, 1989.

Hackney, Sheldon. *Populism to Progressivism in Alabama.* Princeton: Princeton University Press, 1969.

Hale, Grace Elizabeth. *Making Whiteness: The Culture of Segregation in the South, 1890–1940.* New York: Random House, 1998.

Hall, Jacquelyn Dowd. "Broadus Mitchell (1892–1899)." *Radical History Review* 45 (August 1989): 31–38.

———. "The First Southern Conference on Women's History." *Signs* 14 (summer 1989): 902–911.

———. "O. Delight Smith's Progressive Era: Labor, Feminism, and Reform in the Urban South." In *Visible Women: New Essays on American Activism,* edited by Nancy A. Hewitt and Suzanne Lebsock. Urbana: University of Illinois Press, 1993.

———. *Revolt against Chivalry: Jessie Daniel Ames and the Women's Campaign against Lynching.* Rev. ed. New York: Columbia University Press, 1993.

Hall, Jacquelyn Dowd, James Leloudis, Robert Korstad, Mary Murphy, LuAnn Jones, and Christopher B. Daly. *Like a Family: The Making of a Southern Cotton Mill World.* New York: Norton, 1987.

Haltunen, Karen. *Confidence Men and Painted Women: A Study of Middle-Class Culture in America, 1830–1870.* New Haven: Yale University Press, 1982.

Hammack, David C., and Stanton Wheeler. *Social Science in the Making: Essays on the Russell Sage Foundation, 1907–1972.* New York: Sage, 1994.

Hareven, Tamara. *Family Time and Industrial Time: The Relationship between the Family and Work in a New England Industrial Community.* Cambridge: Cambridge University Press, 1982.

Harlan, Louis R. *Separate and Unequal: Public School Campaigns and Racism in the Southern Seaboard States, 1901–1915.* Chapel Hill: University of North Carolina Press, 1958.

———. "The Southern Education Board and the Race Issue in Public Education." *Journal of Southern History* 23 (May 1957): 189–202.

Hart, Hastings. *Social Progress in Alabama: A Second Study of the Social Institutions and Agencies of the State of Alabama.* Montgomery: Brown Printing, 1922.

Hartigan, John, Jr., and Annalee Newitz. "Name Calling: Objectifying 'Poor Whites' and 'White Trash' in Detroit." In *White Trash: Race and Class in America,* edited by Matt Wray and Annalee Newitz. New York: Routledge, 1997.

Haskell, Thomas. "Capitalism and the Origins of the Humanitarian Sensibility, Part 1." *American Historical Review* 90 (April 1985): 339–61.

Hawes, Joseph, and N. Ray Hiner, eds. *Children in Historical and Comparative Perspective: An International Handbook and Research Guide.* New York: Greenwood, 1991.

Hendrick, Burton J., ed. *The Life and Letters of Walter H. Page.* Garden City, N.Y.: Doubleday, Page, 1922.

Higginbotham, Evelyn Brooks. "African-American Women's History and the Metalanguage of Race." *Signs* 17 (winter 1992): 251–74.

Hoffschwelle, Mary S. *Rebuilding the Rural Southern Community: Reformers, Schools, and Homes in Tennessee, 1900–1930.* Knoxville: University of Tennessee Press, 1998.

Hubbard, Elbert. *An Eye-Witness of Child Labor and the South: Are We Coming to This in Alabama?* Birmingham: Alabama Child Labor Committee, n.d.

Illustrated Descriptive List of Celebrated Fire Pictures: Comprising the Series of Six Plates Entitled the Life of New York. New York: Currier and Ives, 1884.

In Memoriam: Howard Gardner Nichols. Cambridge, Mass.: Riverside Press, 1897.

Johnson, Kenneth. "The Peabody Fund: Its Role and Influence in Alabama." *Alabama Review* 27 (April 1974): 101–25.

Johnson, Rossiter, and John Howard Brown, eds. *The Twentieth Century Biographical Dictionary of Notable Americans.* Boston: Biographical Society, 1904.

Johnson, Susan H. "Child Labor and Reform in the Cotton Textile Industry of Alabama, 1887–1919." Master's thesis, Jacksonville State University, 1990.

Jones, Herschel H. *Child Labor in Alabama.* Birmingham: n.p., 1915.

Kaufman, Stuart B., ed. *The Samuel Gompers Papers.* Vol. 5. Urbana: University of Illinois Press, 1996.

Kazin, Michael. *Barons of Labor: The San Francisco Building Trades and Union Power in the Progressive Era.* Urbana: University of Illinois Press, 1987.

Kelley, Robin D. G. *Hammer and Hoe: Alabama Communists during the Great Depression.* Chapel Hill: University of North Carolina Press, 1990.

———. *Race Rebels: Culture, Politics, and the Black Working Class.* New York: Free Press, 1994.

Kennedy, David. *Over Here: The First World War and American Society.* New York: Oxford University Press, 1980.

Kerber, Linda. "Separate Spheres, Female Worlds, Women's Place: The Rhetoric of Women's History." *Journal of American History* 75 (June 1988): 9–39.

Kessler-Harris, Alice. *Out to Work: A History of Wage-Earning Women in the United States.* New York: Oxford University Press, 1982.

Kirby, Jack Temple. *Rural Worlds Lost: The American South, 1920–1960.* Baton Rouge: Louisiana State University Press, 1987.

Kirwan, Albert D. *Revolt of the Rednecks: Mississippi Politics, 1876–1925.* Lexington: University of Kentucky Press, 1951.

Kousser, J. Morgan. *The Shaping of Southern Politics: Suffrage Restriction and the Establishment of the One-Party South.* New Haven: Yale University Press, 1974.

Bibliography

Ladd-Taylor, Molly. *Mother-Work: Women, Child Welfare, and the State, 1890–1930.* Urbana: University of Illinois Press, 1994.

LaMonte, Edward Shannon. *Politics and Welfare in Birmingham, 1900–1975.* Tuscaloosa: University of Alabama Press, 1995.

Larson, Edward J. *Sex, Race, and Science: Eugenics in the Deep South.* Baltimore: Johns Hopkins University Press, 1995.

Laurie, Bruce. *Artisans into Workers.* New York: Hill and Wang, 1989.

Lea, Arden J. "Cotton Textiles and the Federal Child Labor Act of 1916." *Labor History* 16 (fall 1975): 485–94.

Lee, Beverley McElligot. "Control of Children in a North Carolina Milltown: Parents, Professionals, and the State." Ph.D. diss., University of North Carolina, 1987.

Leidenberger, George. "'The Public Is the Labor Union': Working-Class Progressivism in Turn-of-the-Century Chicago." *Labor History* 36 (spring 1995): 187–210.

Leiter, Jeffrey, Michael D. Schulman, and Rhonda Zingraff, eds. *Hanging by a Thread: Social Change in Southern Textiles.* Ithaca: ILR Press, 1991.

Leloudis, James L. *Schooling the New South: Pedagogy, Self, and Society in North Carolina, 1880–1920.* Chapel Hill: University of North Carolina Press, 1996.

——. "School Reform in the New South: The Woman's Association for the Betterment of Public School Houses in North Carolina, 1902–1919." *Journal of American History* 69 (March 1983): 886–909.

Levine, Daniel. "Edgar Gardner Murphy: Conservative Reformer." *Alabama Review* 15 (April 1962): 100–116.

Lindenmeyer, Kriste. *"A Right to Childhood": The United States Children's Bureau and Child Welfare, 1912–1946.* Urbana: University of Illinois Press, 1997.

Luker, Ralph. *A Southern Tradition in Theology and Social Criticism, 1830–1930.* New York: Edwin Mellen, 1984.

Lumpkin, Katharine Du Pre, and Dorothy Wolff Douglas. *Child Workers in America.* New York: Robert M. McBride, 1937.

Markham, Edwin, Benjamin B. Lindsay, and George Creel. *Children in Bondage: A Complete and Careful Presentation of the Anxious Problem of Child Labor—Its Causes, Its Crimes, and Its Cure.* Introduction by Owen R. Lovejoy. New York: Hearst's International Library, 1914.

Mathews, Jean V. "Factoring in Race and Gender: New Facets of Culture, New Aspects of War." *Reviews in American History* 21 (December 1993): 600–605.

Matthies, Susan. "Families at Work: An Analysis by Sex of Child Workers in the Cotton Textile Industry." *Journal of Economic History* 42 (March 1982): 173–80.

McArthur, Judith N. *Creating the New Woman: The Rise of Southern Women's Progressive Culture in Texas, 1893–1918.* Urbana: University of Illinois Press, 1998.

McCluskey, Sybil Talley. "Howard Gardner Nichols and Dwight Manufacturing Company." *Alabama Review* 46 (January 1993): 24–36.

McCurry, Stephanie. *Masters of Small Worlds: Yeoman Households, Gender Relations, and the*

Political Culture of the Antebellum South Carolina Low Country. New York: Oxford University Press, 1995.

McDonald, William Lindsey. *Sweetwater: The Story of East Florence.* Florence, Ala.: Florence Historical Board, 1989.

McHugh, Cathy L. *Mill Family: The Labor System in the Southern Textile Industry 1880–1915.* Oxford: Oxford University Press, 1988.

McLaurin, Melton. *Paternalism and Protest: Southern Cotton Mill Workers and Organized Labor, 1875–1905.* Westport, Conn.: Greenwood, 1971.

Memorial Record of Alabama: A Concise Account of the State's Political, Military, Professional, and Industrial Progress, Together with the Personal Memoirs of Many of Its People. Madison, Wis.: Brant and Fuller, 1893.

Milkman, Ruth. "Organizing the Sexual Division of Labor: Historical Perspectives on Women's Work and the American Labor Movement." *Socialist Review* 49 (spring 1980): 95–150.

Miller, Randall Martin. *The Cotton Mill Movement in Antebellum Alabama.* New York: Arno, 1978.

Mitchell, Broadus. *The Rise of Cotton Mills in the South.* Baltimore: Johns Hopkins University Press, 1921.

Moore, Albert Barton. *History of Alabama and Her People.* Chicago: American Historical Society, 1927.

Moore, D. D., ed. *Men of the South.* New Orleans: Southern Biographical Association, 1922.

Movements, John H., Jr. *Save the Little Americans.* Montgomery, Ala.: Brown Printing, 1913.

Muncy, Robyn. *Creating a Female Dominion in American Reform, 1890–1935.* New York: Oxford University Press, 1991.

Murphy, Edgar Gardner. *Alabama's First Question: Local Support for Local Schools.* Montgomery, Ala.: n.p., 1904.

——. *The Basis of Ascendancy: A Discussion of Certain Principles of Public Policy Involved in the Development of the Southern States.* New York: Longmans, Green, 1909.

——. *Child Labor and Business.* Montgomery: Alabama Child Labor Committee, 1902.

——. *Child Labor and the Public: To the People and the Press of Alabama.* Montgomery: Alabama Child Labor Committee, 1902.

——, comp. *Child Labor in the Southern Press.* Montgomery, Ala.: Executive Committee on Child Labor in Alabama, 1902.

——. *The Federal Regulation of Child Labor: A Criticism of the Policy Represented in the Beveridge-Parsons Bill.* New Haven, Conn.: Tuttle, Morehouse, and Taylor, 1907.

——. *An Open Letter: On Suffrage Restriction, and against Certain Proposals of the Platform of the State Convention.* 4th ed. Montgomery: Alabama Printing, 1901.

——. *Pictures from Life: Mill Children in Alabama.* Montgomery, Ala.: Executive Committee on Child Labor, 1902.

——. *Problems of the Present South: A Discussion of Certain of the Educational, Industrial, and Political Issues in the Southern States.* New York: Macmillan, 1904.

——. *The South and Her Children: A Rejoinder in the Child Labor Discussion, in Response to the* Manufacturers Record, *August 28, 1902*. Montgomery: Alabama Printing, 1902.

——. *The White Man and the Negro at the South: An Address Delivered under Invitation of the American Academy of Political and Social Science*. Montgomery, Ala.: n.p., 1900.

Murphy, Edgar Gardner, J. Howard Nichols, and Horace S. Sears. *Child Labor in Alabama: An Appeal to the People and Press of New England with a Resulting Correspondence*. Montgomery: Alabama Child Labor Committee, 1901.

Murphy, Maud King. *Edgar Gardner Murphy: From Records and Memoirs*. New York: n.p., 1943.

Nardinelli, Clark. *Child Labor and the Industrial Revolution*. Bloomington: Indiana University Press, 1990.

National Child Labor Committee. *Uniform Child Labor Laws: Proceedings of the Seventh Annual Conference on Child Labor, Birmingham, Alabama, March 9–12, 1911*. New York: National Child Labor Committee, 1911.

Newby, I. A. *Plain Folk in the New South: Social Change and Cultural Persistence, 1880–1915*. Baton Rouge: Louisiana State University Press, 1989.

Omi, Michael, and Howard Winant. *Racial Formations*. New York: Routledge and Kegan Paul, 1986.

Owen, Marie Bankhead. *The Story of Alabama*. Vol. 5. New York: Lewis Historical Publishing, 1949.

Owen, Thomas McAdory. *History of Alabama and Dictionary of Biography*. Chicago: S. J. Clarke Publishing, 1921.

Page, Walter H. *The Rebuilding of Old Commonwealths: Being Essays towards the Training of the Forgotten Man in the Southern States*. New York: Doubleday, Page, 1902.

Pascoe, Peggy. "Miscegenation Law, Court Cases, and Ideologies of 'Race' in Twentieth-Century America." *Journal of American History* 83 (June 1996): 44–69.

Patton, James W. "The Southern Reaction to the Ogden Movement." In *Education in the South: Institution of Southern Cultures Lectures*, edited by R. C. Simonini Jr. Farmville, Va.: Longwood College, 1958.

Perry, Robert Eugene. "Middle-Class Townsmen and Northern Capital: The Rise of the Alabama Cotton Textile Industry, 1865–1900." Ph.D. diss., Vanderbilt University, 1986.

Prude, Jonathan. "The Family in Context." *Labor History* 17 (summer 1976): 422–36.

Rafter, Nicole Hahn. *White Trash: The Eugenic Family Studies, 1877–1919*. Boston: Northeastern University Press, 1988.

Rodgers, Daniel T. "In Search of Progressivism." *Reviews in American History* 10 (December 1982): 113–32.

Roediger, David R. *The Wages of Whiteness: Race and the Making of the American Working Class*. London: Verso, 1991.

Royster, Jacqueline Jones, ed. *Southern Horrors and Other Writings: The Anti-Lynching Campaign of Ida B. Wells, 1892–1900*. New York: Bedford Books, 1997.

Sawicki, Jana. *Disciplining Foucault: Feminism, Power, and the Body*. New York: Routledge, Chapman, and Hall, 1991.

Scott, Anne Firor. *The Southern Lady: From Pedestal to Politics, 1830–1930.* Chicago: University of Chicago Press, 1970.

Scranton, Philip. "Culture, Politics, and Acquiescence: Left Historians and Textile Paternalism." *Radical History Review* 28–30 (1984): 482–93.

———. "Varieties of Paternalism: Industrial Structures and the Social Relations of Production in American Textiles." *American Quarterly* 36 (summer 1984): 235–57.

Seaholm, Megan. "Earnest Women: The White Woman's Club Movement in Progressive Era Texas, 1880–1920." Ph.D. diss., Rice University, 1988.

Silber, Nina. *The Romance of Reunion: Northerners and the South, 1865–1900.* Chapel Hill: University of North Carolina Press, 1993.

Simon, Brian. *Education and the Labour Movement, 1870–1920.* London: Lawrence and Wishart, 1965.

Simon, Bryant. "The Appeal of Cole Blease of South Carolina: Race, Class, and Sex in the New South." *Journal of Southern History* 62 (February 1996): 57–86.

Simonini, R. C., Jr., ed. *Education in the South: Institution of Southern Cultures Lectures.* Farmville, Va.: Longwood College, 1958.

Sims, Anastatia. "Feminism and Femininity in the New South: White Women's Organizations in North Carolina, 1883–1930." Ph.D. diss., University of North Carolina, 1985.

Sklar, Kathryn Kish. *Florence Kelley and the Nation's Work: The Rise of Women's Political Culture, 1830–1900.* New Haven: Yale University Press, 1995.

———. "Hull House in the 1890s: A Community of Women Reformers." *Signs* 10 (June 1985): 658–77.

———. "Two Political Cultures in the Progressive Era: The National Consumers' League and the American Association for Labor Legislation." In *U.S. History as Women's History: New Feminist Essays,* edited by Linda Kerber. Chapel Hill: University of North Carolina Press, 1995.

Smedley, Audrey. *Race in North America: Origin and Evolution of a Worldview.* Boulder, Colo.: Westview, 1993.

Steel, Edward M., ed. *The Speeches and Writings of Mother Jones.* Pittsburgh: University of Pittsburgh Press, 1988.

The Story of Alabama, a History of the State: Personal and Family History. Vol. 4. New York: Lewis Historical Publishing, 1949.

Taft, Philip. "A Short Note on the Alabama State Federation of Labor." *Labor History* 16 (summer 1975): 410–11.

Thelen, David P. *The New Citizenship: Origins of Progressivism in Wisconsin, 1885–1900.* Columbia: University of Missouri Press, 1972.

Thomas, Mary Martha. *The New Woman in Alabama: Social Reforms and Suffrage, 1890–1920.* Tuscaloosa: University of Alabama Press, 1992.

Thorn, Cecelia Jean. "The Bell Factory: Early Pride of Huntsville." *Alabama Review* 32 (January 1979): 28–37.

Tolnay, Steward E., and E. M. Beck. *A Festival of Violence: An Analysis of Southern Lynchings, 1882–1930.* Urbana: University of Illinois Press, 1995.

Trattner, Walter I. *Crusade for the Children: A History of the National Child Labor Committee and Child Labor Reform in America.* Chicago: Quadrangle Books, 1970.

Turner, Elizabeth Hayes. *Women, Culture, and Community: Religion and Reform in Galveston, 1880–1920.* New York: Oxford University Press, 1997.

Tuten, James H. "Regulating the Poor in Alabama: The Jefferson Country Poor Farm, 1885–1945." In *Before the New Deal: Social Welfare in the South, 1830–1930,* edited by Elna C. Green. Athens: University of Georgia Press, 1999.

U.S. Bureau of Education. *Report of the Commissioner of Education, 1900–1901.* 2 vols. Washington, D.C: GPO, 1902.

———. *Report of the Commissioner of Education, 1904–1905.* 2 vols. Washington, D.C.: GPO, 1906.

U.S. Bureau of Labor. *Woman and Child Wage-Earners in the United States.* Vol. 1, *Cotton Textile Industry.* Washington, D.C.: GPO, 1910.

———. *Woman and Child Wage-Earners in the United States.* Vol. 7, *Conditions under Which Children Leave School to Go to Work.* Washington, D.C.: GPO, 1910.

U.S. Bureau of the Census. *Census Reports.* Vol. 8, *Manufactures.* Pt. 2, *States and Territories.* Washington, D.C.: GPO, 1902.

———. *Census Reports.* Vol. 9, *Manufactures.* Pt. 3, *Special Reports on Selected Industries.* Washington, D.C.: GPO, 1902.

———. *Census Reports.* Vol. 10, *Manufactures.* Pt. 4, *Special Reports on Selected Industries.* Washington, D.C.: GPO, 1902.

———. *Population.* Pt. 1. Washington, D.C.: GPO, 1901.

———. *Report of Manufacturing Industries in the United States, 1890.* Washington, D.C.: GPO, 1895.

———. *Report on Population of the United States.* Washington, D.C.: GPO, 1891.

U.S. Congress. *Memorial Addresses delivered in the House of Representatives and the Senate of the U.S.* 61st Cong., 3d sess. Washington, D.C.: GPO, 1911.

U.S. House. *Hearings on the Child Labor Bill (H.R. 8234) before the Committee on Labor, January 10, 11, 12, 1916.* Washington, D.C.: GPO, 1916.

U.S. House Committee on the Judiciary. *Constitutional Amendment Giving Congress Power to Regulate Hours of Employees in Factories.* 57th Cong., 1st sess., March 13, 27, April 29, 1902. Supplement H.J. 57A. Washington, D.C.: GPO, 1902.

———. *Uniform Hours of Labor in Manufactories throughout the United States.* 55th Cong., 2d sess., February 18, 1898. Supplement H.J. 55C. Washington, D.C.: GPO, 1898.

Van Vorst, Elizabeth. "The Cry of the Children." *Saturday Evening Post,* March 10, 1906.

———. *The Cry of the Children: A Study of Child-Labor.* New York: Moffat, Yard, 1908.

Van Vorst, Elizabeth, and Marie Van Vorst. *The Woman Who Toils: Being the Experience of Two Gentlewomen as Factory Girls.* New York: Doubleday, Page, 1903.

Walker, Anne Kendrick. *Braxton Bragg Comer: His Family Tree from Virginia's Colonial Days.* Richmond, Va.: Dietz Press, 1947.

Walker, Roger W. "The A.F.L. and Child-Labor Legislation: An Exercise in Frustration." *Labor History* 11 (summer 1970): 323–40.

Walters, Pamela Barnhouse, and David R. James. "Schooling for Some: Child Labor and School Enrollment of Black and White Children in the Early Twentieth-Century South." *American Sociological Review* 57 (October 1992): 635–50.

Ward, Robert David, and William Warren Rogers. *Labor Revolt in Alabama: The Great Strike of 1894.* Tuscaloosa: University of Alabama Press, 1965.

Watson, E. O. *The Church and the Cotton Mills of the South.* Nashville, Tenn.: Missionary Training School, 1905.

Webb, Samuel L. *Two-Party Politics in the One-Party South: Alabama's Hill Country, 1874–1920.* Tuscaloosa: University of Alabama Press, 1997.

Webb, Samuel L., and Margaret E. Armbrewster. *Alabama Governors.* Tuscaloosa: University of Alabama Press, 2001.

Weil, François. "Le Developpement Industriel du Nouveau Sud: L'exemple de Gadsden (Alabama), 1880–1900." *Revue d'Histoire Moderne et Contemporaine* 37 (April–June 1990): 268–82.

Wheeler, Marjorie Spruill. *New Women of the New South: The Leaders of the Woman Suffrage Movement in the Southern States.* New York: Oxford University Press, 1993.

Whisnant, David E. *All That Is Native and Fine: The Politics of Culture in an American Region.* Chapel Hill: University of North Carolina Press, 1983.

Whites, LeeAnn. "The De Graffenried Controversy: Class, Race, and Gender in the New South." *Journal of Southern History* 54 (August 1988): 449–78.

Wiebe, Robert H. *The Search for Order, 1877–1920.* New York: Hill and Wang, 1967.

Williamson, Joel. *A Rage for Order: Black/White Relations in the American South since Emancipation.* New York: Oxford University Press, 1986.

Wingerd, Mary Lether. "Rethinking Paternalism: Power and Parochialism in a Southern Mill Village." *Journal of American History* 83 (December 1996): 872–902.

Wood, Stephen B. *Constitutional Politics in the Progressive Era: Child Labor and the Law.* Chicago: University of Chicago Press, 1968.

Woodward, C. Vann. *Origins of the New South, 1877–1913.* 1951; reprint, Baton Rouge: Louisiana State University Press, 1971.

Wright, Gavin. *Old South, New South: Revolutions in the Southern Economy since the Civil War.* New York: Basic Books, 1986.

INDEX